WHITE AFRICAN

An Early Autobiography

By

L. S. B. LEAKEY

WITH A FOREWORD BY

KIRTLEY F. MATHER

AND

A NEW PREFACE BY THE AUTHOR

SCHENKMAN PUBLISHING COMPANY, INC.
CAMBRIDGE, MASSACHUSETTS 02138

FOREWORD

It was in January 1965 that I had my first opportunity to become well acquainted with Dr. L. S. B. Leakey. Previously I had heard him lecture on two occasions to large and enthusiastic audiences, had shaken his hand in brief encounters, and had read with great interest several of his scholarly reports about his remarkable discoveries concerning the progenitors of man in Africa. Now at last we were to have a leisurely, off-the-record chat. I found him in his laboratory at the rear of the Coryndon Museum in Nairobi, Kenya.

Our conversation ranged widely over his recent finds—fossil remains and artifacts of *Homo habilis* and other fascinating human and prehominid creatures. He told me about his plans for further research in western North America and some of the trials and tribulations he had been encountering. With the assistance of his staff we made plans for me to visit Orlogasailie and Kariandusi, sites of the most important of his earlier excavations in one of the Rift Valleys of East Africa and now under the protection of the Kenya government. All in all, it was a memorable day for me.

Louis Leakey is a "character"—as Harvard students use that term in speaking of their most notable professors. Born in an outpost in the midst of the East African Kikuyu tribe, the son of Church of England missionaries, he is as much an African as a Britisher. He speaks Kikuyu, thinks in Kikuyu, and—as he proudly asserts—even dreams in Kikuyu. But he is also one of the most knowledgeable of the world's anthropologists, and one of the luckiest.

His good fortune—as is almost always the case—is the result of his dedication and persistence. He and his wife and their assistants toiled for at least a month or so in almost every one of twenty successive years in the Olduvai Gorge area before they found the first fossil bones of humankind there, an epochal discovery in the annals of anthropology. And his dedication to the study of ancestral man is an all-consuming fire that drives him relentlessly forward regardless of any obstacle in his way. How this commitment of his life was made and how it came to be so complete, he tells with delightful candor in this book.

FOREWORD

As I had expected, Louis Leakey talks in the same way that he writes: straightforwardly, without circumlocution; candidly and bluntly, with no mincing of words. Those fortunate enough to read this book—and there should be many such—will soon discover that he possesses the hallmark of the truly great scientist, speaking and writing not merely so that he *may* be understood, but, far better, so that he *may not* be misunderstood. Such habits of mind and pen have led some of his colleagues who really do not know him well to think that he is brusque and even domineering, but I found him to be a man of great personal charm, well worthy of my admiration not only as a scientist but as a person.

The book is an autobiography, the personal account of his youth among the Kikuyu and in academic life in England and of the earlier part of his career as an archeologist and physical anthropologist. It is a book of real importance, revealing as it does the motivation and youthful conditioning of a man destined to become one of the most notable characters in a scientific field of increasing relevance to modern man. Above all, it is a delightfully readable book, not to be overlooked even by those who, for reasons I cannot understand, have little interest in prehistoric events. They, too, must be interested in other people and must wonder, now and then, what makes them as they are. Rarely will they find another person who has had such an extraordinary life and can tell his story in so engaging a manner as does Dr. L. S. B. Leakey.

Kirtley F. Mather
Professor of Geology, Emeritus
Harvard University

Cambridge, Massachusetts
6 October 1966

PREFACE TO 1966 PRINTING

This book was written in 1936 at the urgent suggestion of some of my friends, in order to give an idea of the background against which I set out to search for evidence of Early Man in my native East Africa. It deals only with the first 30 years of my life, and ends with my Third East African Archaeological Expedition, during which we visited Olduvai (then called Oldoway) for the first time and found evidence of really early Stone Age cultures. We also found traces of fossil man at Kanam and Kanjera in Kenya, as well as of remains of *Proconsul*, the 25 million years old fossil on Rusinga Island.

It was these discoveries, above all else, that decided my future. But for them I might perhaps have returned to Cambridge University and settled down to teach. But our results had been so exciting and gave such clear indications that we were on the right track in East Africa, that I knew I must devote the rest of my life to the search there.

At the time when the book ends, our first season at Olduvai had led us to accept Professor Reck's claim that the skeleton he found in the Gorge in 1913, was contemporary with the fossil beds. Later, we were able to prove (and Reck to accept the evidence) that his discovery was a burial *into* Bed II, and not contemporary with its formation.

On the other hand, the same first season at Olduvai had yielded stone tools of the Oldowan culture *in situ* in Bed I. These were then the oldest, unquestioned, human cultural remains anywhere in the world, and they still hold that position. To-day, after 35 more years of work at Olduvai, we are preparing to publish a series of seven volumes dealing with our finds there.

At the time *White African* was written, we had, moreover, claimed the Kanam mandible as the oldest known human fossil hominid. The jaw belonged to a creature very much more like *Homo* than scientists expected to have existed in the Early Pleistocene. Consequently, *Homo kanamansis*, as we called the fossil, was rejected by most of my colleagues (partly because it did not conform to the pattern of the now discredited forgery, Piltdown skull and mandible), and it is still not accepted by most of my colleagues. I have never retreated from my position that this jaw fragment belongs with the fauna of Kanam west, and I believe that one day this view will be indicated, by new discoveries.

In 1936, when I wrote *White African*, the age of Early Man in the U.S.A. was usually regarded as about 3,000 B.C., and I found myself in difficulties with some of my American colleagues, on one or two occasions, because I used to tell students that "man must have been in the Americas at least as long ago as 15,000 B.C." I based this view on the distribution of different languages, different cultures and different physical tribal types from Alaska to Cape Horn. The discoveries could not, I felt, be explained without a period of fifteen or more thousand years of development in this Continent. To-day, an age of that order is widely accepted in the U.S.A.; but meanwhile I have been expressing the view that the evidence now available strongly suggests that man may have been in America for considerably more than 50,000 years.

It is not possible for me to believe that at a time when many other mammals were crossing from Asia to America, by the land bridge which existed where now the Bering Straits occur, man alone held back. The fact that the evidence is not yet clear does not mean it will not be found.

I was told, as a young student, not to waste my time searching for Early Man in Africa, since "everyone knew he had started in Asia." Nevertheless I went back to East Africa and searched; we made numerous discoveries which more than justify the time and money which has been spent. I commend to young students the idea of dedicating themselves to finding the evidence that will prove, conclusively, the real date of Man's first arrival in the Americas.

L. S. B. LEAKEY
October, 1966
Nairobi, Kenya

PREFACE

I have frequently been asked to publish some account of the lighter side of my scientific expeditions in East Africa, and in *White African* I have tried to do this.

As my interest in the Stone Age history of East Africa started in early boyhood, I decided to start my story at the very beginning, for had it not been for the circumstances of my birth in the Colony, and for many things that happened in my childhood, and which are recounted in this book, I should probably never have undertaken my research work of the last ten years.

Born as I was among the Kikuyu people, and growing up among them as I did, it was inevitable that I should become deeply interested in this tribe and throughout the book will be found sidelights on Kikuyu custom and Kikuyu outlook.

I have purposely only given a few glimpses of the Kikuyu in this book, because in 1937 I am going to try to write a more detailed study of them.

I have finished off my book with the close of my Third East African Archæological Expedition. Since then a fourth season has been completed and I hope that there will be a fifth and sixth in due course.

But for the very generous help of the Royal Society, the Percy Sladen Memorial Trustees, the Royal Geographical Society, the Rhodes Trust, the Leverhulme Trustees, and the Kenya Government, my expeditions described in these pages would never have been possible and I take this opportunity of thanking them publicly once again. Other scientific societies and many private friends have also helped in many ways and to all of them I express my deep gratitude.

It is hard to find words to express my appreciation of all that my parents have done for me in a thousand ways, all through, and I must thank them especially too, for reading through and checking the proofs of this book and for their help in making the story of my childhood accurate.

L. S. B. LEAKEY.

GREAT MUNDEN, *December* 1936.

WHITE AFRICAN

CHAPTER I

" WE CALL HIM THE blackman with a white face,"
said Chief Koinange on a recent visit to England,
" because he is more of an African than a European,
and we regard him as one of ourselves."

I was very flattered when I heard of this remark (he
was referring to me) for I have always considered
myself more of a Kikuyu than an Englishman in many
ways.

I still often think in Kikuyu, dream in Kikuyu ;
and if my English is not all that it should be in the
narrative which follows, my excuse must be that I would
have preferred to write it in the Kikuyu language.

I was born at Kabete, eight miles from Nairobi
which is now the capital of Kenya Colony. In those
days, Nairobi was little more than a scattered collection of corrugated-iron bungalows, and offices, gathered
for convenience round the railway station ; but to-day
it has theatres and cinemas, gigantic hotels and commercial establishments boasting many stories, race
courses and sports clubs ; and it is linked with all the
other towns by what are called all-weather roads and
by telephone.

When I was born, the eight miles which separated
Kabete Mission from embryo Nairobi constituted a
serious barrier to communications. It was quite an
undertaking for anyone to go to Nairobi and return
the same day, and more usually the journey there and

back occupied two days, whereas now it is possible to go to the capital by car, spend twenty minutes or so shopping, and yet be back at Kabete within the hour. In the old days, of course, the journey had to be made on foot, and the route lay along narrow foot-paths that zig-zagged from one little native village to another, so that the actual distance to be walked was nearer fourteen miles than eight. Nor was it only the distance, and the fact that it had to be covered on foot that made the journey to Nairobi a slow one. Time was of little consequence. So the traveller would stop and gossip at each village as he passed, or pause to rest and take snuff, knowing that there was no need for undue haste, as anyhow he intended to spend the night at Nairobi, and return at his leisure next day.

To-day, in contrast, the Kikuyu people who live around Kabete have been caught up by that mad desire for haste, that seems to be inevitably linked with what we are pleased to call the progress of civilisation. Even those who, having no bicycle or other modern means of accelerated transport, have still to use their own two feet, think nothing nowadays of walking to Nairobi and back before mid-day. There are even those who now go regularly into Nairobi every morning to their work, and return at night. Kabete is in fact rapidly becoming a mere suburb.

The circumstances which led up to my birth at Kabete are themselves not without interest, and so I will briefly summarize them before going on to my own story.

In 1891 the Church Missionary Society appealed for men and women to go out to East Africa and devote their lives to evangelistic work among the natives. Among those who responded to this appeal were my mother and two of her sisters.

In 1936, it is not easy for us to appreciate what such action must have meant. The relatives and friends of the three Miss Bazetts were strongly opposed to the idea. It was well known that very real risks to health, and even to life itself, were involved. Already a number of pioneer missionaries to East Africa had died of tropical diseases, or at the hands of hostile natives. But nothing daunted, the three sisters persisted in their plan, and in due course they landed at Mombasa.

My mother's work was among the Moslem women at the coast, but before three years had passed, the tropical climate combined with generally unhealthy conditions which then prevailed at Mombasa caused her health to break down and she was invalided back to England and told that she must never again venture to tropical Africa. This was a sad blow to one who had sacrificed everything in order to serve in the mission field, and although she had to obey the doctor's orders for the time being, my mother never abandoned the idea of returning to East Africa at some future date.

Then, in 1899 my mother married Harry Leakey who was at that time serving as a curate in a London parish preparatory to going out to East Africa as a missionary.

In December, 1901, after the birth of my two sisters, my father sailed for Mombasa and travelled thence to Kabete, where he had been appointed to take over the work of the newly established station, and a few months later my mother joined him there, taking with her my two sisters and Miss Oakes to help in looking after them.

The mud and thatch hut that served as a home for

them at Kabete was a very simple structure and far from comfortable. Among other disadvantages the roof had not been pitched sufficiently steeply, so that the tropical rain came through it as through a sieve. Even the old tents and tarpaulins which were put over the thatch did not make it entirely waterproof, and as the floor was of earth its condition in wet weather can be imagined.

At first no glass was available to make windows and rough wooden shutters were used to shut out the cold at night, for in spite of being almost on the equator Kabete was very cold at night, as a result of being 6,500 feet above sea level. No fireplace had been made when the house was built by my father's predecessor and so the rooms had to be warmed by a roughly improvised brazier which, in the absence of proper charcoal, often smoked a good deal.

It was in this house that I made my inauspicious entry into the world—prematurely born on August 7th, 1903—at a time of year when dry season thunderstorms combined with the unsatisfactory roof to turn the floor into a sea of mud puddles.

It was nothing short of a miracle that I lived at all, and it is a source of unceasing wonder to me that my parents succeeded in keeping us three children healthy under the conditions which prevailed. One would have expected it to be at least a whole-time job for my mother and Miss Oakes, and yet my mother found time to devote several hours a day to helping my father in the work of the station. Both of them were busy too, learning the Kikuyu language, and in the meantime the few pupils who began to collect at the mission had to be taught to read and write in Kiswahili, the language of the coastal people and one which my mother had mastered before she had been invalided home.

The site of Kabete mission was very beautiful. Sufficient land had been acquired (about sixteen acres) by purchase from the local families to provide building sites for church, school and mission house, and in addition room for garden plots and building sites for such of the mission adherents as were ostracised by their families on account of their change of faith. The surrounding country had a population density of about 250 people to the square mile (to-day that figure has been doubled) and so a considerable part of it was under cultivation. The rest was mainly bushland, which, far from being unused, was the equivalent of pasturage, as I shall show in another chapter.

Here and there stood isolated patches of virgin forest, reminders of the not very distant past when the whole of this region had been forested. In these islands of trees were hidden most of the villages, so as to conceal them as much as possible from raiders. The Kabete district was only a few miles from the boundary between Kikuyu and Masai territory and so was well within striking distance of raiding parties from over the border. At the time of which I am writing, however, raids and counter-raids had ceased as a result of the establishment of Pax Britannica.

Beyond the stream that bounded the mission property on one side, the ground rose steeply, and the hill so formed was bisected by a valley through which ran the Bogojee stream which descended to its junction with the Mathare over a series of waterfalls. These all had beautiful maidenhair and other ferns growing where the spray formed perpetual rain, and the sun made little rainbows. The various Bogojee waterfalls were to be the scene of many a happy afternoon for us children, and each of us pretended to own one fall : it was our dominion over which we ruled, ordering the fairies and unseen population to do our bidding ; but I must not anticipate my story.

Not unnaturally, the birth of an English baby at the Mission was a source of great excitement to the Kikuyu people all around and everyone wanted to see me. At first, owing to my premature birth, I had to be kept swathed in cotton wool, but as I grew stronger and began to be taken out in my pram, and lie on the verandah in a cot, the people had an opportunity to satisfy their curiosity, and look at the new white baby.

The natives' desire to see me was not without its trials for my parents and our friend Miss Oakes, because custom and belief demanded that having admired me they should spit upon me in order to prove that they had not in any way bewitched me or cast the spell of an evil eye upon me. Naturally my parents who did not believe in the power of the evil eye or of witchcraft, regarded the risks of infection which were inherent in this custom as far more dangerous to me than any of the dangers envisaged by the natives. And so they did all in their power to check this form of tribute. They were not always successful, however, and from time to time I had to be rushed indoors and washed and changed after some wellwisher had aimed with more than usual accuracy.

The custom, which is closely linked with that of spitting on the palm of the hand before shaking hands, owes its origin to the deep-rooted belief in black magic which is common to the Kikuyu and many other African tribes.

It is believed that the surest way to kill someone is to take some part of him—a piece of his hair, a paring from toe or finger nail, or some spittle—and with it make black magic. The victim will then die by supernatural agency.

As a corollary to this belief, it follows that the best way to show your friendship to, or faith in, another person is to give him some part of yourself wherewith he may kill you should he so desire. Hence, if you are about to shake hands with a great friend, or with an influential member of the tribe, or even with a stranger to whom you wish to show respect or humility, you spit upon the palm of your hand, and then shake hands with him, thereby transferring some of your spittle to him and so putting yourself at his mercy.

Similarly, if you have been admiring someone's children or their flocks and herds it is incumbent upon you to prove that you have not surreptiously cast an evil eye or other spell upon them, and so before leaving you expectorate upon them, a gesture which proves your good intentions. Should you omit to do so, and the children or animals which you had admired were then to die or sicken, you would at once be suspect.

This idea of spitting at other peoples' animals or children, and of spitting into the hand before greeting a friend, is quite unintelligible to most Europeans to whom the act of spitting denotes hatred and contempt. It is therefore fortunate that the Kikuyu had come to realise something of the European's attitude to such behaviour before the white population became as numerous as it is to-day. Otherwise the custom might have been the cause of much ill-feeling.

Even to-day in the more remote parts of Kikuyu and Masai-land (for the custom was by no means confined to the Kikuyu) it is not uncommon to find old men who spit into their hands before they shake hands with you ; and to refuse the proffered greeting because of this would be discourteous in the extreme.

Very soon after his arrival at Kabete, my father was given the nickname of " Giteru " by the people.

" Giteru " means big beard, and his hirsute face was a constant source of amusement because the Kikuyu favoured hairless faces. To-day quite a few of them have beards and an even greater number moustaches, as they have begun to copy Europeans, but the fact that they and many other African tribes never used to allow hair to grow on their faces or on any other parts of the body has given rise to the quite baseless theory that the African negro is by nature a hairless race.

This error is propagated in many text-books upon the races of mankind, and is due to the fact that the early travellers and other observers were insufficiently acquainted with native custom and belief.

So far as I can judge from my own observations, the native races of Africa are neither more nor less hairy than the European races. Some individuals are by nature more hirsute than others, while a few (as also occurs among European races) never develop much facial or body hair.

As far as the Kikuyu are concerned, the facial and pubic hair is consistently removed by means of special depilating tweezers (nowadays safety razor blades are becoming increasingly popular) while the hair on arms, legs and chest was removed by the following curious and somewhat painful method. The hairy parts were coated with clayey mud which was allowed to dry before being scraped off. When this was done the dry mud pulled the hair out by the roots. Kikuyus have frequently laughed at my own hairy body and offered to give me a " mud-shave."

In course of time, after constant depilation the hair tends to give up the unequal struggle and the time comes when practically no hair will grow at all, even if it is left unplucked for weeks at a time.

In connection with my scientific expeditions in East

Africa, I have sometimes taken parties of Africans into districts where there has been no human population. Under such circumstances they seldom trouble to depilate (just as we often neglect to shave when we are in remote places) and they soon develop a normal growth of hair on their bodies, as well as beards. As soon, however, as the expedition starts on its way back to the inhabited areas they remove all their body hair again lest they should be held up to ridicule.

This digression about African hairiness arose from my statement that my father was given the nickname of Giteru—the big beard. Mother, on the other hand, was always addressed as Bibi (pronounced beebee). This word, which is of Swahili origin is really a term of respect and honour, and is the feminine of Bwana. It corresponds to the English ' Madam.' Nowadays the Europeans in Kenya have taken the word and shortened its vowel sounds so that they pronounce it ' bibby.' They use it as though it simply means ' woman,' and they consequently greatly resent it if an African (using it in its correct sense) addresses a white woman as Bibi, and they insist upon the use of the word Memsab instead. This word is a corruption of the Indian Memsahib. On the other hand the Europeans are equally resentful if the Africans do not use the word Bwana when they address a white man !

It is this sort of fantastic inconsistency that makes it so difficult for the African to understand the European. Perhaps not unnaturally the white man's attitude is often (privately of course) regarded as that of an illogical fool.

CHAPTER II

IN THE ORDINARY COURSE of events a missionary working for the Church Missionary Society was expected to spend four years in the field before returning to England on furlough, but in my father's case ill health prevented this and so in February, 1905, we had to leave Kabête and I started on the first of my many journeys between East Africa and England.

When we sailed, we were accompanied by a Kikuyu boy who after having spent a few years at the Mission school had been baptized by the name of Stefano. Stefano was the son of one of the Kikuyu elders who lived near Kabete mission, and my father's object in taking him to England was threefold. It would be very useful indeed to have someone who spoke Kikuyu on his first furlough in England as it would thus be possible for father to keep up his knowledge of that far from easy language during his year of absence from the country and the people. Secondly, if a Kikuyu boy could be taught English properly he would be absolutely invaluable later on in helping with the difficult task of translating the Bible and Prayer Book into his own language. Thirdly, on board ship, during the voyage home, and later in England he would be immensely useful helping to look after my sisters and myself.

It was, of course, an experiment that might have proved unsatisfactory, but the boy was very keen to go and it seemed well worth trying. People argued against it that it would make the boy swollen-headed and that when he at length came back to his own people he would find it difficult to return to his own simple life after having enjoyed the comforts of England. But these fears were unfounded, and when Stefano came back to Kabete once more, speaking excellent English and having enjoyed his stay in England immensely, he reverted to his ordinary life among his own people quite easily and to this day I have never met a more humble and unspoiled African than he is. This is all the more remarkable in view of his subsequent career. After coming back from England Stefano became chief assistant to my father in all his work on the language. He learnt to be a very efficient typist, and for years he earned a bigger salary than any other native at Kabete. But all the time he was humility personified. He used to preach sometimes in church on Sundays and help in many of the activities of the Mission, but never did he make any use of the fact that he alone of all the Kikuyu tribe had been to England—the white man's country. In fact, so little did he refer to this episode in his life that few of his friends and relations, let alone more casual acquaintances, ever learned from him more than a little of what England was like.

When father next went on leave to England, Stefano obtained a post as chief interpreter in the High Court in Nairobi. It was a highly paid and very responsible post and he might well have been excused had it made him a little "swollen-headed," but his humility remained always the same.

Of that, my first stay in England, I cannot remember any details at all, and in December, 1906, we once more returned to Kabete. Owing to health reasons my father had stayed in England much longer than the ordinary furlough period of a year, but now his health was fully restored, and he was able to take up his work once more.

Almost the first task that he undertook, over and above the ordinary routine work of the station, was the demolition of the ramshackle and rapidly decaying mud and thatched house in which I had been born. Before leaving for England in 1905 my father had started building a stone bungalow with a corrugated iron roof and wooden ceiling. This had been completed in our absence, and we now moved into it. It was here that my brother Douglas was born in 1907, and this same house still serves as the home of the missionary-in-charge at Kabete to-day.

Compared with our earlier home it was luxurious in the extreme, and I remember that throughout my boyhood I thought of it as the most comfortable and well furnished house in the world. But to my mother, used as she was to all the comforts of her old home in Reading, even this lovely new stone house must at times have been a real trial, but she never let us see it.

It was about this time that Miss E. Laing came from South Africa to be our governess. Owing to urgent business, father was unable to go to the station to meet Miss Laing, so he sent one of our reliable native men with four others to meet her and to carry her the eight miles to Kabete in a hammock, which was the commonest means of transport and the most suited to the conditions of the time. The four hammock bearers were in tribal dress and at least one had a spear and the others short swords and Miss Laing never tired of telling us in later years of the utter terror which invaded her mind when she found that she was expected to trust herself to this party of " wild men." She imagined herself being carried out and murdered or made to serve as food for a cannibal feast. To us these men whom we knew personally seemed so harmless that it had never occurred to my father or mother that anyone could possibly be frightened of them, but to an English girl whose only knowledge of Africa had been gained in the South it must indeed have been a terrifying ordeal.

By this time my uncle and aunt, Mr. and Mrs. Burns, were established in Nairobi, and we used occasionally to go in to visit them. This meant hammocks for my mother and for us children and horseback for my father, and in addition there had to be people to carry in our luggage the eight miles to Nairobi, for it was out of the question in those days to think of going to Nairobi and back in a day; and usually a visit to Nairobi meant a stay of several days, as it was not worth expending all the energy and trouble involved by the journey simply for one night.

The luggage was carried by Kikuyu women and, indeed, all heavy load-carrying in those days was women's work. If timber or iron or cement had to be fetched from Nairobi, or if anything was to be carried in, a message was sent out to the nearby villages the night before to the effect that there would be load carrying work available next day. Invariably far more women and girls than we required would arrive next morning clamouring for the work and from them the necessary number would be selected. Kikuyu women and girls are trained from their earliest childhood to load carrying. Little girls of four or five start by carrying their infant brothers or sisters on their backs, and they also accompany their mothers and older sisters to the fields or to the river and come back carrying a little load, which becomes bigger and bigger as they themselves grow older. The method of load-carrying adopted by Kikuyu women is to support the weight by a strap over the forehead, the load itself being carried on the back. In order to do this satisfactorily, the strap is adjusted so that the bottom of the load rests on the top of the hips, and the carrier walks in a slightly bent position. I am writing this chapter in Edinburgh, and to my very great surprise I find that this identical method of load-carrying is in use here, and every day I see women passing down the street with heavy baskets on their backs, but with the weight partly taken by a strap over the forehead.

The weight which a Kikuyu woman will carry by this method is almost beyond belief. I myself have weighed loads of just over two hundred pounds which Kikuyu women had carried for a distance of over seven miles ! Another remarkable thing in the days when they acted as bearers for us to and from Nàirobi, was the way in which they would wrangle with each other, not for the lightest but for the heaviest loads. They took a very deep personal pride in their physical strength, and even pregnant women would think nothing of carrying a load of about sixty pounds into Nairobi, eight miles away, and then walking back home to prepare the evening meal for their families.

Again and again in Kenya protests had been made by scandalised Europeans against this habit of " making the womenfolk into beasts of burden," but I can say without hesitation that there was seldom any coercion involved. The women have been accustomed to load-carrying from early childhood and they scoff at the idea of letting the men folk carry the loads for them. It is easy to understand that, to the white man, the sight of a man walking along carrying nothing but a spear in front of a line of women and girls bent down under heavy loads, is intolerable. But (at any rate in olden days), it was necessary that the man or men should be unencumbered by loads and free to use their weapons at a moment's notice. While I do not want to suggest that the custom of letting their women folk do all the load-carrying should be indefinitely retained by the Kikuyu, I do maintain that load-carrying was not and is not the hardship that it is commonly thought to be.

From our earliest years my sisters and I became completely bi-lingual, and we learnt to speak and think in the Kikuyu language as easily as in English. We were constantly with Kikuyu people. All the house staff were Kikuyu boys or girls, and an African nurse whose name was Mariamu used to help in bathing us and putting us to bed, and also used to take us out for walks.

Mariamu used to thrill us with Kikuyu folk-tales and fables that we considered to be much more exciting than " Little Red Riding Hood " and " Jack and the Beanstalk," and I think that the best thing I can do is to give a translation of two of the stories which I remember most vividly.

" Once upon a time a lion and a hyæna and a hare met together and they decided to go down to the plains and make themselves a big communal garden and plant it with all kinds of food ; so they went, and they dug up the ground and they planted the seeds and went back to the forest to wait for harvest time.

" And when harvest time came the hare and the lion and the hyæna met together again, and got ready to go down to gather the crops. And the lion said to the other two, ' Let's make an agreement ; let's agree that if any one of us stops unnecessarily on the way down and fails to give an adequate reason, the other two shall kill and eat him.' And the hare said ' Yes ' and the hyæna said ' Yes,' and so it was agreed. And they set off. And after a little while the hare got tired, because his legs were shorter than the legs of the lion or the hyæna, so he stopped to rest. And the lion said, ' Hare has stood still. We must kill and eat him.' And the hare said, ' No, wait a moment. I've got a good reason. I'm thinking.' And the lion and the hyæna said, ' Oh ! What are you thinking about ? ' And the hare said, ' Oh, I was just thinking about those two rocks over there. The one is larger than the other, and the other is smaller than the big one ! ' And the lion and the hyæna who were very stupid said, ' Ah, yes. Hare was thinking about important things : he had a good reason to stop.' So they did not kill and eat him, but went on. And presently the hare was tired again, and he stopped ; and again the lion and hyæna said, ' Hare has stood still, let's eat him.' ' Oh, no,' said the hare, ' I've got a good reason. I'm thinking again.' ' Oh,' said the other animals, ' what are you thinking about this time ? ' And the hare said, ' I was just trying to think what people do with their old garments, when they get new ones.' And the lion and hyæna said, ' Yes. Hare was thinking about something important, we won't eat him,' and they went on. And after a time the hyæna* wanted a rest, and so he thought he would do as the hare had done, so he stood still. And the lion and the hare said, ' Ah ha ! Hyæna has stood still. Let's kill and eat him.' But the hyæna, trying hard to remember how the hare had managed, said, ' Oh, no ! Wait a minute, I'm thinking.' And the hare said sharply, ' Thinking ! What are *you* thinking about ? ' And the hyæna, who was a stupid animal, said, ' Oh, nothing.' So the hare and the lion said,

---

* The hyæna is both hated and feared by the Kikuyu because it eats human flesh, and so, in nearly all fables, it is made the object of derision.

' That's not a good reason for stopping ' and they killed and ate him, and went on together. And the lion hurried a lot, and presently the hare—tired once more—stood still again, and the lion said, ' Well, hare, you've stood still, I'm going to kill and eat you.' ' Oh, no,' said the hare, ' wait a minute. I had a good reason. I was thinking.' ' What were you thinking about ? ' said the lion. ' Well,' said the hare, ' do you see those two holes in the rocks over there ? I was just thinking that my ancestors used to run into one of those holes and out of the other and I was wondering if I could do the same.' And with that he rushed off and into one hole and round behind and out of the other, and in again and out again, and then he came back to the lion and said, ' Can you do that, Lion ? ' And the lion, who was very proud and did not want to admit that he could not do anything that hare could do, said, ' Oh, yes, I'll show you.' And so the lion rushed off towards the hole and he dashed in and he stuck. Then the hare came up quickly behind him and said, ' Lion has stood still. I'm going to kill and eat him.' ' Oh, no,' said the lion, ' no, no, no,' but he was too frightened—because he was stuck—to think, and could not give any reason, but just went on saying ' no, no, no.' So the hare, who could not of course kill the lion, started nibbling at the lion's buttocks. And the lion, thinking he saw a chance of saving himself, said, ' Oh, Hare, please, Hare, if you must eat me, come round and start at my head ; you make me feel so ashamed starting at that end.' And the hare said, ' Oh, no, Lion, that would make me shy, and anyway, I don't think I want to eat you.' And with that the hare left the lion stuck in the hole and went off to the plains and got in the harvest and had the whole lot to himself because he was very clever although so small."

In the other story the hare comes off worst, but the moral is the same, namely, that wisdom is better than any physical power or ability.

" A hare and a chameleon both wanted to marry the same maiden and they went to woo her, and the maiden wanted to marry the hare, who was beautiful, and not the chameleon, who had such ugly eyes and was a bad animal. But because she feared to anger the chameleon by giving this decision herself, she decided on a plan which she thought would certainly result in what she wanted, but which would work in such a way that the chameleon would lose his suit by his own failure. So she said to her suitors, ' You shall run a race, and whoever wins shall marry me.' And they both agreed to this, and so the maiden went and took a stool and put it some way away and then said to the two of them, ' Race, and whoever sits down on the stool first shall marry me.' And the hare was pleased because he knew that he could run faster than the chameleon. And so he agreed. And the chameleon agreed too, because he knew he was cleverer than the hare. So they got ready to race and just as they started the chameleon put up a hand and held on to the hare's tail. And the hare ran very fast and came to the stool and sat down. And the girl came up and the hare said, ' Look, I've won.' But just then they heard a squeaky voice from underneath the hare, and the hare got off the stool, and then they saw that the chameleon was on the stool, and he claimed that he was on the stool before the hare and that the hare had sat on him. And the maiden and the hare could not understand how it had happened, but as it was obviously true, and the agreement had been made, the chameleon married the girl."

By the time that our new stone house at Kabete was finished, the number of natives who had become adherents of the mission had increased so much that it became necessary to have a new and larger building to serve as church and school, and so my father set to work to erect a new wood and corrugated-iron church.

During his furlough my father had collected enough money from friends of the mission to purchase all the materials for the new church, and these were shipped to Mombasa, and then railed to Nairobi. The local authorities kindly agreed to send the trucks to a point on the railway only two and a half miles from the mission station, provided that the whole consignment was cleared within an hour of arrival. This formidable task was gladly undertaken and achieved by about 150 mission adherents.

In those days the Kikuyu who accepted Christianity did so in the face of much persecution, and nothing but a very deep, earnest faith could have supported them in the trials which they endured. Scarcely a week would pass without fresh evidence of the depth of the opposition which the majority of the Kikuyu felt towards this new religion. Boys who started to attend school and service would be caught by their parents or guardians and severely beaten and dragged home, only to return again as soon as they were free. Young men who came to the mission were scoffed at and taunted, and usually disinherited from all their family rights in land and property.

For girls it was even more difficult, and those who dared to come to the mission were often treated abominably. Because of this, girls had frequently to be given sanctuary at the station. At first, when there were only a few of them, they were given sleeping quarters in a room on the verandah of our own house, for only so were they safe from being kidnapped and carried off at night to be tortured for their faith. Even then they did not always escape, and I shall never forget how one poor girl was carried off and, when found at last, she had been beaten almost to unconsciousness and then hung up by her ankles to the roof of her mother's house with her head in the smoke of a fire. After she had been rescued, she was asked if she wanted to come back to the Mission, and in spite of threats from her mother and father that they would treat her in the same way again as soon as they could catch her once more, she came back to the Mission, so great was the hold of the teaching of Christ.

When I was six years old, two things happened which I can still recall with the utmost vividness, so deeply were they impressed upon my young mind. Mother used to have a bottle of permanganate of potash crystals from which she would occasionally take a grain or two and put them in warm water to make a disinfectant solution to bathe our cuts and scratches. I used to watch the water turning pink with the greatest interest and I longed to see what would happen if a much greater quantity of the crystals were put in. At last my opportunity came. One day I came into the dining-room and saw the bottle standing on the sideboard. There was no one about, so I decided to seize my chance and make the experiment. Going to the pantry I climbed up to the shelf and took down a small enamel cream jug and hurried with it to the place where our drinking water was kept, dipped the jug in, and filled it. Looking round to make sure that I was still unobserved, I went back to the dining-room and emptied about a dessertspoon full of crystals into the cream jug and watched with joy as the water turned not pink but a dark purple red verging upon black. Unfortunately for me, I then heard someone coming, so I rushed out and poured the mixture away and put the jug back, but in doing so I spilled a few drops of the solution on the sideboard cloth, where they left a horrid tell-tale stain, that burnt right into the material. Also unfortunately for me, the mixture had been so strong that the interior of the jug was irretrievably stained a dark brown. Naturally both the burnt cloth and the stained jug were discovered before long, and I could see by her face that my mother was very angry. She asked me if I had done it, and I lied boldly and said, " No." But she was sure that it must have been my work and told father when he came in at lunchtime. He too, asked me and I denied knowing anything about it. Certain that I was lying to them and minding that far more than the damage to the jug and the cloth, they both pleaded with me to own up. But I was adamant, and in the end I received the first real spanking of my life—for lying and being deceitful, but I never admitted that I had done it. So ended my first " scientific experiment " which had been carried out from a burning desire to see for myself what would happen.

The other incident that I remember most vividly, although it happened when I was so young, was nearly losing my sight. I and my sisters were playing one day under an acacia tree which was covered with a mass of creeping passion-fruit plant. We were climbing about in the branches when a small bit of dead leaf got into one of my eyes. It hurt considerably and I rushed into the house and it was taken out and my eye bathed with a boracic solution. But the bit of dry leaf must have been somehow infected with a germ, for in a day or two my eye was completely blocked up and the infection spread quickly to the other eye, so that I became temporarily blind.

Very fortunately for me, there was a Dr. Marsh living

not many miles away, where he had taken up farming, and I was taken over to him, and after several weeks of fearful pain I gradually recovered.

Soon after I had recovered, my parents' furlough became due, and on Boxing Day, 1910, we left Nairobi by train and were soon on board the steamer *Gaika* bound for England. On this occasion we were again accompanied by a Kikuyu boy—Ishmael Ithongo. While we were in England, Stefano was to start work in Nairobi as a High Court interpreter, and it had been arranged with the authorities that when my father returned to Kabete again he would once more have Stefano's services for his translation work. In view of this, the Government requested that another boy should be taken to England to learn English so as to be able to take Stefano's place as High Court interpreter when my father returned from leave.

As soon as we reached England, we all went to Reading to stay with my grandmother. We reached Reading on a Friday, late in January, 1911, and on the following Monday my two sisters and I went to school for the first time. Shortly afterwards my father acquired a house in Boscombe and we moved into what was destined to become our English home for several years after the war.

My parents had only meant to be in England for the one year of their furlough, but certain unavoidable circumstances soon made it certain that we could not hope to return so soon, and so it was decided that we should remain in England for at least two years.

Before going to Africa, my father had been a school-master, and as he hated the prospect of having nothing to do for any length of time, he accepted the suggestion of a Mr. Vernon Peek that between them they should start a new preparatory school in Boscombe, and in

January, 1912, I and three other boys became the first pupils at Gorse Cliff School.

I enjoyed the life at Gorse Cliff very much, chiefly, I think, because when it started there were only four of us, so that as the school grew I was able to grow accustomed to mixing with large numbers of other boys of my own age, gradually instead of suddenly finding myself feeling like a fish out of water, as I had done at the previous school.

Unfortunately, my mother's health became very much worse and she had to spend several long periods in a nursing home, and it was not until May, 1913, that at last we were able to sail for Africa once more. By then I and my sisters had acquired a good grounding in the ordinary preparatory school subjects, and as my parents naturally did not want us to lose the benefits of this they decided to take out someone to teach us. They chose Miss B. A. Bull, a London graduate who had specialised in classics, and she came back with us to Kabete.

CHAPTER III

WE RETURNED TO KABETE in May, 1913, when I was not yet ten years old, and if the Great War had not broken out, I should in the normal course of events have gone back to England to a public school when I was thirteen. I should presumably have passed through school in the usual way, and become a typical produce of the public school system, and this book would never have been written.

But the War did break out and as a result I remained at Kabete until late in 1919, and it was the events of those six years which have moulded all my subsequent career.

They were happy years, and full of incidents. As soon as we were once more settled in at Kabete Miss Bull began her duties as our tutor. For classroom we used a long side verandah of the house. It was cool and shady but not an ideal schoolroom for there was too much to distract our attention. Closing in the verandah from the view of curious passers-by was a hedge of mukungugu, a shrub which is grown by the Kikuyu people for the purpose of supporting the vines of the yam plants in their gardens, but one which makes an ideal garden hedge. Between the hedge and the verandah was a small patch of flower garden with beautiful roses (which flowered all the year round), luxuriously growing verbena, and thick bushes of plumbago. This flower garden and the hedge behind it were the happy hunting ground of a number of chameleons, as well as the resort of many birds, some of which nested regularly in full view of the verandah.

It was exceedingly difficult to concentrate upon the declension of a Latin noun if, out of the corner of one's eye, a chameleon could be seen slowly and deliberately climbing up a stem to get within tongue's reach of a blue-bottle fly sitting at the top. Would the poor hungry reptile get within range before the fly moved on ? Would we be watching at the right moment to catch a sight of the long sticky-tipped tongue as it shot out at its target, or would we miss that and only look again in time to see the jaws opening and shutting as the blue-bottle became a meal ?

One day a whole lesson was completely spoilt— from Miss Bull's point of view—by a terrific struggle between a chameleon and a brilliant green tree snake. The snake had seized the chameleon by the back, but the chameleon was a great fighter and it bit and struggled and defied the efforts of the snake to get a better grip until at last, losing patience, Miss Bull called to a native boy to come and kill the snake and stop the fight. It was a harmless snake and we children protested vigorously. By the time the fight and argument were over the hour allotted to that particular lesson had passed. Such distractions as these made lesson time pass very quickly indeed but I fear they were not very good from the point of view of our studies.

After tea Miss Bull used to take us out for a walk (or perhaps it would be more accurate to say that we used to take Miss Bull for a wild scramble) and our favourite walk was to three waterfalls which were visible from the house. The first of these three falls we called Gibberish. It was the highest and most spectacular of the three and had a great big, wild fig tree growing at the bottom on one side. This tree was so old that it was hollow at the bottom, and you could climb into the hole. Gibberish was my sister Julia's " country " over which she was " queen." When we were in her territory we others had to take our orders from her. Julia's " Prime Minister " was a " Mr. Nobody," and as soon as we arrived the first thing to be done was for my sister Julia to go to the " Palace "—the hole in the tree—and get the news of what had happened since we were there last. After whispered conversations with " Mr. Nobody," the " Queen " would come out and tell us all the news, and then we'd go off to explore, and collect maidenhair ferns and wild flowers to take home to my mother. Before leaving the waterfall the same ceremonial of an audience with " Mr. Nobody " in the hole in the tree had to be gone through and " Mr. Nobody " was given his instructions to protect the kingdom till we came again.

The second waterfall was regarded as Gladys' kingdom. It was much less spectacular and its only interesting feature was a natural bridge beneath which the water flowed. This was " Cattish," and the " Prime Minister " of Cattish lived in a cave under the natural bridge. Below Cattish was the third fall, which was my kingdom ; it went by the name of " Doggish." Occasionally we visited all three waterfalls on the same afternoon, but more usually we only went to one " as there was so much to do."

Towards the end of the six years which I am writing about at the moment, we outgrew these " fairy " games, but in spite of this the waterfalls still held their attraction over us, and they became the scenes of other activities as we shall see.

Miss Bull did not stay very long with us at Kabete, and in her place we had a Miss Broome from Natal.

Miss Broome was young and as fond of scrambling

walks as we were, so that she joined in them as one of us, instead of being a rather unwilling onlooker. As a teacher she was also much more successful from our point of view, and we three children loved her dearly.

Unfortunately, after the war had been in progress for some time Miss Broome decided that her duty lay in nursing the wounded, and much to our sorrow, left us. So attractive had she made our lessons, however, that we had come to like Latin and Algebra and the other subjects instead of hating them, and from then until we went back to England in 1919 we taught ourselves as best we could.

My father was, of course, fully qualified to teach us, and he tried to give us a little time each day to supervise our studies, but as the work of the station was already very much more than one man could really manage, he naturally could not spend much time with us.

If our lessons suffered after Miss Broome left us we made up for it by gaining a great deal of general knowledge in our free time.

Not far from the house father had planted a lot of black wattle trees and this plantation was one of our favourite retreats. We called it " The New Forest," and as it was beautifully shady we could spend even the hottest hours of the day there without fear of sunstroke.

When I was eleven I built a hut down at the bottom end of the plantation. It was a one-roomed hut with a floor area of about eight feet by ten, and we used to have great fun in it. Each of us had our own small garden where we grew flowers and also sweet potatoes, maize and peas, and one of our joys was to cook potatoes down in my hut.

Later on, when I was thirteen, I started building

myself a three-roomed house. I earned money with which to buy the materials by trapping wild animals for their skins, and by trapping birds and beasts for zoos. But I will tell of these activities in another chapter.

Having decided on a site for my new house, I started building operations in earnest when our holidays started. I engaged two native labourers to assist me, and then I negotiated with a neighbour for some trees from which I could cut building poles. This done, I and my two men then went and felled the trees and when they were cut and everything was ready, I enlisted the help of my African playmates to help me in bringing the poles to the site.

In language and in mental outlook I was more Kikuyu than English, and it never occurred to me to act other than as a Kikuyu. I was nearly grown up in my own eyes and in the eyes of my native companions (I was in fact only just over thirteen), and as they were beginning to plan building themselves their own bachelor quarters, I naturally did likewise.

By Kikuyu custom a man who wants to build himself a house must initiate the work by himself or with the help of a little hired labour, but once the preliminary work is done, he has the right to call upon members of his age group and his friends to come and help him in his work, and when it is finished he then provides a feast for those who helped him, but there is no other payment. When the ground for the house had been cleared and the poles had been cut, I therefore called upon the members of my age group to come and help carry the poles and erect the structure of the house. This done, we went into the bush and cut small straight withies which were to be used in making the walls. Meanwhile my two hired men

were set to cut down dry banana leaves called
" Matharara," and also dry banana bark. The former
were for the walls of the house and the latter for the
roof. In all the work my age group friends helped me
and eventually the house was ready except for doors
and windows.

My ambition in building this, my second house,
had been to live in it, but my parents decided that it
was not sufficiently damp-proof and well-built for that
to be really safe, and so I was only allowed to use it
as a day room and study. That, however, did not
satisfy me at all, and so I began planning a third and
much better house.

This, my third house, which I built when I was
fourteen, had wattle and daub walls—lined with a
layer of plaster made from a white pipeclay. It was
fitted too with proper doors and windows, and in it
I lived until we came back to England three years
later.

I wanted freedom and independence, I wanted to
possess things of my own, and so I worked for them
and built my house. It was a good house although
most of my readers, if they could have seen it, would
have called it a hovel. Save that it was much smaller—
it only had three rooms—it was a far better house than
the one in which I had been born and which had
been my parents' home for four whole years.

In my own house I slept and worked and, in fact,
did everything except feed ; for my parents insisted
that I should still feed with the family, which was
essentially sound.

The Kikuyu boys who had helped me in my house
building, naturally called upon me to help them in their
turn, and I well remember my mother's anger when
I came home late one afternoon having been away on

one of these jobs all day without letting her know where I was going. I had been far too busy helping one of the members of my age group to think about meals and had not realised that by failing to turn up for lunch I would cause my parents much anxiety.

In some of our activities I became the leader of my age group although in others I was content to be led. Most, although not all, of those I was mixing with were adherents of the Mission, and I organised them into a junior football team. Our first match was played when I was thirteen, and we challenged the junior team of the Church of Scotland Mission eight miles away. They were a bigger and heavier crowd than we were, but we were more accustomed to working as a team and we beat them.

Like the rest of the team I always played barefooted, and I never found any difficulty in kicking the ball with my bare toes. It is all a matter of practice, I suppose, because when years later I tried again after having been in England for some time I found I could no longer do it without considerable pain.

On their part the boys of my age group taught me to play their own traditional games, of which the game of spearing the hoop was far and away the best.

Our leader in this game was always a boy called Magua. The game is usually played with about six aside, but the numbers can be increased or decreased a little without spoiling the game or offending against the rules. Each player is armed with a long wooden sapling sharpened to a point at one end and, the captains having been chosen, they pick their sides. A small hoop with a diameter of about a foot is then produced and the teams take up their positions in a long line, each player standing about 10 yards from the next. The players of one side are one end of the line and those

of the other side at the other end with each captain
at the outside end of his line, like this

0   0   0   0   0   ⁺0   0   0   0   0   0   0   0   0
captain   captain

The captain of one side then takes the hoop and walks
to about the point marked with a cross on the diagram.
This point is near the inside end of his own line of men.
He may go as far forward as he likes, and about 15
or more yards in front of them at his discretion, but
his decision will depend upon the skill of his own team
and the question of whether or not he wants to effect
a rescue of some of his own side who have been captured.

He then bowls the hoop in such a way that it rolls
very fast along the front of the opponent's line at
anything from 15 to 30 yards distance from them.
At this small fast-moving target each of the opposing
side in turn throws his wooden spear, the object of
course being to stick the spear through the hoop and
into the ground.   As soon as this has been achieved by
one of the opponents, the captain of the side which
bowled the hoop chooses one of his own side who has
to go and take up his position exactly at the point where
the opponent was standing when he scored his hit.
From this point the player must throw his spear so that
it too lands inside the circle formed by the hoop as it
now lies.   That is to say, he has to throw at a stationary
target, which should be easier to hit than a moving one,
but is not, unless you have had a great deal of practice.

Should the thrower miss, the captain tells another
of his team to try, and the man who missed becomes a
prisoner and is placed at the far end of his opponent's
line beyond their captain.   Of course, sometimes the
second thrower misses too, and, if so, he also becomes

a prisoner, and the third player must try. If by any
chance every single one of the players of one side fails,
then they would all be prisoners, and the game would
be over at once, but I have never actually seen that
happen in the first round.

When one of the players has succeeded in transfixing
the stationary target, the captain of the other side in
his turn bowls the hoop, and the same process is gone
through. If one or more prisoners has been taken, at
the next throw the captain of the side does everything
in his power to bowl the hoop in such a way that all
the opposing team will miss it and it will reach the
prisoners. If he succeeds in doing this, and the
prisoners can themselves spear it (they, and only they,
are allowed to move forward out of the line and approach
more closely to the line of the hoop to do so) they have
the right to escape, but they are only considered free
if they manage to run fast round their captors and
touch one of their own team.

The moment, therefore, that a prisoner spears the
hoop, members of his own side run to meet him while
his opponents try to catch him before he can escape.

The game ends when one or other side has made all
the others prisoner, and if at any point the captain
of a side elects to try the standing throw himself and
is made a prisoner, one of the others becomes deputy
captain until he can be released.

The game, of course, goes back to ancient tribal days
and was a form of training for both hunting and war-
fare. To be proficient every player must be able to
hit a small target with his spear either when it is
moving fast or when it is stationary, and the two things
require a very different action and form of skill. A
player must also be a fast runner, or he can never escape
once he has been captured.

Among others this game formed a *part* of the preparation of the boys for the initiation ceremony which would transform them from boys to men. The training included not only skill with weapons (we were taught sword play with single sticks, and we were taught how to throw a club accurately in a game called "throwing the club") but also it involved teaching in the rules of behaviour of the tribe, the sexual laws and customs, etc. ; but I do not propose to discuss intricate anthropological matters in this book.

I did not undergo by any means all of the training, nor did my companions, for already as a result of their being Mission adherents the training was being to some extent modified.

Most of the boys in the group were probably older than I was, but as none of them knew their ages it was not possible to be certain. The whole question of the age of Africans is a very interesting one, and I am convinced that in the past we always considerably underestimated their ages. My reason for stating this is based upon observation of boys and girls born at Kabete Mission, whose date of birth was registered in the Baptismal register. Judging by appearances, I have formed the opinion that they must be about eleven or twelve years old and then, when I have looked them up in the register, I have found that they were actually thirteen or fourteen.

Similarly, I know a Kikuyu boy and a girl who were both born on the same day as I was, and when we were about seventeen they were taken to be much younger than me. On the other hand, five years later, when I went back to Kabete, the boy still looked younger than I did, whereas the girl—who had married at eighteen—had aged a lot and by that time looked several years older than her real age.

This boy—his name is Ndekei—has for the past ten years worked with me on my scientific expeditions in East Africa, and last year I asked an European who had had long experience of Africans and who happened to be visiting our camp, if he could guess at Ndekei's age and he put him down as four years my junior.

In this connection too, we have other very interesting information which shows that natives often live to a very great age and that we Europeans tend to under-estimate their ages. When my father went to Kabete in 1901, Kavetu, the father of Stefano who went with us to England in 1905, was already the father of a number of children and had been married for about thirty years. As he could not have married until he had served seven years as a warrior after initiation, he must have been initiated at least 37 years before 1901. Moreover, from what we know now of the age at which initiation used to take place in boys, he was probably about 18 years old when he was initiated. In other words, Kavetu must have been fully 55 in 1901, and be over 90 now. He is a great grandfather and as a result of many illnesses is very weak now. I have not infrequently met men who had lived to be great grandfathers, and I know of one who was a great great grandfather when he died, so I think we may safely conclude that it is not uncommon for Kikuyus to live at least to the age of 90, as many of Kavetu's contemporaries are still alive.

My old friend, Karugi, who kept the braziers alight to warm the room when I was born, was a young newly married man of about 26 in 1901, so that he must be about 60 now, but he still thinks nothing of walking 16 miles in a day, while two other men of his age group—both grandfathers—recently walked 50 miles with me in a single day each carrying a thirty-pound load !

After Miss Broome had left us to do war nursing, I began to help father in taking some of the classes in the boys' school, and I learnt a lot myself while doing so. The boys of about my own age who composed the majority of my class were very quick to learn, and quite as intelligent as English boys of their own age would have been under similar circumstances.

During the last few years there has been a good deal of discussion concerning the mental ability of the natives of Kenya, and one of many views that has been put forward is that they are inherently inferior in mental qualities to the white men.

I find myself unable to agree with this view. Under present conditions it is, of course, inevitable that the outlook and general knowledge of the African native is more limited than that of the white man who makes his home in Kenya, but that does not seem to me to be in any way due to an inferior quality of brain, but to be mainly due to the accidents of environment and opportunity.

At the present time even those Africans who pass through the native schools in Kenya are inevitably less educated than English boys who pass through the European schools. This can be attributed to a number of things. In the first place, the education available to most of the natives in Kenya is of a very elementary character. They learn to read and write in their own language and are taught a little elementary mathematics, geography and history, and possibly some hygiene. Comparatively few are taught any English and the number that acquire a really good knowledge of that language form only a minute percentage of the total native population.

As far as Englishmen are concerned, not only is the education which is available to us at school much wider in its scope and more elaborate in detail, but also it opens the doors to a very great deal that we may describe as indirect education. By reading books, articles and newspapers we learn probably much more of the things that go to make us into intelligent members of European society than we do from actual school lessons. Similarly, we have the immense advantage of all the education in its widest sense that we derive from daily contacts with our parents, relatives and friends. In the ordinary way the native of Kenya has none of these advantages. It is therefore not at all surprising that when his intelligence and general mental alertness are judged by English standards, he does not compare favourably with the white man.

Proofs of the very real mental ability of the natives of Kenya is amply demonstrated by their achievements in a wide range of activities in spite of the handicaps I have mentioned. They are to be found occupying such varied posts as typesetters for newspapers, telegraphists, mechanics, etc. This they are doing in spite of having started with very little education in the narrow, and still less in the wider sense.

In connection with African education in Kenya, it has even been suggested (but not categorically stated) that possibly education of European type may be the cause of the alleged increase of insanity among the natives of the Colony. I do not believe that this has any foundation in fact. That there is an increase in the number of mentally deficient *adults* is, I think, correct ; but I suspect that the true explanation is to be found in the laws which we have imposed upon the native population and not the meagre education which we are providing for them. Among most tribes in the past, children who were mentally afflicted were killed, so that it was very rare to come across an insane person. Even adults who became insane in later life were commonly either put to death or expelled from the tribe and left to starve.

According to British law the killing of insane people is murder, and is punishable as such. In consequence during the past thirty years the practice of killing insane people has been slowly but surely checked. The natural result is that there is a marked increase in the number of cases of insanity, and it has become necessary to provide asylums for mentally deranged natives.

I will not discuss here the ethics or humanitarian aspects of this grave problem, but I must protest against the insinuation that it is education which is the cause of increasing insanity, and against the possible attempt to use this view to justify the denial of education to my African friends.

Although I was only eleven when the Great War broke out in 1914, I can remember the terrible shock that the news caused us. At once the country was filled with all sorts of alarming and untrue rumours. The Germans had crossed the border from German East Africa, had captured the railway line and were advancing upon Nairobi ; A German battleship had bombarded Mombasa and blown the town to bits ! Nairobi was likely to be attacked from the air ! A German Zeppelin had been seen (people were positive of it) flying over on its way to German East Africa ; and so on.

One of the first things that happened was that all able-bodied men rallied to Nairobi to volunteer, and a force was hastily recruited to defend strategic points along the German-British boundary.

Next came the demand for large numbers of natives to act as " carriers " in the campaign in German East Africa. To a large extent these " carriers " were conscripted against their will, and I can vividly remember the scenes which occurred. Natives would throng to the Mission begging my father to intervene and prevent the " Makanga " or native tribal police (who were only carrying out their orders) from forcing them to go off as " carriers." In particular, young men who were attending school strongly resented the fact that again and again the Makanga singled them out for this conscription and left their own " heathen " friends unmolested.

Then came the formation of the Volunteer Carrier Corps, which was organised by some of the missionaries. This was a very different proposition, and hundreds of mission natives volunteered at once, and many of my own friends (not those of my age group, who, like myself, were still too young), left home to go to the war zone.

Soon after the first party of volunteers had gone to the front letters started coming back to their relatives at Kabete asking for various things to be sent to them and we were kept busy helping illiterate relatives to decipher their letters and then addressing parcels containing the presents that were to be sent back.

The most constant demand was for snuff and for books. The Kikuyu are a great snuff-taking people, and they soon found that snuff was not provided with their rations, and, what was worse, that it was often quite unobtainable in the districts where they were serving, so they wrote home for snuff, and their relatives came to us for help in securely packing it and forwarding it to the fighting area.

The books that were in demand were school books

and religious books, so that, in their spare time, the mission volunteers could continue their education, and also their preparation for baptism.

Most of the white officers in charge of the Volunteer Carrier Corps were missionaries, and before long one of them sent us a whole series of lantern slides illustrating the life of the Corps at the front.

My father entrusted me with the first showing of these slides to an audience of friends and relatives, wives and children, sisters and sweethearts, at Kabete. The slides, of course, did not show people recruited from our area alone, and I shall never forget the pleasure that was expressed every time some local person was recognisable in one of the pictures. A Kabete man who had volunteered was renowned as a clown, and was in particular remarkably clever at walking on his hands. One of the slides showed him entertaining his companions at one of the base camps, and this slide was applauded again and again.

The Carrier Corps was seldom right up at the firing line, but the casualties were nevertheless very severe, chiefly as the result of illness. Lists of those who had died came through from time to time, and the relatives had to have the sad news broken to them. In addition, men who had been invalided back to the hospitals, and thence home, began to come back with harrowing tales of the conditions under which much of the work had to be done. In spite of these facts, fresh detachments of volunteers were still coming forward, although a great deal of conscription was also necessary in order to keep the Carrier Corps up to the requisite strength.

Towards the end of 1918, the influenza epidemic that swept the world burst upon us at Kabete, and in a short time the people all round us were dying in hundreds. It was simply awful. The medical services available to the natives were completely inadequate, and all of us at Kabete were kept busy trying to help as far as we could. Supplies of quinine and other drugs rapidly ran out, and we had to send urgently to Nairobi for more. One of the chief causes of the very high mortality rate among the Kikuyu—in some cases the whole population of a village was wiped out—was the natives' own attempts to cure themselves. Among the symptoms of the disease was appalling pain in the form of headaches and aches all over the body. In the ordinary way, the standard Kikuyu remedy for such pains was " cupping " and they naturally tried this out, but with disastrous results, for the bleeding lowered their vitality and resistance to the disease, and probably caused far more deaths than would otherwise have occurred.

As soon as we at Kabete realised this, we started an extensive campaign to try to explain that as far as the aches which accompanied influenza were concerned, cupping was a very dangerous remedy. But it was not at all easy to convince the Africans of the truth of this, for often the patient did get some relief from his pain as a result, and death did not follow until some days later, so that cause and effect were not at all obvious.

Just when the worst was over, but while there were still hundreds seriously ill or only convalescent, the news came through that the Armistice had been signed, and the war was over. There had been previously one or two false rumours of the end of the war which made us hesitate to believe the news, but once it was confirmed, we set to work to spread the tidings far and wide, by messengers.

I shall never forget how I myself ran all over the countryside from one Kikuyu village to another, telling them that the war was over, that their friends and relatives would soon be home again, and that there would be a thanksgiving service that evening at the Mission. But again and again the news was received in stony silence, because of the influenza. The people were so weak and so afraid that the disease which was harassing them would kill them as it had already killed so many, that the news of the end of the war hardly meant anything to them.

One man who was still seriously ill, and whom I tried to cheer up, expressed very poignantly what many of the others felt but could not put into simple language. He said: "What does it matter that the war is over now, when my son comes home he will find his mother and his wife and me too, dead?"

CHAPTER IV

Owing to the density of the native population all round Kabete there were comparatively few large wild animals in the district, but there were plenty of small beasts and many birds. In the early days, two elephants that were presumably trekking from one forest zone to another did pass through Kabete district, and next morning my father was called to see the tracks which they had left, but that was the only time wild elephants came anywhere near us. Lions were exceedingly rare, too. Occasionally a stray lion would wander into the district from the less populated Masai country a few miles to the south east, but it seldom stayed, for there was very little satisfactory cover.

Once, just after the beginning of the war, two lions came into the neighbourhood and stayed for about a week, causing a good deal of trouble while they were there. But, foolishly, they did not confine their activities to killing native cattle ; one day they killed a fine bullock up at the Government Veterinary Research Laboratory, about two miles from our house. When the partially eaten carcase was found next morning the officials at the Research Station built a thorn hide near the remains and two of them decided to go and spend the night there waiting for the lions to return, when they would shoot them. Just before sunset one of the junior workers at the Laboratory announced that he would go and sit in the thorn

shelter until his seniors came later in the evening.
He was told that he could do so but that he would
merely be wasting his time, and had much better come
and have a " sundowner" instead. However, he
persisted, and within a few minutes of sunset and before
it was really quite dark he made out the forms of two
animals approaching the carcase. Thinking that they
were probably large hyænas that would eat up much
of the meat before the lions came back later on in
the evening, he fired, and to his surprise and joy found
that he had killed a magnificent black-maned lion.

Next morning we heard the news down at the
Mission, and my sisters and I went off to see the lion;
and that, with one exception, was the only wild lion
I ever saw in Kenya, dead or alive, until I was twenty-
six years old. Moreover, so far as I know, my father
has only once seen a wild lion, in spite of having spent
most of the past thirty-six years in the country. This
was on an occasion when we all had a magnificent
view of a lioness chasing an antelope, when we were
travelling in the train from Nairobi to Mombasa.

Leopards were a little more common than lions
in the Kabete district, but they were very seldom
seen. Once when I was very young my father was
asked by the natives of a village about two miles away
to come and shoot a leopard that was making a habit
of killing their goats. He took his rifle and was led
by a small boy of about thirteen to a valley where the
leopards spent most of their time. Arrived in the
valley, the lad led my father to a small cave in the
cliffs and told him that this was the leopard's lair.
To prove it, the little boy then crawled into the dark
hole and presently emerged dragging two very small
leopard cubs ! My father always says that he was
worried enough when he saw the boy go unarmed

into this cave, but he thought that probably it was a mistake anyhow, and that it was not the leopard's lair at all. When the boy came back with the cubs, he was horrified at the thought of what would have happened if either of the parent animals had been at home. I imagine, however, that this boy knew quite well that the leopards were not in the cave at that time. Probably he and his companions who herded the goats and sheep in the valley had been to the place on many occasions, and they knew that the parent leopards always growled when anyone came near. I don't say this in order to detract from the boy's bravery in any way, but simply to suggest that perhaps he was not quite as foolhardy as he appeared to be.

The cubs were brought back to the Mission, and at first we intended to keep them as pets. But my father was afraid that if we kept the cubs alive the parents would come round and possibly be dangerous to us children, so he decided to kill them. Next day he discovered that had he kept them alive he could have obtained £10 each for them from a man in Nairobi!

I think that probably my father was very wise in deciding against allowing us to have these leopard cubs as pets. Many people in Kenya have had lion and leopard cubs as pets, but there is always a danger involved.

Both lions and leopards if caught young enough can be made very tame, and the danger lies in just that very fact. Their owners who have brought them up, and have become attached to them, are apt to forget that one day some quite trivial incident may infuriate their pets and that they will then be at their mercy. Not a few tragedies have happened in this way, and I firmly believe that it is unwise to try and make pets of either lions or leopards unless you definitely make up your mind that as soon as they grow up they must no longer be kept, even in semi-freedom. In view of this it is hardly worth having them as pets at all, because nothing is more awful than having to condemn pets that have had a free early life to subsequent perpetual imprisonment. Many a lion and leopard that has started life as a family pet in Kenya has ended up behind bars in a zoo, and I know of nothing that makes me so unhappy as seeing such creatures kept under these conditions.

I am afraid I have by no means always thought this, and in the past I have helped to supply wild animals for zoos, but I now wish I had never done so.

In connection with keeping lions as pets, I have known several very amusing things happen in Kenya. Some of our friends once had a lion cub as a pet, and when it was more than half grown it was still free and used to roam about the garden and the house as it chose. One day a visitor came to call, knowing nothing of the existence of this pet. As she was walking up the drive to the house, she suddenly saw a lion emerge from the shrubbery and approach her. Thinking it was a wild one, she let out a shriek for help and made a dash towards the house. The lion, thinking it was a game, rushed after her, and as she reached the verandah she looked back and to her horror saw it was catching her up. Still thinking she was being chased by a wild lion, the lady rushed for the room of a door which opened from the verandah, pushed it open and went in, but before she could shut it behind her the lion too was pushing against it, so, in terror, she left it and dashed for another door at the far end of the room, knocking over tables and chairs as she did so. The lion thought this was a magnificent game, and followed hard, so that at the next door the same thing happened.

Some of the family witnessed the chase up the path and on to the verandah, but they were at first so convulsed with mirth that they could not intervene. Fortunately for the visitor, they pulled themselves together after the lion and the visitor had disappeared indoors, and the lion was called off, but not before the visitor had almost collapsed with terror.

On another occasion several years later, I was playing tennis with some friends who had a young tame lion. My partner in the game was a girl who, like myself, was a guest, but she apparently had not been told about the pet lion. Suddenly I saw her throw down her racquet and rush headlong for the house, shouting ' Lion ' ! Looking round, I saw the lion cub coming out of a rose bed near the tennis court close to where the girl had been standing !

Although we children at Kabete never had either a lion or leopard as pet, we had plenty of others, both domestic and wild.

We always had dogs, and more often than not they were mongrels ; but to my mind there are few purebred dogs that are as faithful or as useful as mongrels can be. I know, of course, that to many dog lovers this is a very heretical view, but our own various mongrel dogs live in my memory and prejudice my point of view.

For instance, there was Toronco, the first. She was a cross between a bob-tailed sheepdog and a Great Dane ! She was of large build, steely grey in colour, with a fairly shaggy coat and a long tail, but it would have been hard to find a better watchdog at night, or a more loving and faithful companion by day. She had only one vice. The long flapping leather skirts of the Kikuyu women always aroused her anger, and many a time and oft did she receive a beating for chasing Kikuyu women and biting at their skirts.

Trusty was another mongrel. She was Toronco's daughter, and her father, as far as we ever knew, was an Airedale. She was short-haired, khaki brown in colour, and much smaller than her mother, but, like her, a very good watchdog and hunter.

Between them Toronco and Trusty accounted for a number of wild cats and other animals that used to raid our fowlyard, and one of my earliest and most thrilling hunts was with those two dogs when I was about twelve years old.

The most curious looking mongrel that we ever had was Trusty's successor, Polly. His mother was a pedigree spaniel and his father a dachshund! He had the body build of spaniel but on a more elongated scale. His ears took after those of his mother, but, owing to their being covered in very short hair like his father's, they had a most comic effect. His legs were short and his feet turned out like a dachshund's, but in spite of this he was a very good runner. I've seldom seen a more comic sight than that of Polly winning a dog race at a local gymkhana which was organised at Kabete Veterinary Laboratory to amuse a number of soldiers who were in a convalescent camp there during the war.

All sorts of dogs were entered for the race, big dogs and little dogs, long-legged dogs and short-legged, and Polly beat them all! Polly was an excellent retriever and used to get wildly excited at the very sight of a shot-gun, but he was also a great coward where all wild animals were concerned.

All these dogs of ours were very great friends with the cats, of which we had almost too many. Each of us children had our own especial cat, and all of them, save the old mother and one other, were black.

One of the great troubles with the cats was the problem of protecting their kittens from the attacks of the awful ' siafu ' or biting ants ; in fact, the siafu were the chief menace to all our pets.

I remember one day being awakened by one, my sister's cat, Cinders, miaowing horribly outside my bedroom door. I got up and opened the door and she quickly led me to the box where her kittens were. To my horror, I saw that the whole box was a solid moving mass of siafu and no kittens were visible at all, although the cries coming from the black mass and also the convulsive movements in the box showed that the kittens, who had not yet got their eyes open, were there.

I rushed for help, and with my sisters and my father we got the kittens out and first of all dipped them again and again into a pail of water to get the ants off. Having thus got rid of the worst of the ants, we spent the next hour or two each with a kitten, from which we had to remove the remaining ants one by one. These ants have such strong nippers that, if you simply pull at them, the body comes away and leaves the head and nippers still sticking to the flesh. How those poor kittens ever survived their ordeal I do not know, but in the end they recovered.

On another occasion a regiment of siafu attacked one of the litters of puppies, and we had to rescue them in a similar way ; while once, when they got into the hen house, they killed a number of sitting hens, who valiantly stayed on their nests, preferring to be eaten alive rather than desert their task of incubation.

These siafu must account for the death of thousands

of young birds and animals throughout Africa every year, and they are one of the reasons why rabbits, even if they were introduced, would almost certainly never be able to establish themselves and become a plague as they have in Australia.

Siafu live underground in a great nest, and from this the army sallies forth in long and regular lines in search of food. If you follow along their paths carefully, you can always find their nest, but it may be as much as a half mile away from the place where you first notice the path. Seeing that they forage so far from home, these ants—unlike many others that never stray very far from their nests—work in a most methodical manner. As the line of worker ants advances on its march, the big warrior ants take up their position on either side of the path, and stay there looking for all the world like policemen lining a road during some ceremonial procession through the streets of London. The army moves on and on, and the throng of ants that move along the path formed by the warriors includes many other warriors that are moving forward to take up their position on the sides as the regiment of workers moves slowly forward. Ahead of the main body go scouts, and as soon as they locate anything like a carcase of a dead animal or a nest of young birds, or the lair of some young and helpless animal, they seem to call the army towards them. Once such a food supply is located the workers start biting off little bits and hurrying back along the path towards the nest, only to return again for more.

Meanwhile from all along the route, scouts are also sent out on either side in search of further food supplies, and if anything further is located a path is made to it and lined by warriors, and a part of the regiment is diverted to this new spot.

When food enough has been obtained the regiment retires in a well-organised way, and in the end all that is left is a well-beaten and quite clear track which has been trodden down and imprinted upon the ground by the feet of thousands of passing ants.

Just after the end of the war I heard that one or other of the Zoos in England (I can't remember which) was offering £5 for a queen siafu ant alive, and I decided to try and obtain the prize.

I found a nest of siafu not far from our house, and proceeded to make plans to raid it and get the queen out alive. In order to do this without being too badly bitten, I clothed myself in Wellington boots drawn over long trousers and tied tightly to prevent any ants (as I fondly hoped) from finding their way in. I also covered the outside of the boots with paraffin which in the ordinary course of events will keep siafu off. I had my hands protected with gloves, also soaked in paraffin, and I had a quantity of paraffin available to sprinkle over the warrior ants if they were too troublesome.

Thus prepared, I set to work to dig down into the nest in search of the queen ant. At first all went well, but as I got deeper down and near the centre of the nest, the ants seemed to realise that their queen was in danger, and after that I was quickly routed. The warriors no longer seemed to mind the smell of paraffin at all, and very soon swarmed up my boots and all over my clothes. I found that my clothing was no protection either, for the ants found their way in at a number of points, and in a short time I was being horribly bitten all over my anatomy, and, what was worse, I was so well fastened up that I could not get my hands inside my clothing to remove the ants that were biting me. At first I tried to carry on with my task and ignore the pain, but before long I was nearly driven mad and had to rush away, hastily remove every stitch of clothing and pull off hundreds of warrior ants. After that I did not try again, and I held these ants in much greater respect! I am convinced that if anyone did win that £5 they more than deserved it.

In addition to cats and dogs we children had at one time and another an enormous variety of wild pets. All round Kabete a little bush antelope, known as a duiker, was very common, and natives frequently used to bring in young duiker to the Mission. The first three or four of these that we tried to rear died after only a few days, but in the end we discovered how to nurse them satisfactorily and we had several that eventually grew to maturity,

They used to live in the large fowl run with the fowls, and one of our tasks each morning was to get food for them. They were particularly fond of young rose shoots, but of course we could not feed them with those except for a rare treat, or our garden would soon have been ruined. They were also very fond of mulberry leaves, of sweet potato vine and of a small creeping plant which the natives call " Mukengeria ", all of which were available in plenty around Kabete. These duiker were exceedingly tame, and could perfectly well have been allowed to wander at liberty in the garden, but we never dared let them do this because of dogs.

Our own dogs would probably have been all right, but we were always afraid that visitors would bring dogs which would immediately kill our pets, and so they had to live in the semi-captivity of the large fowl run.

One of our male duiker unfortunately developed a most unexpected habit. He took to killing fowls, and then chewing their heads off. How he actually killed them we never actually discovered, for he was never caught in the act, but in the end he became such a menace in the fowl run that we had to build a special new enclosure to which he and the other duiker were transferred.

Another most interesting and unusual pet was a colobus monkey. One day when we were at lunch we heard a party of natives approaching the house, all talking most excitedly, and we went out to see what the noise was about. As the crowd came nearer we could hear from time to time a sound that was half-way between a grunt and a roar, and each occasion that this happened the crowd would break up a bit, only to gather round a central figure once more. Presently the cortege arrived at the house, and we saw that the central figure was a man who was holding a colobus monkey by its tail, and was thus dragging it along. The poor beast was very tired and exhausted, but he strongly resented the treatment that he was receiving and every now and then would summon up enough energy to make a grab at one of the crowd who came within reach, making the angry roaring noise which we had first heard as he did so.

My father immediately went off to the carpentry shop and hastily improvised a cage out of an old packing case, and into this the colobus was put. We then offered him some water, which he drank greedily. We planned at first, to keep him only for a few days until he recovered his strength (for he was quite worn out) and then to release him. Meanwhile we tried to discover what he was doing in this district, for the nearest forest of the type favoured by the colobus monkeys was many miles away. Then we noticed that he was an exceedingly old male, and we came to the conclusion

that he had been driven out by some younger and
stronger male and had been wandering aimlessly
about in search of a new patch of forest.

Had we released him anywhere near Kabete he would
have found no forest for sanctuary, and in travelling
through the thickly populated country would have
almost certainly been killed for the sake of his
much prized skin, so in the end we decided to keep
him, especially as he became very tame even in the
first two days and did not seem in the least anxious
to escape. He lived for about eight months, and
became a great favourite among our many pets.

We were really rather surprised at his living so
long, for colobus monkeys have a reputation for being
exceedingly delicate and usually pine away in captivity,
but I am certain that, had he not been so very old,
Christopher would have lived much longer, and that
his death was not in any way due to his new mode of
life.   Of all simians other than the great apes I think
a colobus monkey has the most human face. Christopher
Columbus, as we called our pet, looked just like a
rather wizened old man.   His face was white but the
top of his head was black, giving the appearance of
an elderly gentleman wearing a skull cap.   The long
white hair on his back looked, too, very much like the
hood of a University don, and in fact his general
appearance—but for his tail—was that of an elderly
and rather benign professor.

Besides the colobus we had other monkeys at various
times, including a Sykes monkey and a black-faced
monkey, but neither of them ever became so tame,
and there was always a risk of their biting us without
any apparent reason.   The only other time that I had
a really tame simian was years later when I reared a
baboon from the time it was a few days old, but that

is part of another story and I will not anticipate here.

Throughout the six years that I am dealing with at present, I had a number of field mice, which occasionally bred, and which were very tame. But as pets they were not very amusing, for they liked sleeping all day and only coming out of their nest into the open part of their cage at night. I could, however, always persuade them to show themselves to visitors by squeaking to them repeatedly in a particular manner. When I did this they would at first answer the squeaks from inside the nest, and presently emerge to see if I had any titbits for them.

Another pet that we had that was entirely nocturnal in habit was a little galago, commonly known in Kenya as a " bush-baby ". The galagos are allied to the lemurs of Madagascar and are much more common in East Africa than is generally believed. But they are seldom seen, as during the day they retreat to holes in trees, or failing that curl themselves up into a ball in some tree top. Our galago was obtained by my father from some natives at a station near the coast on one of his occasional journeys thither on Mission business. It was not until a year or two ago that I discovered that galagos are also far from uncommon round Kabete, where, however, they are so seldom seen by the Kikuyu that they have no special name for them, and when they do come across them call them by the name they give to the ground squirrel.

Another very common little animal in some districts is the tree hyrax, but like the galago it is seldom seen alive. Only once did we have one in captivity, but it did not survive long, which was a great pity, as they make excellent pets.

The tree hyrax is very well known to the Kikuyu

and it is very important to him. When our little fellow
died, we were immediately besieged with offers from
the natives to purchase his carcase, and I strongly
suspect that after we children had sternly refused
and had given our pet a decent burial in the pets'
graveyard, he was dug up and carried off by one of
the native workmen. The reason why the natives
wanted this carcase so much was that the Kikuyu
believe that the hyrax is imbued with magical properties,
which are highly valued in connection with certain
cattle diseases. In this case the immediate reason
was that there had been a bad outbreak of contagious
abortion among the herds of goats and sheep round
Kabete, and the Kikuyu firmly believed that even a
small quantity of the stomach and entrails of the
hyrax, if sprinkled over the herds, would result in the
abatement of the disease.

In addition to the animals I have mentioned, we
also had as pets at various times a serval cat, hares,
Thompson's gazelle, and some genet cats. Among
the latter was a female which I caught as an adult in
one of my box traps and which gave birth to a litter
of kittens. The interesting thing was that one of
the kittens was coal black, while the other three were
spotted like their mother, but in two of them the spots
were arranged quite differently from those of the third.
Certain over-zealous zoologists have tried to make
different races and even different species of genet cat
upon the basis of skin colour and spot pattern, and
upon this basis the one litter contained two species
and three races, which fact should be a severe warning
to zoologists.

As far as my own observations go, the genets are
nearly as variable in coat-markings as the domestic
cat, and skin colour and pattern of markings cannot

be safely used as criteria of species or even of races.

One of the Mission adherents of those days, named Joshua Muhia, was a very keen hunter and trapper. This was an unusual thing to find among the Kikuyu, except in small boys, for the Kikuyu to-day are essentially an agricultural community. But some Kikuyu men had in the past married girls of the Wanderobo hunting tribe when they first came down into the Kabete district of Kikuyu country, and Joshua undoubtedly had Wanderobo blood in his veins, which probably accounted for his occupation.

He was frequently called in by the other Kikuyus to trap porcupines and duiker which were damaging the fields, and when I was about eleven I formed a great friendship with him, and started going off with him on his trapping and hunting expeditions. From him, in the years that followed, I learnt an immense amount not only about the methods of trapping all kinds of different animals but also of their habits, their tracks and their calls. As a result I became an ardent trapper and hunter myself.

For most animals and birds we had various forms of noosed spring trap and I learnt to make and set all the different variants of this trap, as well as how to make the ropes and strings necessary for the nooses from nature's own materials.

It is surprising how easy it is to make cord and string from the barks of various trees once you know how to, and also know which plants will yield the right kind of bark for what you want. Round Kabete there are over a dozen different plants whose bark is excellent. Having peeled the whole bark off a straight branch or sapling, the next thing to do is to separate the inner layer of the bark which is soft and pliable from the outer which is stiff and which, when it dries, becomes brittle. Having peeled off the inner bark—to do this quickly and satisfactorily a special process is required— you chew it until it is soft and frayed, and then proceed to turn it into string or cord according to your needs. This is done in a most ingenious way, by rubbing it between the palm of the hand and the thigh. Although I can do it easily, I find that I cannot adequately describe the method in words, so I will not try to do so.

Almost any of the spring noose traps that I learned to make could be easily made without the help of a knife (not even a stone knife would be necessary), and I am convinced in my own mind that it was probably by similar methods that early Stone Age man obtained much of his food supply. I am quite sure that if necessity ever arose I could catch enough birds and small game to live on, without any weapons at all, provided that I was in a country where birds and small game were fairly plentiful.

Another way of catching certain kinds of game without weapons is by stalking them when they are resting during the day in their lairs. Animals like duiker and hares usually have a favourite place to which they return every day to sleep, and long use makes these places into regular forms. Nearly always there is one particular path leading to these forms, although if disturbed the animal can of course escape in any direction.

One simple and primitive way of catching such animals is to make a low fence of pliable branches round three sides of such a form, leaving the normal line of entry open. If this is done skilfully, the animal will suspect nothing and return to its lair next day quite happily. The hunter then stalks up slowly on hands and knees until only a few yards from the dozing and unsuspecting animal, and when he is near enough he makes a violent dash to the form. The animal tries to escape on the far side, finds itself temporarily hindered there by the rough fence, which must not be solid and impassable, as if it were it would be noticed and suspected. All that is necessary is something that cannot be easily negotiated, so as to cause a slight delay. Finding its way of escape blocked, the frightened animal turns to another side, but this momentary delay in escape is sufficient providing the hunter is quick, and he thus has time to throw himself upon his prey.

I was sceptical of my own ability to use this method until I tried it, and caught a duiker, and I think that in that moment when I hurled myself upon the animal I experienced one of the most exciting sensations of my life. I was only thirteen, but I suppose that deep-rooted wild animal instincts were aroused in me, and I was thrilled as I have never been since.

The various Kikuyu methods of trapping that I learnt from Joshua were mostly designed for catching antelopes, hares, porcupines, rats and moles and various kinds of birds. None of them was much good for trapping carnivores such as wild cats, jackals and mongooses, for the Kikuyu had no use for these animals, nor were they pests that attacked either crops or flocks, and so they were left alone.

But all these animals were a menace to our fowls, and, in addition to hunting them with the dogs, my father and I designed traps to catch them. The traps which we made and used were various forms of a box trap which did not in the least hurt the animal that entered them. We had to design the traps like this because we had so many cats and dogs about that there was always the risk of some of them being caught. In fact, on a number of occasions when visiting the traps near the house in the morning I found one of our own pets sitting inside the box trap quite calmly waiting to be let out.

At first I only did this sort of trapping to protect our fowls, but soon I found that I could sell the skins of wild cats, jackals, mongooses, genet cats, etc., in Nairobi, and after that I started trapping over a much wider area, and some of my traps were as much as three or four miles away from home.

At this time I was living in my own house, and I used to get up just before dawn and start out on my round to inspect the traps, and one particular incident in connection with these rounds I shall never forget. It was all due to the fact that Africans reckon the hours of the day differently from us, and that at Kabete we sometimes had the clocks showing the time in the native way and sometimes in the English way. The Kikuyu starts to count the hours of the day from when the sun rises and the night from sunset, and since he lives on the equator where there is little or no variation all the year round this system works very well. Seven o'clock in the morning is 1 o'clock. Eight o'clock is 2 o'clock, and so on, and 6 o'clock at night is of course 12 o'clock, after which comes the first hour of darkness with 7 p.m. as 1 o'clock once more.

Usually the clock in my house was kept in Kikuyu time and I used to get up when the clock showed 11.0 so that I was ready to start on my rounds by what would be 5.15 a.m. in our English terminology.

One night I woke up suddenly, and looking out through the window saw to my surprise that it was quite light, in fact it looked as though the sun was very nearly up. Glancing at my clock I saw that the hands pointed to 5.30 and as it was so light outside I thought that I must have set the clock by English time, and that it was almost sunrise. I must have overslept badly I thought, and I leapt out of bed, got into my clothes, picked up my club and spear and dashed out and started off on my round. It was not until I had gone about a mile that I realised that it was getting no lighter, and that nowhere was there any sign of people stirring from their villages. Then I heard a hyæna close by, and I realised all of a sudden that it was midnight and that it was the light of a full moon in a cloudless sky that I had mistaken for the coming dawn. I admit I became frightened. Actually, there was nothing to be frightened of, for there were few if any dangerous beasts in the district, but it was rather a shock finding myself (I was fourteen at the time) all alone out on the bush paths in the middle of the night, and I turned and ran home as though a thousand devils were chasing me.

In addition to trapping wild animals I also did a lot of bird trapping. My father had built us a large aviary in which I had all kinds of birds as pets, and then one day I saw an advertisement in the press that a man wanted to buy African birds for a Zoo in India, and I sold him most of those I had. Finding I could sell them, I trapped more, and I later sold a second collection to the same man, and I also did some business with the representative of a firm called the " World's Zoological Trading Company," who bought birds, and also genet cats and mongooses, etc., from me for cash.

One of the animals that I was particularly anxious to trap was the rare melanistic serval cat, for I had heard that a good price was being offered for one of these for a Zoo in England, but I never succeeded, although I got news of these animals several times from the natives, and set my traps in the areas where they had been seen. Once one of them did get caught in a big box trap, but the only evidence I had of this was the footprints outside the trap which showed that a serval cat of some sort had entered, and a quantity of black hairs all round a hole in the wire netting which formed the top of the trap, where he had bitten a hole and then squeezed his way out.

Another animal that I always wanted to trap was the aard-vark, or African ant-eater. Aard-varks were fairly common round Kabete, and any morning you could find the fresh holes which they had dug in search of the nests of " white ants " or termites upon which they principally feed. My desire to trap or kill one of these animals was due to curiosity more than anything else, and looking back upon it I am ashamed that I ever wanted to kill such a harmless and rather useful animal. However, the fact remains that as a boy I had a hunting passion, which had nothing to do with reason or logic.

One day some of our workmen came in and reported that they had seen an aard-vark disappear down a hole near the vegetable garden down in the valley, and we decided to dig it out. But we little knew what that involved. The aard-vark has exceedingly powerful claws on its forelegs, and it can dig quite as fast as a man with a spade, so that the more we dug the further he burrowed in and we were no nearer to him after several hours of hard work.

Quite senselessly, and without reason, our blood was up. I suppose it was our pride that was hurt by the idea of being defeated by a mere animal. The fair thing to do would have been to acknowledge defeat and let the better side win the day. But human nature is not like that, and in desperation we got a jam tin with some gunpowder and a fuse and put it down the hole and set it off. The explosion was too far from the aard-vark to hurt it, but it frightened it badly, so that for a quarter of an hour it stopped digging, and in that time we caught up with it and got it, and so my curiosity was satisfied.

The aard-vark is commonly supposed to be toothless but it is not. It has, on the other hand, the most remarkable dentation imaginable, for, unlike the teeth of other mammals, its teeth have no enamel at all. We sent the skull to the museum in Nairobi and kept the skin, while the flesh was eaten with relish by some of our natives. This was a rather curious thing, and one which even now I have never succeeded in explaining. Once they are grown up and initiated the Kikuyu are forbidden by their laws and customs to eat the meat of wild animals (to-day that taboo is rapidly disappearing and when on safari Kikuyus will eat the meat of most wild game except zebra and carnivora), but buffaloes, eland and aard-vark are not included in the taboo. As far as the two former animals are concerned they are so like cattle in some ways and their flesh is so like beef that the exception is easily understood, but I have never succeeded in eliciting a sound explanation as far as the aard-vark is concerned. Its Kikuyu name, incidentally, is " Nyama," which is the same word as that for meat, but the only reason that I can get either for the name or for the fact that aard-vark meat is not taboo is " it was the custom of our fathers."

In those days the Museum at Nairobi was in a small building near the centre of the town, and it was entirely run by a private Natural History Society known as the East Africa and Uganda Natural History Society. Just before the war the Committee decided to have a full-time assistant curator, and a Mr. Arthur Loveridge was appointed to the post. Loveridge was primarily a specialist in snakes and reptiles, but his duties included collecting for all departments of the Museum.

He used to come out to Kabete a good deal and stay with us, and I felt for him a kind of hero-worship. He stirred my growing interest in birds to a greater zeal, and from him I learnt how to skin birds for museum specimens, how to blow eggs, and what was more important, how to classify birds. He used to give me, from time to time, long lists of the Latin names of the birds to be found in the district and I became an ardent ornithologist, and at thirteen I had firmly made up my mind that I was going to be an ornithologist all my life, when something happened which changed all that, and diverted my chief interest to the subject which is now my profession —archæology. Even now, however, I have never quite deserted my first love, and on all my expeditions the study of birds has its place, even though it be but second.

CHAPTER V

BROUGHT UP AS I was on a Mission station among a native people whom I had learned to love dearly, it was perhaps hardly surprising that I planned to make my life's work that of a missionary, but at a very early age I had also decided that my main hobby in life would be that of an ornithologist, and in this I received every encouragement from Mr. Loveridge.

Then at the end of 1915 a cousin of mine in England sent us as a Christmas present a book called *Days Before History*, by H. N. Hall. This book told the story of the later Stone Age people of Britain, in simple language for children. It was a fascinating story, and its effect was to make me immediately interested in the Stone Age, and I started hunting around Kabete to see if I could find any " arrow-heads " or " axe-heads," for those were the two principal Stone Age weapons mentioned in the book, and of course they were described as being made of flint.

Had I known what flint was, I might never have found any stone implements at all in those early days, for I was looking for " flint " arrow-heads, and I should in consequence almost certainly have overlooked the many Stone Age implements of obsidian. But it so happened that I had no idea of what flint was like and knew only that it was blackish in colour. And so I started hunting all round Kabete for any black material that might prove to be a flint arrow-head.

Almost at once I found in road cuttings and other places where the surface soil was removed, bits of black looking material, which I immediately concluded was flint, and as I did not really know what an arrow-head would look like I decided that the best thing to do was to collect every single piece of this black stuff that I could find. My parents were rather sceptical about this collecting, and assured me that this stuff was not flint, whatever else it might be, but I kept it all with religious care hoping that one day someone would be able to advise me about it.

Then one day I ventured very hesitatingly to show it to Mr. Loveridge. I had not done so before, as I knew that his interest was in birds and snakes, and I'd thought he might laugh at me. He told me that although he did not really know anything about stone tools, he did know that the black stuff was obsidian, and that it was often made into arrow-heads and other tools. He even went further and assured me that some of my specimens were certainly implements as far as he knew. I was delighted beyond words. He told me that in the Museum in Nairobi there were a few good arrow-heads made of this obsidian which had been sent in by some settler, a member of the Natural History Society, and he promised to show them to me next time I went in to Nairobi, and also to find out as much about them as he could.

Once I had received this assurance that my " bits of black stone " as my father called them, were really things that had been made by Stone Age man, I started collecting with doubled keenness. Wherever I went on my hunting and trapping expeditions either with Joshua or by myself, I had my eyes watching the ground half the time, and I picked up every bit of obsidian I saw.

Mr. Loveridge told me that I ought to keep a record of where they came from, and so I started a catalogue, and on each piece of obsidian I stuck a little piece of sticky paper with a number which corresponded with an entry in my catalogue.

And so at thirteen I embarked upon a study of the Stone Age in East Africa, and I firmly made up my mind that I would go on until we knew all about the Stone Age there. I was still interested in birds, but—I argued to myself—the birds were already being studied by Dr. van Someren, Mr. Loveridge and others, so I would undertake a new line of study.

Mr. Loveridge had looked up all the references which he could find and he showed me passages in one or two books, which indicated that there were all sorts of other types of tool to be looked for in addition to arrow-heads and axe-heads. Neither he nor I were at all clear what these other things would look like, and so I decided to keep every single piece of obsidian I could get, until such time as I could get expert advice.

In some of the periodicals and books which were in the Museum Library I found references to Stone Age man living in caves. Hall's book, *Days Before History*, had not told me this, as he was only dealing with the Neolithic and Bronze Age periods when men lived either in huts of wattle and daub, or in pit dwellings, or in some cases in houses built upon artificially constructed islands in lakes. I now decided to hunt for caves and explore them, but I had no idea then, that if I was to find any Stone Age relics in caves I would have to dig for them. I imagined that I should just find things lying about on the floors of the caves and so I was for the most part very disappointed.

The first cave which I explored was one at our

" Gibberish " waterfall, which we discovered entirely by accident. One day my sisters and I were scrambling over the rocks and among the bushes above the falls, when my sister Julia very nearly fell down a deep hole. We all rushed to see it, and after we had cleared away the surrounding bushes we found that it was very deep and we could not see to the bottom. We called to some Kikuyu goat herds who were near, and asked them if they knew of this hole, and they replied in the affirmative. Sometimes, they said, a goat or a sheep fell down it, and if it did it was never recovered because a big snake and all sorts of wild beasts lived at the bottom in a cave there.

It seemed to us highly improbable that any wild animals could get up and down this hole and we said so, and the boys countered this by saying that there was another entrance to the cave at the base of the waterfall.

We all scrambled down the path to the bottom of the fall, and the boys then pointed out to us a long-familiar hole near the edge of the water. We were already aware that this led into a " den " where at one time a lot of hyænas had lived, and we also knew that since the hole had been partially blocked up the hyænas had abandoned this lair.

The goat herds now assured us that the hole at the bottom and the one at the top of the cliff both led into " a big cave," and we at once decided to explore it. The only tracks of animals which were visible at the lower entrance were those of porcupines and of a mongoose, so we decided that there was nothing to be frightened of.

As we had come to the conclusion that the only way to get into the cave was to descend down the " chimney," I spent most of the next morning making

a rope ladder, and in the afternoon we all went over
to Gibberish, taking a lamp and a spear and accompanied by two Kikuyu men.

Father had made us promise that one of the men
should go down first with the lamp and a spear, just
in case of wild animals, but when they saw the hole
they became so frightened that it was with difficulty
that we at last persuaded one of them to venture into
the unknown. I must admit that it was not very
pleasant for him. He was firmly convinced that at
the very least there was a gigantic python living at
the bottom, while to his superstitious mind the
possibility of ogres was also very real. The hole was
so narrow that there was only just room to climb down
the rope ladder, and inevitably his unprotected legs
and lower portions of his anatomy would reach the
bottom first, which was certainly not a pleasant
prospect if a python or an ogre were lying in wait
there ! He descended very slowly and at last we heard
him give a sigh of relief as he reached the bottom and
found himself unattacked.

We were wild with excitement to know what he had
found, and he called up to say that there was a great
big cave " as big as a big house," and that it was very
frightening but that he could see no wild animals.

After he had climbed back to the daylight I
descended with my sister Julia. We found that from
where the " chimney " ended the floor sloped steeply
away down to the far corner, where a small ray of light
could be seen coming through the hole near the water's
edge. My other sister joined us and we then explored.

We found no traces at all of human occupation
which was disappointing. This was chiefly because,
in my ignorance, I had expected to find things lying
all over the floor just where they had been left, and

we did not then think of digging. On a later visit, after a careful search I did find one small obsidian flake (it had been brought to the surface, as I proved years later, by the burrowings of a porcupine), and that was enough to convince me that men had once used this place as a home, and so stir my imagination.

After the discovery of Gibberish cave I set to work to try and find other caves in the district, but without very great success. At one place I had an unpleasant adventure. I found a long, narrow, round hole running straight into the face of a lava cliff near another waterfall. I got a long stick and pushed it in but could not touch the end of the hole, and then I put some dry grass on the end of the stick and set it alight and pushed that in. By means of this simple illumination I could see that just beyond the point where my stick reached the tunnel turned sharply to the right and I imagined that there would be a fine big chamber beyond. I was determined to see round that corner, and I crawled into the hole, which was so narrow that all I could do was to move along it lying on my stomach. It was impossible even to kneel, so that I had to progress by putting my hands forward as far as possible, gripping the rough, uneven floor of the hole, and then dragging my body forwards.

I had matches with me and a sheath knife, and when I got to the place where the passage turned abruptly to the right and looked round the corner, instead of finding a chamber, where I could turn round and face the open again so as to get out, the passage just came to an abrupt end, and I was stuck. Very fortunately for me I was accompanied by two natives, and but for them I do not know what I should have done. In order to extricate me one of my companions had to come in on his stomach behind me and seize my ankles and pull, while the other one who was outside pulled him. In this way I was dragged back rather like a cork out of a bottle neck, and a very painful process it was.

It was about this time that I took up bee-keeping, not ordinary English bee-keeping, but bee-keeping by the African method.

One of my Kikuyu friends, Gicuru, was a renowned bee-keeper, and he promised to initiate me into all the secrets of bee-keeping if I acquired some hives. Kikuyu hives are made by hollowing out short blocks of tree trunk, and so the first thing for me to do was to negotiate for a suitable tree which we could cut down and make into hives.

This was not such an easy thing as it sounds, because I naturally had to observe all the Kikuyu rules governing etiquette in such matters. In the first place suitable trees—I wanted a big and very old tree—were all owned by elderly men, and as a young man I could not negotiate directly with my seniors in matters of this sort. Then again, even after I had arranged with an elderly friend of mine to carry out negotiations for me he was not allowed by etiquette to go round asking owners of trees if they would allow one to be cut down. To do so would be to insult them. He had rather to make casual conversation with people who might possibly let me have a tree to cut down and say that he had heard that I was in need of a tree and then leave it at that. If anyone so informed had a tree to dispose of he would then have to make the opening suggestion and so initiate negotiations.

After a time my friend was offered a tree which suited my purpose as it was within reasonable distance of Kabete and was large enough to make all the hives which I required in addition to such other hives, stools, etc., as custom demanded I should have made. For instance, in return for the right to cut down a tree for making hives it is an understood thing that the first hive made as well as the first two stools must be given to the owner of the tree. The man who carried out the negotiations had to be rewarded also by the gift of a stool from the tree.

The next thing was to find a skilled hive-maker, for the task of hollowing out a log of solid wood into a barrel is not one which everyone can perform. Fortunately I had not far to seek, for Joshua, my trapping friend, was also a wood-worker, and he gladly undertook the task of making the hives and stools from my tree.

He and I cut down the tree together, and then cut up the trunk into sections. For the hives the sections had to be about two feet six inches long and for the stools about one foot. Joshua himself was to receive no direct fee—that again is Kikuyu custom—but he had the right to select any one of the hives which he made (other than the first, which became the property of the owner of the tree) and also to take blocks from which to make stools for himself. In addition to this he was entitled by custom to use one of the blocks destined for hive-making, to make a mortar for his wife.

When all of the sections of the tree trunk had been used up I found that I had six hives and three stools for my own use, and my next task was to place the hives in suitable places and in this and all other things pertaining to bee-keeping, I was instructed and helped by Gicuru.

The Kikuyu have many curious customs and ideas connected with bee-keeping, and all of these I learnt with great interest. First of all, my six hives had to be branded with my mark. It is so long ago that I forget now exactly what the mark chosen for me was. As one of the biggest Kikuyu bee-keepers in the district, Gicuru knew the private marks of almost every bee-owner round about, and he made sure that I had a mark that was not likely to be confused with any other.

Kikuyu bee-hives are all placed in trees, and any Kikuyu has the right to put a hive in a tree that looks suitable without even consulting the owner of the tree or of the land. As the hives of any one man are thus scattered all over the countryside often miles from his own land and his own village, it was obviously essential that there should be some means of deterring dishonest people from taking honey from other men's hives. This means was provided by the use of magical ceremonies which were performed whenever a new hive was put into position in a tree, and as long as everyone believed in magic this provided an adequate safeguard against theft, as it was regarded as certain that a thief would be automatically punished by sickness or other material disaster.

One of the inevitable and *in some ways* unfortunate results of the coming of the white man is a growing sophistication and disbelief in magic, and in consequence theft is on the increase. Under the old tribal conditions there was no need to have police for preventing thefts and other deliberate crimes *within the tribe*, for either by means of magic or by the direct intervention of the ancestral spirits of the injured party every criminal knew that he would be punished ; and fear of various forms of supernatural punishment were a far more real deterrent to the potential thief or criminal than the fear of discovery by the police is or is ever likely to be. After all, the would-be criminal argues, the police are only human, and so there is a chance of escaping them by human cunning, but when punishments were enforced by magic and by the spirits they could not be eluded by any natural means.

Having branded my hives with my special mark, the next task was to find suitable trees for them. The Kikuyu have two ways of putting up a hive; by the " ndumbi " and the " mbogoro " methods. The first of these consists of finding a tree where there are two natural forks sufficiently near to each other to be able to support the hive securely. But more than just the presence of two forks is necessary, for once the hive is in position it must be so placed that it is easily accessible for the purpose of taking the honey, since a " ndumbi " hive is never moved. As it is not easy to find good places for putting hives by the " ndumbi " method, the " mbogoro " one is more usual. For this method a stout " mbogoro " has to be cut from some tree whose wood is very hard and rot proof. The shape of the " mbogoro " is shown in the accompanying

diagram; at one end it has a hook, and at the other end an inverted V. From this end ropes or leather thongs are securely fastened to the two ends of the hive, and it can then be hung in a tree by the simple process of putting the hook end of the " mbogoro " over a branch.

When the time comes to take the honey from a hive set by this method, the bee-keeper climbs up and unhooks the hive and lowers it to the ground, takes the honey from it and then hoists it up again into position.

Two of my hives we set by the " ndumbi " method and the other four by the " mbogoro " technique, and the setting of each hive had to be accompanied by the correct procedure.

When we went to put up a hive, we took with us a bunch of leaves of a sweet-smelling plant called " Kirara na Ithe." Having arrived at the foot of the selected tree, we lit a small fire and put these green leaves on to it, and as soon as they began to smoke we opened one end of the new hive and placed it over the smoke, so that the whole interior of the hive was fumigated with the sweet-smelling smoke from the " Kirara na Ithe " leaves. Then the whole of the interior and exterior of the hive was rubbed with the withered leaves, and the hive closed up again, the remains of the leaves being stuck into a little hole at the front end. The hoisting of the hive and setting in position could then take place. When this had been done, we had to stand at the bottom of the tree and whistle a special tune " to call the bees," and next utter a curse formula to protect the hive from thieves.

As a missionary's son I was inclined to ridicule this whistling for the bees and all the other rites, and I insisted that one of the hives should be put up without any such procedure. Gicuru assured me that it would never be occupied by a swarm unless the correct ritual was performed, so I said, " We will see."

In three weeks' time the five other hives each had a swarm in occupation, but this one had none. So I told Gicuru that I would get a swarm for it by English methods. He laughed, and wanted to know how we did it. So I told him that our practice was to find a swarm and introduce it into the hive. Very soon after this I had the good fortune to find a swarm one evening. It was hanging in a great black mass on a tree a few miles away, and early next morning while it was so cold that the bees were numb and still, I took that swarm and put it into my empty hive, confident that they would take up residence. But as soon as the sun became warm they all swarmed out and flew away. Eventually I let Gicuru perform the ancient rites at this hive and the very next day a swarm arrived and occupied it. I do not suggest that the whistling, etc., was necessarily responsible for the arrival of the bees ; I do not know ; but I record the fact as a very suggestive coincidence.

CHAPTER VI

IN THE SUMMER OF 1919 it was at last possible for
my parents to go to England on leave once again.
Owing to the War their normal tour of four years
had lengthened out into seven and both my parents
were very weary from the effects of their prolonged
stay in Kenya. To me the idea of giving up the free
life I had been living and going to school in England
was far from pleasant, and yet a part of me was very
keen to go, for I had by this time developed an ambition
to go to Cambridge and take a degree in Anthropology
if I could, and I knew that if I wanted to do so I must
go to school and prepare myself for the University.

With immense care I packed up all my specimens,
chief among which was my collection of obsidian flakes
and tools. By this time I had acquired a good deal
more knowledge of the subject and I was certain that
some were " stone implements," while all of them
seemed to me to show at least some indications of
having been humanly chipped.

My father was, even now, not at all convinced that
most of my collection was anything but " mere bits of
broken bottle glass," for obsidian is a natural black
glass produced by volcanic activity and to the casual
observer looks just like bottle glass.

The fact that so many of the implements of Stone
Age man in Kenya were made of this obsidian had a
curious result, and one which was very fortunate for me.
At a much later date I learned that in 1912 two American

archæologists had visited Kenya in search of evidence of prehistoric man. They intended, if they found sufficient evidence, to carry out detailed investigations and had they done so they would have been in the field before me, and the whole course of my subsequent scientific career would probably have been entirely different. In their search, these Americans visited the Nakuru and Naivasha lake basins—areas which were later to give me such valuable results—but they could find no trace of " flint workings " and decided that there was nothing of interest in the district.

I believe that they actually stayed at a hotel at Naivasha where the whole surface of the ground round about is as I now know, covered with obsidian flakes and tools which are washing out of the old lake deposits there. Had the Americans not had their minds firmly fixed to the idea that they were looking for " flint implements " they would certainly have picked up and examined some of these flakes and soon realised that they were in the presence of a rich prehistoric site. As it was, the close proximity to a hotel where beer bottles were so common, led them to think that the black stuff on the ground was broken bottle glass, and in consequence they never examined it.

Besides my rock specimens and my obsidian flakes and implements, I packed and took home to England the collection of bird skins which my sister Gladys and I had made, as well as my collection of birds' eggs, but already my interest in ornithology had been almost entirely replaced by prehistory, and in the end, after lying uncared for in drawers at our home in Boscombe for many years, the birds' eggs and skins were given away.

By the time we sailed for England many of my age-group friends were thinking about getting married, and

it was with a sad heart that I bade them all good-bye.
My best friend, Ishmael Gatenjwa, was engaged to
be married to Naomi Wairimu. She had worked
as bedroom girl for us for some years, and I knew
her well and liked her very much. Unfortunately for
Ishmael, Naomi's parents were against the marriage and
almost the last thing I did was to go and see both of
them and wish them the best of luck. The objection
to their marriage was based on the age-old Kikuyu
fear of breaking a death-bed curse. Naomi's grandfather had had some serious difference of opinion with
Ishmael's grandfather and on his deathbed he had
uttered a curse to the effect that he would come from
the spirit world and give serious trouble to all his
family if they ever allowed any of his descendants to
marry into his enemy's family. Ishmael and Naomi,
who were both Christians, had no fears about the
effects of the curse and as they were very much in love
with each other they wanted to get married as soon as
possible. But the curse had been uttered in such a
way that it would affect not only the two who married
but all the other members of the family if they allowed
the marriage to take place, and in consequence Naomi's
family, who were all heathen, were most antagonistic
to the marriage, and they were trying to persuade
Naomi to marry another Christian boy who was also in
love with her.

Naomi, however, would have nothing to do with
this other lad, who was of an age group older than
Ishmael's, and it was in discussing the whole question
with an older Kikuyu man that I first learned of the
Kikuyu unwillingness to make a girl marry against
her will. Any Kikuyu will, in certain circumstances,
do all in his power to persuade a girl or woman to marry
someone, but it is only seldom that such persuasion

is carried to the extent of a forced marriage if the girl is adamant. It would be idle to deny that cases of forced marriages do sometimes occur, and such cases are frequently quoted by Europeans as proving that the Kikuyus treat their womenfolk more as chattels than as human beings. Quite apart from other considerations the Kikuyu people fully realise that a " forced marriage " is seldom satisfactory.

In the end the opposition to Ishmael's marriage with Naomi was overcome, and they have been happily married for many years now. Moreover the fact that the death-bed curse of Naomi's grandfather did not take effect has very considerably modified the opinion of the local non-Christian natives, and they have decided that Christians can ignore such curses with impunity, not only to themselves but also to their relations.

After an uneventful voyage we arrived at Southampton and went straight to our house at Boscombe, and immediately my father started negotiations to get me into a public school. Through the help of friends who were connected with the school, a place was found for me at Weymouth College, and at the beginning of the January term of 1920 I entered my public school when I was sixteen and a half years old.

Seldom, I suppose, has any boy gone to a public school in such curious circumstances. During the preceding seven years I had hardly seen more than three or four English boys of my own age and all my friends were Kikuyus. Although I had been studying regularly throughout that time, first under Miss Bull and then under Miss Broome, and finally under my father, I had had a remarkably free and independent life.

In some ways I was extremely shy and unsophisticated while in others I was very grown up. I had, after all, built myself a three-roomed house and lived in it for over two years.   I had employed labour of my own and earned money by trapping in order to buy materials for my house.   I had helped my father in the teaching work at the Kabete school and had run and organised the Kabete football club.

My start at Weymouth was not auspicious.   I had hardly been in the building an hour before the school bully had seized me and locked me into a dark coal hole attached to the boiler house.   Instead of meekly submitting I fought and kicked, but the bully was joined by some others, and I was forced in and left there until I was rescued by one of the prefects.

I was chosen as a fag by a prefect who was known to Miss Oakes, who had been my mother's help and nurse when I was born.   Having secured me as his fag he told me he had been asked to look after me, and as he was scarcely six months older than I was, and in many ways far younger than me, I resented this very much.   However, fag I had to be, and if I was going to be a fag I decided I would do it thoroughly.

Until I went to Weymouth I had always played Association football and I found it very difficult, at first, to get hold of the Rugby code.   No one explained to me what I was expected to do or what the idea of the game was, and I simply found myself put down to play in a practice game as a forward.   At Kabete I had always played football either bare-footed or in gym shoes, and my new football boots felt like a ton of lead.   I wandered about the field being cursed by my own side and my opponents and it was only with difficulty that I began to get an idea of what I was expected to do.   Eventually I began to take an interest in the game, but it was not until a year later when G. S. Conway, the Captain of Cambridge and an

English International, came down to coach us at the invitation of his uncle, the Headmaster, that I really began to see the possibilities of the finer points of the game.

Unlike most of the other boys at school I hardly made any friends, although there were a few boys whom I liked much better than the others. The difference between my outlook on life and theirs seemed always to present an almost insuperable barrier, and I regarded almost all of them as appallingly childish.

The school had a fairly strong field club which, however, took little interest in pre-history and much in bird life, and so for a time my interest in birds was greatly revived, although I was never tempted to start making a collection of British birds' eggs.

Near the school was the Lodmoor swamp which provided an extraordinarily fine place for bird study and in the company of one or other of the boys with whom I was more or less friendly, I spent many hours with a pair of field glasses watching the habits of different kinds of waders and ducks. It was in this that I found far more in common with some of my fellow pupils than in any other of the many school and out-of-school activities.

I knew absolutely nothing about British birds when I went to Weymouth, but I got to know most of those to be found in the district both by their flight as well as by their song and plumage.

When I left Kenya to come to England, I had, for my age, a very fair knowledge of Latin, French and Mathematics, but in all other subjects I was appallingly weak. Owing partly to my age and partly to the standard of my knowledge in these three subjects, I was put straight into the Fifth form, and as a result I soon found myself in very great difficulties. Of Greek

I knew nothing at all, and was not even sure of the letters of the alphabet, but I was plunged straight into a class that was doing translations from Xenophon.

The headmaster very kindly gave me some special coaching, but I was never able to get level with the other boys in the class, so far as Greek was concerned, and I always dreaded the hour devoted to it. At the same time my pride made me want to catch up, and so I spent long and weary hours over a Greek grammar trying to master the tenses and the declensions of the nouns. I must have learnt something, for when later I was moved up into the Sixth form I was never bottom of the class in Greek so far as I can remember, but what I learnt I learnt only with a very superficial part of my mind, for whereas I can still read Latin I find that nowadays I cannot even remember all the Greek letters.

Until I went to Weymouth I had never attempted to write an essay, and in fact I did not know what " writing an essay " meant. At the end of the first English lesson of the term, our English master gave us several subjects from which we were to choose one and write an essay on it by the following week. I remember very vividly going up to him afterwards and asking him what an essay was, and his look of horror when he realised that I quite honestly did not know.

In time I came to like writing essays, although I was always in difficulties because of the subjects which were commonly set.

Once, I remember, we were told to write an essay on " The Theatre," but as I had never been to a theatre in my life and had no idea what a theatre was like, this was difficult. I avoided the issue by taking an idea from Shakespeare's " All the world's a stage

and all the men and women merely players," and I
then wrote my essay on " All the school's a stage and
all the boys and prefects merely players," and went
on " At first the new boy in the bully's hands. . . ."

When the first summer term came round I found
myself faced with new difficulties in connection with
games. I had never played cricket except for one
term when I was nine years old and I could not
remember anything that I had learnt then. No one
explained the rules to me and I simply found myself
put down to play in a " second set " game.

I was utterly miserable. I did not know where to
stand or what to do, and I was embarrassed by the
very obvious fact that little boys of thirteen were
regarding me as an object of scorn and derision. A
more unorthodox batsman would have been impossible
to find ; but after I gained a little confidence I could
usually make a few runs, and before I eventually left
I was playing for the second XI and for my house.
In spite of this I simply hated cricket, and avoided
playing whenever I possibly could. My quick tempera-
ment hated the inactivity of the game, for even in
fielding, which was the part of the game I enjoyed
most, one often had to wait for long periods before a
ball come near enough to be caught or chased. I have
often wondered whether I would have liked the game
if I had been properly taught, but I think not. Cricket
seems to me essentially a game for typical Englishmen,
and I am anything but typically English.

Being so near to the sea in summer the whole school
used to go down periodically to swim, but here as in
so much else, I found myself terribly handicapped by
my African life. In Kenya there are very few rivers
which are big enough to swim in, and those that are,
as well as some of the lakes, are full of crocodiles,

while other lakes are too alkaline or too much fouled by
bird life to be fit to swim in. In consequence, I arrived
at school unable to swim, and no one seemed to think
it was necessary to try to teach me. All the boys
had learnt to swim during the preparatory school stage
of their lives. I suppose I could have gone to one of
the masters and asked to be taught to swim, but I was
too unreasonably proud to go and admit that I could
not do what almost every boy could do so well, and
I felt rather bitter that no one offered to teach me.
It made me feel rather like an animal that had been
wounded, and with which the herd would have nothing
to do in consequence of its helplessness.

Long before I acquired a study I amazed the headmaster by going to him and begging for permission to
sit up late in one of the classrooms and work after the
others had all gone to bed. I was strongly determined
to learn all I could and make sure of being able to go
to Cambridge. My ambition, of course, was to get a
scholarship, but that was never realised, for among
other reasons I was past the age limit of almost all the
available scholarships before I had reached a sufficiently
high standard. This worried me terribly, because I
knew that without the help of a scholarship it was going
to be very difficult to finance my studies at the
University.

During my last year at school, we had a change of
English masters, and I got on better even with the
new master, Mr. W. A. B. Tunstall, than with his
predecessor, whom I had liked very much. Mr.
Tunstall was from St. John's College, Cambridge, and
at tea in his room I often discussed the question of
my going up to Cambridge. He urged me to try to
get into his college, and promised me letters of introduction when the time came for me to go up for

interviews. At first the idea did not please me at all, for I had made up my mind that, if possible, I would go to Peterhouse, my father's old college, or failing that, to Corpus Christi, where many other Leakey's had been before me.

While I was still at school, I often used to wonder why it was that I fitted so badly into the life of the place, why I made so few friends, why I was so unpopular. But, looking back, the thing that surprises me far more is how I managed to fit in as well as I did. Used as I was to comparative freedom, accustomed to organising my own life to a considerable degree, I found myself in conditions where most of my natural abilities were of no use to me, and where everything had to be done according to the rules and ideas of other people—rules which seemed to me fantastic. If I wanted to go shopping in the town I must have a pass ; if I wanted to go for a country walk on Sunday I must wear a straw hat and a dark suit. Unless I had special permission I must go to bed at a given hour whether I was tired or not, and whether I had finished the work that I was doing or not. It was all so very stupid from my point of view.

I was being treated like a child of ten when I felt like a man of twenty, and it made me very bitter. I was not understood as an individual nor treated as such, and so I was not happy.

CHAPTER VII

WHEN I WENT TO Weymouth College in January, 1920, I had firmly made up my mind that I wanted to go to Cambridge, and I hoped that I should learn enough at school to enable me to win a scholarship at one of the colleges.

One day at the beginning of 1922, I went to discuss the matter with my headmaster, Mr. R. R. Conway. I told him that I was determined to go to the University and that I wanted his advice about the possibility of getting a scholarship.

He appeared to be rather surprised at my saying that I was planning to go to Cambridge, but he was very nice about it, and told me to sit down and talk it over. The first question he asked me was what subject I intended to take for my degree and I had to admit that I really did not know, because I was quite ignorant of anything about the rules and regulations concerning degrees at Cambridge, and I wanted him to tell me and give me his advice. He then explained to me the details of the Tripos system and pointed out firmly, but gently, that he really did not think it was much use my going up. He reminded me that I could not expect to take the Classical Tripos as my Greek was far too weak ; that I had no hope of doing anything in Modern Languages, as I only knew French, whereas two languages were required ; and that for the rest he really did not think that either in Mathematics, Science or History I had any chance at all.

He added that I could of course take the course for the Ordinary as distinct from the Honours degree, but he did not think that that would be in the least worth my while. On that one point I agreed with him heartily.

He then wanted to know what funds I had available. When I told him that I had a certainty of only £60 for one year and that I should have to find the rest as best I could, he simply shrugged his shoulders and said that that settled the matter. It would, he thought, be much better to give up the idea altogether and try to get into a bank !

I was furious. I was quite determined that I was going to go to Cambridge and was going to take an Honours degree, so I told him that I'd thought of taking Anthropology, if that was possible, and asked him what he thought of that. Upon this he looked up various University regulations and said that, as far as he could see, I could only take the Anthropology course as a second part of a Tripos, and that I had to take an examination in some other subject first, and he did not see that I had any chance at all.

I went away utterly miserable, for I saw all my most cherished dreams falling to the ground ; but my despondency did not last long. I was quite determined, and I felt convinced in my own mind that if I tried hard enough I could find a way of achieving what I wanted.

After thinking matters over I went to the Headmaster again, and told him that I wanted a few days' leave of absence from school so that I could go up to Cambridge and interview the tutors at some of the colleges and find out more for myself, and he consented to allow me to do this. Father had given me letters of introduction to his old college, Peterhouse, and the English master, Mr. Tunstall, had given me letters to the tutors of his college, St. John's, and so in due course I went up to see what I could do.

I went to Peterhouse first of all, and the tutor there was exceedingly kind, but although he made me an offer of a college grant towards my expenses if I came into residence, I refused to commit myself until I had my other interviews.

I next went to St. John's College, where I saw Mr. E. A. Benians, who has since become the Master. I had a long talk with him and again explained my whole position. He was very helpful and friendly. I think he saw at once that I was determined to come to Cambridge somehow, and he gave me every kind of encouragement, although he did not attempt to gloss over the difficulties. Among other things he told me that although I was too old to take a scholarship examination, I was eligible for a sizarship for which an examination would be held in the summer, and he suggested that I sit for it. For this I should have to offer four subjects, but need only take the papers in three of them, while I would be allowed to put in " a certificate of competent knowledge " for the fourth. This was very cheering, but I had still not solved the problem of what subject I could offer for Part I of the Tripos.

After further discussion Mr. Benians gave me a copy of the *Students' Handbook* and suggested that I should take it away and look through it, and see if it gave me any ideas, and come and see him again later.

I took it away and proceeded to go through it with great care and when I came to the section dealing with the Modern Languages Tripos I suddenly saw that I had a chance after all. At that time—the regulations governing this Tripos have since been altered— a candidate for Part I of the Modern Languages Tripos had to offer two modern languages, and I suddenly conceived the idea of offering French with Kikuyu as my second language. After all, Kikuyu was as much a modern language as German or Swedish, and the regulations said nothing at all which implied that the languages must be European.

I went back to Mr. Benians and told him that I had decided to take the Modern Languages Tripos and that I would offer these two languages. I don't think I shall ever forget the look on his face when I made this suggestion, and he was not inclined at first to take it seriously. However, I argued my case strongly, and pointed out that there seemed to me to be nothing in the regulations which could be interpreted as a ruling against an African language, provided that it was spoken by a reasonably large population, and provided also that the University could be satisfied on one or two other points, such as the possibility of obtaining competent examiners.

After a certain amount of further discussion Mr. Benians consented to forward my suggestion to the proper authorities, and promised to let me know the result in due course. He warned me, however, not to be too optimistic. In due course I heard that the University had agreed to allow me to take Kikuyu for the Tripos. I immediately went to see Mr. Benians again and suggested to him that, if the University authorities were prepared to accept Kikuyu as a degree subject, I would like to offer it also as one of my four subjects for the sizarship examination. Seeing the look of grave doubt on his face, I hastily added that, of course, I would not expect the College to examine me in Kikuyu, but that I would submit a " certificate of competent knowledge," which the conditions of the sizarship examinations permitted.

To this plan Mr. Benians consented, and so in the summer of 1922 I again went up to Cambridge to sit for this examination. In addition to Kikuyu I offered Latin, French and Mathematics, and somehow—I've never quite known how—I succeeded in answering the questions set sufficiently well to be awarded a sizarship of £40.

I had been required to provide two certificates of competent knowledge in Kikuyu, and these I obtained from East Africa without much difficulty, although I doubt if quite such curious certificates have ever been offered before in a connection such as this. One of them was given to me by Dr. J. W. Arthur, head of the Church of Scotland Mission at Kikuyu. He had known me since I was a baby, and he knew of course that I could speak the language like a native ! The other was a typewritten statement dictated and signed by a Kikuyu chief !

In October of 1922 I at last found myself in residence at St. John's College, and I felt that I was well on my way to realise my ambition, although I knew that it was still doubtful if I should be able to obtain the necessary funds to enable me to stay up the three years necessary to get my degree.

My first year at Cambridge passed very happily and very quickly—much too quickly for my liking. After the restrictions of school life, I was once again free ; I had my own rooms ; I could cook for myself, and I could do as I liked. I was so keen to do well in my examinations that I worked long hours every day, but I soon realised that my chances of success were much smaller than I had once optimistically hoped. My chief difficulty was French literature ; I felt reasonably happy about translation and composition, but I soon found that I not only knew nothing about French literature, but, what was worse, I was not interested in it in the very least ; and because I was not interested in it I could not remember anything that I read about it or was taught.

Although I could ill afford the extra expense I decided to take special coaching, but even with that to help me I knew I was not really learning anything, and I became very despondent. So far as Kikuyu was concerned, I had been nominally placed under the care of Mr. W. A. Crabtree, of St. Catharine's College. He did not actually know the Kikuyu language at all, but he knew Luganda, a somewhat similar East African language, and as the University regulations demanded that I must have a " Supervisor," he was chosen for that purpose. After a little time I received instructions that, as I was not attending any lectures in Kikuyu and as the University authorities considered that I ought to do something to prevent myself from forgetting the Kikuyu language, I was to start teaching the Kikuyu language to my supervisor. I used to go regularly, therefore, to his house and solemnly give him lessons in lieu of attending lectures. This I enjoyed very much, for we had many very interesting discussions upon the structure and origin of the Bantu group of languages, of which both Kikuyu and Luganda were examples, and I learnt a lot from him, in addition to teaching him my language.

When the summer term arrived I started working harder than ever, for the examination time had almost come and I was very seriously worried lest I should fail in the French literature papers. Nor was my fear unfounded. When the examination was over I was certain that I had failed in some of the papers, and this was unfortunately confirmed when the results came out. This was a very serious blow for me indeed, for among other things it meant that I was not awarded a scholarship that I had hoped for, and I simply did not know where I was going to find the money to pay for my second year.

Apart from this financial aspect, my failure did not really matter very much, for I had attempted to do a two years' course in one year and, as the regulations then stood, I was eligible to try a second time at the end of my second year, and neither my tutor nor my coach was really surprised at the result, for they had both warned me that what I was attempting was almost impossible.

My next problem was how to pass the long period of the summer vacation without spending any of my money, and if possible not only spending nothing, but earning something towards paying off outstanding bills. I had applied for several tutoring jobs which I had seen advertised in *The Times* and other papers, and I had also asked some of the educational agencies to try and secure me a post, but with no avail. I was beginning to get really desperate when I heard that a cousin of mine, who was a doctor's wife, wanted someone who could cook to go with her and her family to North Wales, and I applied for the job. Mrs. Ridge had taken a house near Portmadoc for the summer holidays, and was going there with her children and some of their cousins, and it was arranged that I should undertake the cooking and housekeeping, and in return for that I was to have my board and lodging free, as well as a small salary.

I have always liked cooking and housekeeping and I thoroughly enjoyed myself.

I was getting very worried as to how I was going to meet the expenses of my second year, when I heard of a fund which was devoted to helping the education of missionaries' sons who themselves hoped to be missionaries. I immediately put in an application and received a grant which, with the £40 sizarship which had been continued for a second year, and a contribution from my parents, made it possible for me to enter upon my second year of study.

One of my greatest ambitions was to be a Rugby football Blue, but although I had played for the college 1st XV all through the preceding season I had not even been awarded my college colours, so that my chances were fast receding into the background. Then, during the October term of 1923, my chance came. The university captain was looking for a fast wing forward and he and several members of the University XV came to watch a match in which I was playing, and several of us were told that this was going to be considered as a kind of trial. I was playing the game of my life when somebody accidentally kicked me on the head, and I had to be carried off the field suffering from concussion. As soon as I felt a little better I foolishly insisted on returning to the game and received a second blow which forced me to retire altogether.

That evening I had a most terrible headache. Instead of going to bed I tried to work and next day my head was worse and I had to go to my doctor, who ordered me to leave Cambridge for at least a week or ten days, and take a complete rest. I was most loth to do so, but my head was too bad to be able to do any work, so I arranged to go and spend ten days with an uncle and aunt in Norfolk, and on the very morning that I left Cambridge I received an invitation to play in a match for the University and of course I had to refuse.

But, as the proverb says, " It's an ill wind that blows nobody any good," and I little thought when I was kicked on the head what a great effect that incident was going to have on my whole career.

After I had been away about ten days I returned to Cambridge, but as soon as I tried to do any brain work my head started aching most terribly, and then I temporarily lost my memory. My doctor then said that I must give up all ideas of working at Cambridge for at least a year and must go and live an open-air life somewhere.

This was terrible news. I had just enough money to live at Cambridge and study, but I had absolutely no money to spare for taking a whole year's holiday, and I was desperate. But something had to be done, and I set to work at once to make all kinds of enquiries for some post which involved an open-air life. By chance I heard of the existence of the Percy Sladen Memorial Trust, and I applied to the trustees for a small grant to enable me to go out to Kenya and spend my enforced holiday making a preliminary examination of the archæological possibilities of the country. I knew that if I could get out to Kenya I could live there almost for nothing, and I had badly wanted to make a preliminary examination of a number of sites which I hoped to investigate more fully in the future.

The trustees at first seemed inclined to consent to my plan, but they eventually decided that, as I had not yet had any training in archæology, they would not be justified in giving me the financial aid which I had asked for, so that plan had to be abandoned.

It so happened, however, that in connection with this scheme I had been in touch with an old family friend who was then in England, Mr. C. W. Hobley. While he was a Government official in Kenya, he had been a prominent member of the Natural History Society, and had himself collected a certain amount of information about the Stone Age in East Africa.

Through Mr. Hobley I heard that the British Museum of Natural History was planning to send an expedition to Tanganyika Territory to collect fossil remains of Dinosaurs, and were looking for someone who had had African experience. I got into touch with the authorities and asked to go up for an interview, and as a result I was chosen, and told that I must be ready to sail in three weeks' time.

The only other member of the expedition was the leader, Mr. W. E. Cutler, who had made a great name for himself as a collector of fossil reptiles in America, and who was acknowledged to be one of the very best field collectors of the day. I felt that I was therefore exceedingly lucky, as under him I should gain very valuable practical experience. Mr. Cutler had never before been in Africa, and that is why the Museum authorities wanted someone to accompany him who was used to dealing with natives and who was acquainted with camping conditions in Africa.

Had it not been for my accident I should certainly not have applied to go on this expedition, and I should therefore never have had the really valuable practical training in methods of fossil collecting and preservation which I received from Mr. Cutler, and which has proved immensely useful to me in my subsequent research work.

Nor was this the only very great advantage that I gained from being appointed to this expedition. During the whole year that I was away from Cambridge I not only had all my living expenses paid, but also earned a small salary which was later invaluable as a contribution towards my expenses when I eventually returned to Cambridge to continue my interrupted studies. My luck had certainly turned in a most unexpected manner.

CHAPTER VIII

IT WAS ON JANUARY 29th, 1924, that I received the official invitation of the British Museum authorities to be a member of their East African Expedition and I immediately went to London to accept the offer in person and to find out details of what my duties would be and when we were to sail.

The main object of the expedition was to be the collection of fossil bones of ancient reptiles from an area which had been partially worked by the Germans before the war. In addition to this it had been decided that we were to collect birds and small mammals, as the region in which we were to work was poorly represented in the Museum collections. I was to be responsible for this part of our work and also for the supervision of the labour gangs that we were to employ. I had obtained a certain amount of practical experience in the dispensary work at Kabete, by helping my parents, and as we were not going to have any doctor with our party I was to be in charge of medical stores, and to do what I could.

Mr. Cutler and I were due to sail on February 17th, but our departure had to be postponed until February 28th, partly because of a dock strike in London which interfered with the loading of our stores and equipment, and partly because Mr. Cutler was not able to be ready by the earlier date.

As representatives of the British Museum we travelled first class, and to me this was a new experience, for although I had been backwards and forwards from East

Africa many times with my parents, I had never travelled anything except second class. The journey was quite uneventful and we reached Mombasa on March 17th. As leader of the expedition, Mr. Cutler would have a certain amount of business to attend to at Dar-es-Salaam, the official capital of Tanganyika territory and next port of call, so I obtained permission to disembark at Mombasa and go for a few days up-country to see my parents before rejoining Mr. Cutler. I wanted to take the opportunity of engaging a personal servant from among my Kikuyu friends, and also to obtain maps and information about the district to which we were going from a friend of mine, Captain Wood, who had spent some time there during the War. I had a very enjoyable ten days, and then left again for Mombasa and Dar-es-Salaam, accompanied by a Kikuyu boy called Nahashon.

Nahashon had never been away from his home before, and the train journey to Mombasa thrilled him considerably, but his interest in that was quite eclipsed by the sight of the steamer in which we were to sail to Dar-es-Salaam. He immediately asked me for paper and pencil and wrote a long letter describing " the floating village," as he called it, to his brothers and friends at Kabete.

Having arrived at Dar-es-Salaam I found that Mr. Cutler had experienced considerable difficulties in getting all our equipment into the country, for we wanted to avoid paying Customs duty, and the Customs authorities had proved somewhat unhelpful. As we were an official expedition I was convinced that the matter could be arranged, if handled properly, and one of Mr. Cutler's difficulties was, of course, that he was not accustomed to the way things are done in Africa. This was exactly the kind of thing for which I had been appointed to the expedition, so I immediately offered to see what could be done.

I had letters of introduction from friends in Kenya to one or two people in the Government service, and I went off and interviewed one of them in the Secretariat and asked him for his advice. He was exceedingly helpful and after looking through vast numbers of rules and regulations governing all questions concerning Customs duty, we found a paragraph which laid down that the kit, equipment and tools of Land Commissions " and other such commissions at the discretion of His Excellency the Governor " could be imported free. Armed with this information I set to work to draft a letter to the Governor asking him that, *for Customs purposes*, the British Museum Expedition should be considered as " a special Commission." I then took the letter to Mr. Cutler for his signature as leader, and handed it in to the proper quarter, and in due course we were given the permission which we required.

As a result of the dock strike which had originally delayed our departure from London, a good deal of our stores and equipment had still not arrived at Dar-es-Salaam, and so Mr. Cutler decided that I should proceed alone to Lindi to make preliminary arrangements there, and if possible go inland to Tendaguru and build a camp, while he waited at Dar-es-Salaam to check all our equipment on arrival and then bring it on with him to Lindi.

I had to wait several days for a boat, as Lindi is a very small port which was only visited regularly at six weeks' intervals, though cargo boats occasionally put in there. I was fortunate enough to find a Dutch cargo boat had just decided to call at Lindi on its journey south, so that I did not have to wait for the small coastal passenger steamer, the Dumra. In due course I arrived outside Lindi harbour about mid-day, but as the tide was unfavourable and the entrance to the harbour is blocked by a sandbar, we did not drop anchor inside until just as it was getting dark at 6.15 p.m.

I had never been at Lindi before, but I had been warned that it had no hotel, and had been advised by friends in Dar-es-Salaam to get in touch with the Provincial Commissioner, Major Cadiz, to whom I had been given a letter of introduction. When we had anchored I sent this letter ashore together with a note asking if he could possibly put me up for the night. After a time a verbal message came back in the affirmative, so, after having had dinner on board, and having found out that the ship was not sailing until next day, I decided to go ashore but to leave all my heavy luggage and my native boy on board until the next morning.

It was really rather foolish of me not to sleep on board myself and wait until daylight to go ashore. But the cranes which were loading sisal were making an appalling din, and I knew that I should not sleep. Moreover in view of the message I had received I imagined that Major Cadiz was expecting me.

Having landed, I enquired of some natives where the Provincial Commissioner's house was, and was directed to follow a track along the shore until I saw the lights of a house, which I would come to " in a few minutes." I set off at a fast walk and had gone some little distance when suddenly I fell with a crash and found myself lying at the bottom of a very muddy and thorny ditch. I scrambled out and scraped off as much of the foul-smelling mud as I could, and went on, and after a few more yards turned a corner round some bushes and saw the lights of the house that I was looking for.

Believing that I was expected I walked boldly up the steps and called " *Hodi !* " which is the East African equivalent of knocking on the door, and presently some-one came out and asked what I wanted. I explained who

I was and why I had come and it turned out that I was not expected at all, but that the verbal message had been very much distorted *en route*. Major Cadiz had told the messenger to say that he could NOT put me up for the night, but that if I would come and see him next morning he would put an empty Government building at my disposal. The boy to whom the message had been given had passed it on to someone else, and he in his turn had passed it to someone who was going on board in connection with the lighterage work, so that it was hardly surprising that it had become considerably altered in the process.

But I had arrived ; and as there was no boat available to take me back to the steamer at that hour of the night, Major Cadiz took pity on me, and, as he could not give me the accommodation himself, he took me across to the Postmaster, who very kindly gave me a bed for the night.

I had had as fellow passengers Mr. and Mrs. Wyatt. Mr. Wyatt had come down to take over duty from Major Cadiz who was going on leave, and he and his wife were staying temporarily with the District Commissioner, Major Anderson, as Major Cadiz and his family were in the midst of packing up all their possessions preparatory to leaving.

Like myself, the Wyatts had left all their luggage on board, intending to take it off at their leisure next day, but as I was getting into bed, Major Cadiz's son came round to say that a message had just been sent from the ship to ask Major Wyatt and Mr. Leakey to come at once and take off their luggage as the Captain had decided to sail at 7.0 a.m. next morning.

I hastily went and consulted with Major Wyatt, and we eventually decided to do nothing then, but to go on board at dawn next morning instead, which we did. We then found that the ship was not really going to sail until mid-day, but that it was going to go out across the sand-bar on the morning tide and then anchor and continue loading cargo from lighters. So as we were on board we had breakfast, and did not finally get our luggage off until 1.0 p.m., when we brought our possessions ashore in one of the empty lighters.

I had come down to Lindi without any camp bed or mosquito net, as these things were among the kit to be provided by the Museum, and when I had left Dar-es-Salaam they had not yet arrived from London. In view of this I went to see the Government storekeeper to discover whether I could borrow what I required from the Government stores, and I succeeded in obtaining the temporary loan of a camp bed and mosquito net, with which I installed myself in the empty house which had been put at my disposal.

I next went to the Indian shops and bought some stores, hand lanterns and cooking pots, and by evening I was more or less comfortably camped in the house, which was a two-storey building which had been the German club-house in pre-war days. It had not been inhabited for a very long time, and was therefore in a bad state of repair, but it suited my purpose admirably, and I stayed in it for five days while I made my preparations for the journey to Tendaguru.

Before we left England we had been provided with some of the German literature dealing with their scientific work at Tendaguru before the war, and when I came down to Lindi Mr. Cutler had given me this together with rough copies of some of the German expedition maps and some photographs showing the actual hill which had been the site of their main camp. We wanted to camp on this same site, for it was said to be near to the only available drinking water in the area, and also to be right in the centre of the richest part of the fossiliferous deposits.

From the maps I knew the approximate position of Tendaguru hill, and from the published papers I knew that the Germans had had as their native headman an old Arab called Boheti, and I was determined to secure his services as a guide if I could. I accordingly made enquiries in the native quarter of Lindi, and also from the Government officers, and after a day or two Boheti came to visit me. He was not in very good health and said that he did not think he could come up with me and show me the site, but he gave me a helpful description of how to find it. He said moreover that possibly later on he would be willing to come and show us some of the principal spots from which the Germans had excavated some of their best fossils, but for the present he could not act as my guide.

Owing to the lack of water the Tendaguru district is very sparsely inhabited, but he told me that there were a few scattered villages in the vicinity of the old German camp site, and he thought that once I got somewhere near I should probably be able to find someone who could show me not only the site of the old camp, but also the position of the only water hole.

The Government officers next informed me that the headman or Jumbe of the administrative sub-district in which Tendaguru was situated was in Lindi on official business, and so I asked to see him. Jumbe Ismaeli told me that he did not know the exact whereabouts of the old Tendaguru camp as he had not been in the district in the pre-war days, but he agreed that I should accompany him when he started back for his district ; he further promised that before he went to his home he would come with me and help me to locate the site I was looking for and also assist me to get local men to build the camp.

This was excellent, and after a further two or three days at Lindi, which I spent in getting together fifteen porters, engaging a cook, and making arrangements with the Government officials about the forwarding of my letters, etc., I set off on April 17th on my safari into the interior. My object was to locate the site of the old German camp and build a new camp there for ourselves, so that everything would be ready for us to start excavation work as soon as Mr. Cutler arrived. Although I had spent so much of my life in East Africa, the country and conditions here were entirely new to me, and I felt that I was starting on a great adventure.

I roused my boys at 5 a.m. and, as we had packed almost everything on the previous evening, there was little to do, and by 6 o'clock, after a quick cup of tea, we set off. Jumbe Ismaeli and I headed the party, then came the porters each with a load of from 50 to 70 lbs. weight on his head, while my gun-bearer, cook, and Nahashon, my Kikuyu boy, brought up the rear.

For the first half-mile our track led through the coconut palm plantations which cover the narrow coastal plain, and then we entered the bush-covered hill country that lies at the back of Lindi harbour. After about a half-an-hour's march we reached the top of a high ridge and, looking back, we caught our last glimpse of the sea, while ahead of us was a great flat-bottomed valley with more ridges beyond.

All the way the track had been very slippery, for it had rained heavily during the night, and the soil was very clayey, but the difficulties we had encountered were nothing compared with those of the next hour. The track descended the hill almost vertically to the valley below, and walking down it was rather like trying to walk down a greased slide. In spite of the aid of nailed shoes and a stout stick, I fell heavily several times, and it will always be a mystery to me how the porters with their heavy loads ever negotiated that slope at all. However, we all reached the bottom safely, if somewhat bruised, and we then started the worst hour of our whole safari. Before us lay a flat-bottomed valley and winding across it and threading its way through reeds over ten feet high was a winding native track. Owing to the rains, the whole flats were little more than a swamp, and at every step we sank into the black mud half way up to the knees, or, treading on a hidden stone, would slip and fall into the mire. The distance across this flat was scarcely a mile, but it took us over an hour to get to the other side. By that time we were all covered from head to foot in black, slimy mud, and I had lost one of my shoes.

Fortunately, we found a small pool of clear water on the far side, near which were two native huts and a small patch of cultivation, so I called a halt and we rested and washed ourselves, and then pressed on once more, after we had all enjoyed a very refreshing drink of green coconut milk.

By 1 o'clock the heat of the sun which had emerged from the clouds had become terrific. I called a halt again, and we all had some food under the shade of a big thorn tree ; after that, another hour's march brought us to the little native village of Nkanga, approximately seventeen miles from Lindi. By this time the porters were completely exhausted and as both food and good water were available here, we camped for the night.

Jumbe Ismaeli had sent a messenger on the previous day to tell the inhabitants that a Mzungu, or white man, would be passing through in a day or two, and as we walked into the village the elders came to meet me, and informed me that they had built me a small grass rest hut so as to save me from having to put up the tent.

Before we reached this hut, which was on the outskirts of the village, men and women came out bringing presents of rice, eggs, bananas, sugar cane, manioc roots and a fowl, in return for which I gave them presents of beads and some cotton cloth, and also attended to their ailments.

Next morning we were up early and started off just before sunrise. The track led through lightly wooded country, and the soil was very sandy, but being damp it was firm underfoot, and made walking easy. Later on in the year, at the height of the dry season, the same section of the journey to Tendaguru was a most unpleasant one, as the dry, loose sand made walking very tiring and was also exceedingly hot underfoot.

After we had marched about nine miles we reached a small village called Noto, and here I halted with the intention of giving the porters a short rest before continuing our safari, but while I was sitting under a big mango tree resting, Jumbe Ismaeli and one of the other men came up and asked leave to put up the tent and prepare camp for the night. As it was only 9.0 a.m., I was astounded by their suggestion, but they pointed out that from here onwards we would have to leave the track, which led in the direction of Jumbe Ismaeli's own village, and, instead, march across country, and, as they pointed out, we did not know how far we would have to go before we found water or reached any other village. As the men were already tired we should be unwise to start off into the unknown until next day.

I was most reluctant to accede to their request, but as we had no tents for the porters to sleep in, and since the rainy season was not yet over, I appreciated the necessity for trying to reach another village for our next halt, so I had to admit that they were probably right. We therefore put up my tent and I then called on some of the local elders, and requested them to build me a small rest hut at this place, so that I would not have to take the tent with me on my march back to the coast, when I went to meet Mr. Cutler later on. They promised to do this for me, and then in their turn they made a request of me. As it was early in the day, and I was going to spend the whole day here, would I please go out and see if I could find any game to shoot, as they had had no meat for a long time, and would very much like some. I at once consented, for it would mean that I would see something of the country round about, so I set off with a local guide and my gun-bearer, but although we roamed for miles we saw no game at all.

Next morning we again started just before sunrise, and we began to march across country in the direction in which they said Tendaguru lay. I had checked up the information given me by the local natives with my maps and compass, and was satisfied that the direction was right. The country here was covered in long grass, all of it over four feet high and some of it as much as fourteen feet high—elephant grass, it is called—and since it had rained heavily during the night we were all soaked to the skin before we had gone more than a few hundred yards.

Here and there in the grass were patches of thorny creepers and stinging nettles, which made it very unpleasant to be the leader of the long line of men, so those of us who had no load took it in turn to go ahead, and each of us was badly scratched by the thorns and stung by the nettles. After about three hours of very slow marching we came to a patch of forest and after passing through this for about two miles we quite suddenly and unexpectedly came to the edge of an abrupt slope. Looking away to the north-west I caught sight of a small conical hill which reminded me at once of some of the photographs of Tendaguru Hill which I had brought with me from London.

I called a halt, opened my luggage, and took out the photographs, and with them and my maps I was soon quite certain that my objective was in view. It looked about ten miles away and probably was not much more as the crow flies, but we had to walk rather more than twenty miles in order to reach it.

After allowing the porters to rest for about an hour, we continued on our way, and when we got to the foot of the steep slope we suddenly came upon a native pathway, by the side of which two men were resting. We made enquiries from them and learnt that there was a village called Tapahira about eight miles further on and they consented to hurry on ahead and tell the inhabitants that we were coming. So when we eventually arrived there at about 1.30 a.m. we found a band of about twenty men busily engaged in putting up a small grass rest house for me.

As we approached the village I had seen tracks of many species of game including eland, buffalo and sable antelope, so as soon as I had eaten some lunch I went off in the hope of shooting something that would provide meat for my own men and for the inhabitants of Tapahira, but I had no luck, and when I returned in the evening my sole bag consisted of two pigeons, which I gave to one of the local men in exchange for a dozen hens' eggs.

Next morning—Easter Sunday—we got up earlier than usual and were on our way by 5.0 a.m. The scenery now changed and instead of the lightly forested country that we had passed through during the later part of our march on the previous day, we were now in open grassland with occasional thorn trees and a little later this open parkland gave place to more wooded

country with a few dense patches of bamboo.   Unlike
the bamboo of the Highland zone in Kenya Colony the
bamboo here grew to no more than thirty feet high, and it
was very rare to find a stem of more than two inches in
diameter.

We were now heading once more straight across
country in the direction of Tendaguru Hill, and the
going was very bad.   Again and again it was necessary
to stop in order to cut down overhanging branches, so
that the porters, with their loads on their heads, could
get through, and every now and then we had to make a
wide detour round a more than usually dense patch of
thorn bush.

Presently we came to the top of a little cliff, from
which a plain stretched for miles across the country,
and here we halted while the men tried to find a convenient point at which to descend it.   Tendaguru Hill
was very plainly visible from here, about three miles
away, and I sat down on a stone to have a rest and study
the hill with my field glasses.   After a time I noticed
that the stone on which I was sitting seemed to be
unusually square, and when I examined it more closely
I found that it was a square block of concrete with an
inscription on it.   It proved to be the boundary stone
of a former German " Forest Reserve ", although the
woodlands through which we had passed hardly seemed
to be worthy of the name of forest.   I now pushed on
ahead of the porters accompanied only by my Kikuyu
boy and a local guide who had come with me from the
last camp, and in less than an hour I was standing on
Tendaguru Hill.

Before very long the porters arrived, and I told them
to put down their loads and scatter and see if they
could find any trace of former European occupation,
as I wanted something which would confirm my belief

that I had found the right place. Before long, one man
came in with a very rusty old sardine tin, and another
with a broken beer bottle, and with these objects as
clues we very soon located the actual spot upon which
the original German camp had stood just ten years
before.

We set to work at once to cut down the grass and bush
and clear a site on which to erect the tent, and when
this had been done the porters sent a deputation to me
asking that they might be paid off and allowed to start
back to Lindi. I called all of them together and
informed them that I was willing to sign on any of them
who wished to remain, as permanent employees of the
Expedition at the rate of fourteen shillings a month
and food rations, and three of them agreed to remain
with me. The others were then paid their wages for
the safari, and each given a small bonus, and while they
prepared a meal for themselves before starting back,
I hurriedly wrote some letters, including one to Mr.
Cutler, at Dar-es-Salaam, to tell him that I had located
the site and was starting to build a camp. If the men
hurried back to Lindi—and I felt sure they would—
these letters would just get there in time to catch the
weekly post to Dar-es-Salaam, which in those days was
sent regularly by runner for a distance of two hundred
and sixty-nine miles.

As we had approached Tendaguru Hill some of the
men had noticed a pool of rainwater in a small depression,
and as we did not know how soon we should locate the
spring that was supposed to be near the hill, I sent off
the three porters who had elected to stay with me with
some cans to go and bring in a supply. Meanwhile
Jumbe Ismaeli came to me and said that he was going
to see if he could find any local natives—for he had seen
the smoke of a fire some miles away—and at the same

time he requested me to fire my rifle into the air two or three times, so that if any natives were within earshot they would know that a white man had arrived in the district.   At about 4 p.m. Jumbe Ismaeli returned to camp accompanied by a few local natives who brought with them eggs, bananas and other presents.

Instead of accepting these as gifts and giving them something in return, I explained that, as we were expecting to be here for six or even eight months, I wished to start purchasing everything which we might require from the beginning, and as I had no idea of what the correct local prices were I asked Jumbe Ismaeli, who was the headman for the whole of this sub-district, to tell me what I should pay.

Accordingly I wrote down a list of prices at his dictation, and when expressed in terms of English money the prices worked out as follows :

> Eggs, a hundred for 1s.
> Bananas, one hundred and fifty for 1s.
> Locally grown rice, ½d. per pound.
> Fowls for slaughtering, 4d. each.

Jumbe Ismaeli had brought a signalling drum from one of the villages to which he had been, and at sunset he proceeded to beat out a long message which I could hear being taken up and repeated in the distance.   I asked him what message he was sending out, and he replied that he was informing the people of his district that a white man had arrived, and telling them to come next morning to greet me.   He added that he had told them to bring their knives and axes with them so as to help me start building a house.

It was with a strange mixed feeling of pleasure, triumph, expectation and loneliness that I retired to my

tent that night.   I was more than fifty miles away from
the nearest white man, in the heart of a district known
to be inhabited by lion, leopard, elephant, and many
other kinds of game.   I had only a few natives with me,
and although I was but twenty, I was undertaking a
responsible job for the British Museum and had already
achieved the first part of it.   I looked forward to the
next few months with the greatest of interest.

Next morning I was up at dawn and went out with my
gun-bearer to see if I could find any game, and when I
got back, empty-handed, at eight o'clock, I found that
about thirty natives had arrived in response to the
message sent out by drum the preceding evening.
After a very hurried breakfast we all set to work to
clear a large space at a point where there was a fairly
flat terrace on the hillside, and when that had been
done I sent most of the men off to cut poles, collect
bark fibre for lashing together the framework of the
house, and bamboos to serve as rafters, and while these
gangs were away, I and my personal boy and the gun-
bearer measured out the plan of the house, and then
started digging post holes.

I had decided to build a three-roomed bungalow
which would provide a bedroom for each of us and a
living-room in the middle and the ground plan was
like this :

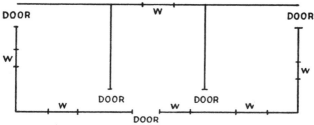

The total length of the house was 36 feet and the width
12 feet, giving each room 144 square feet of floor space.

Everybody worked very hard and by 2.30 p.m., when we stopped work for the day, as the men wanted to go home to their villages, we had already erected almost the whole framework of the house.

Next day a number of women came to work, as well as most of the men who had come on the previous day, and I set them to cut grass ready for thatching, while we continued the building work. On the third day we had completely finished everything except the thatching of the roof, and the task of tying the grass to the lath framework of the walls. By the time we knocked off work on the fourth day, only a few more hours' work remained to be done, so that by midday on the fifth day, I was able to move into my new quarters.

CHAPTER IX

HAVING BUILT THE HOUSE in which Mr. Cutler and I were to live for the next six months, I set to work to erect store houses and a kitchen nearby. I also started clearing a big area at the foot of the hill where I proposed to build the huts which our workmen would occupy.

While the work was in progress I spent several afternoons hunting for the place from which the German expedition had obtained its water supply in 1914. Eventually we found a small dry watercourse about a mile from Tendaguru Hill and when we followed down stream we came to a place where there were several large rock pools, and a little further on there was a very slight trickle of water along the bottom of the rocky bed. The stream bed was very overgrown with bushes, but after cutting some of them away we found the spot where the water was seeping out from the rocks. After a little work we succeeded in making a small reservoir just below this point and for the first few months this supplied us with all the water that we needed, but as the dry season advanced the supply became less and less and finally dried up altogether, and we then had to get our water from a much greater distance.

On May 6th I left Tendaguru to return to Lindi as I was expecting Mr. Cutler to arrive on the little coastal steamer the *Dumra*, which was due to call at Lindi on the 9th, and I had promised to meet him and help to get all our equipment and stores up to Tendaguru.

As it was only a little more than a fortnight since I and my men had come up, the track of our cross-country marches was still clearly visible, and as we went, we cut away more bush here and there so as to make the path still more definite.

We camped at Tapahira the first night and then went right through to Nkanga, thus doing the next two stages in a single day. At Nkanga I found a native messenger who had been sent by the Provincial Commissioner at Lindi, and who was on his way to Tendaguru to bring me a letter from Mr. Cutler. In this he told me that he was unavoidably detained at Dar-es-Salaam and would therefore not be able to come on the *Dumra* on the 9th. He gave me instructions to complete the camp at Tendaguru and then to " make a road from Tendaguru to Lindi."

I did not know exactly what he meant by " make a road," for the distance from Tendaguru to Lindi was over 50 miles and it was obviously impossible to make a road for wheeled traffic over that distance in so short a time. I decided, therefore, that as I was now only 17 miles from Lindi, I would go in and talk the matter over with the Provincial Commissioner.

When I reached Lindi I found several more letters from Mr. Cutler and discovered that what he wanted me to do was to have an eight-foot wide trail cleared all the way to Tendaguru so that in marching up with all the heavy loads which comprised our equipment we should be able to travel reasonably fast. He also had the idea that we might need to use the trail for lorry transport later in the season, when we had heavy cases of fossils to move, but I decided that until he had seen the nature of the country for himself and could appreciate what such a plan would cost, I would do nothing except general clearing.

I was in Lindi when the *Dumra* arrived and found that she had brought down a large number of cases of plaster of paris for our work at Tendaguru, so I asked the Provincial Commissioner to try and get me fifty porters for May 18th, on which date I planned to be back in Lindi again. Having received his promise to do so and obtained his authority to get the natives of the various villages between Lindi and Tendaguru to work at clearing the track for a wage of 6d. per man per day, I started back again for our camp.

I was anxious to get through as quickly as possible, so after spending the first night at Nkanga, I pushed on as rapidly as I could, leaving my porters to follow at their own speed. By marching almost without a pause I was able to reach Tapahira Camp by 2.30 p.m. Here I had a meal and a rest and then, leaving instructions that when my porters arrived they could spend the night there and come in on the next day, I started off again and arrived at Tendaguru Hill at 8 p.m. having marched 39 miles in the day.

Work had proceeded in camp according to plan and already a number of huts for our labourers had been erected and a good path had been cleared from camp to the water hole, and the next thing to do, therefore, was to see that the clearing of the trail to Lindi was carried out. So, after two days' rest, I marched back to Tapahira and having seen that the men of that district were working well on the bush-cutting, I went on to Noto and Nkanga and so back to Lindi once more.

When I arrived at Lindi I set to work to open all the crates of plaster of paris and make it up into 50-lb. loads ready for porterage. The porters I had asked for duly appeared, and were sent off in charge of a head man, and I myself decided to remain in Lindi as Mr.

Cutler was due to arrive on the 24th, and I expected that he would want to start off for Tendaguru straight away.

In this, however, I was mistaken, for Mr. Cutler decided that he wanted to spend about a week or ten days in Lindi discussing matters with the Provincial Commissioner and also studying the local geology to see whether it would throw any light upon the problems that we were to deal with at Tendaguru ; accordingly I once again set off for camp alone, taking with me a large number of the loads of equipment. I again accomplished the journey in two days, and after two more days in camp I started back for Lindi.

Even after I had arrived there several more days had to be spent in clearing the remainder of our goods through the Customs, and dividing the things up in one-man loads and eventually on June 11th, Mr. Cutler and I started off, just eight weeks after I had made my first march along that route. During those eight weeks I had travelled backwards and forwards a good many times, and an eight-foot path had been cleared along the whole distance, while Tendaguru Hill had been transformed from wild bush to a neat encampment with accommodation for a hundred men.

The journey with Mr. Cutler was not without its amusing incidents. He was exceedingly interested in all the new plants he saw and started collecting specimens straight away. After a while we came to a district where a small climbing bean was very plentiful and he wanted to collect not only its flowers and leaves but also some of the seed pods. This particular bean happened to be one that I knew well and I warned Mr. Cutler to leave the seed pods severely alone, or, if he must have them, to handle them with very great care, as they are covered with very small hairs which are very lightly attached to the pods, and which cause excruciating pain to the human skin if they come in contact with it.

Unfortunately Mr. Cutler did not heed my warning, and while I was not looking he had apparently picked a number of the pods and tied them up in his handkerchief. When we reached Noto camp we were all very tired and hot and sat down under the shade of a mango tree to rest, and Mr. Cutler proceeded to take the pods out of his handkerchief and then wipe his face and neck with it. In a moment the little hairs were all over him and he was dancing about in agony, yelling like a madman and cursing like a trooper. Fortunately I had some soothing lotion in the medical chest and after a little time was able to alleviate the pain, but not before he had sworn to do no more botanical collecting in Africa.

In another incident our headman Juma played the chief rôle. Included in the equipment supplied by the Museum, there was a very nice small-bore, single-barrel, collector's gun, and I had loaded this with dust shot and given it to Juma to carry. During the war Juma had been a soldier in the German army and he was very proud of this and constantly boasted of his marksmanship. He had never seen a collector's gun before, and imagined that it was a rifle, for it was quite unlike any shot-gun he had ever seen. As we marched through the forested patches between Noto and Tapahira Juma, who happened to be ahead of everyone, suddenly found himself face to face with a snarling leopard. In an instant the gun went to his shoulder and he fired at almost point blank range—with dust shot ! Thinking he was using a rifle he was astounded that the leopard did not fall down dead, and he came rushing back to us to warn us to be careful as there was a charmed leopard in the road which was invulnerable, and which must be an evil witch-doctor in the guise of a beast, waiting to kill us.

We reached Tendaguru easily in three days, for Mr. Cutler was a very good walker, and on June 15th we started in earnest upon our work of collecting fossil reptiles. From then until the end of October we never went to Lindi again.

After a few days of preliminary reconnoitring Mr. Cutler selected three main sites for excavation and after that our work was carried out with almost routine regularity and hardly varied from one week to another.

I had recruited about one hundred labourers, of whom only a few were local men, while the vast majority were members of a tribe living over a hundred miles away, the Wangoni, while a few had come from even further and were Wayao from Nyasaland. Every year large parties of men from these tribes come to places like Lindi in search of work. I had made it known as soon as I arrived at Lindi in April, that we were going to employ a large staff, and since news in Africa travels quickly, by the time we were ready to start excavation work we had had applications for employment from far more men than we could take on.

At 5.0 every morning, except Sunday, I used to get up and go outside our house and beat loudly upon the signalling drum which Jumbe Ismaeli had originally used to announce my arrival in the district and which I had acquired for the sum of three shillings. At 5.30 the drum was beaten again and all the men would file up from their camp to the store shed near the house. Here I took roll call, and issued the men with their tools and gave the head men of the different gangs their orders for the day.

The workmen then started off for their sites where

they were excavating, while I attended to the sick parade, for almost always a few of the men were down with malaria or some other complaint. As soon as sick parade was over, I would set off to one or other of the three sites on which work was proceeding, and then return to camp for breakfast about eight. Directly after breakfast Mr. Cutler and I would start out. Usually he and I would go to the same site and spend the day in preserving the bones with shellac and then setting them in plaster of paris, for our native workmen only removed the overlying deposits, and all the actual work of preserving and taking up the fossils was done by us.

I had never done this work before, but Mr. Cutler was an excellent teacher and from him I gained the most valuable practical training, which has proved immensely useful to me in my subsequent career.

At each site we had three gangs working, a small gang who dug with the picks, a larger gang who shovelled the debris into baskets, and a big gang engaged in carrying these baskets of debris away to a dump. The Museum had supplied us with a number of wheelbarrows, and I had tried to make the men use them, but they simply hated them, and after finding them on several occasions carrying wheelbarrows half full of soil on their heads, or in other words using them in their traditional manner as though they were baskets, we abandoned them, and used baskets instead.

Owing to the distance of the sites from the camp the men had elected to work continuously from 5.30 to 2.0 p.m. and then knock off for the day, so we used to set an alarm clock in camp before we left and when this went off at 2.0 p.m. the cook would get out the signalling drum and sound it. Although none of the excavations was less than three miles from camp, the notes of the drum could be heard quite distinctly at every site and as soon as they heard them the men would knock off for the day and hurry back to camp to get a meal and then rest.

Mr. Cutler and I would then leave the site where we had been working, and separate, each of us going to one of the other two sites to see how the men had progressed in the work they had been set to do. We used to get back to camp for lunch at about 4.0 p.m. After this very late lunch I had to inspect the work that the native bird collector had done and write the labels and enter the specimens in a catalogue, while Mr. Cutler was usually busy working on some of the smaller fossil specimens which were brought back to camp for treatment.

Just before sunset the headman of each gang of ten would come up to the storehouse to receive the rations for his men next day. These included an allowance of water for cooking and drinking, for very soon after we had started work in earnest the water hole near the camp had dried up completely and we were having to get all the water for ourselves and our men from a distance of ten miles.

There was actually a little water very much nearer than that, but this was the supply of the local families, and they had begged us not to use it, for, as they pointed out, if it was used by all the people in our camp who numbered over a hundred and twenty (some of the men had brought their wives), it would soon be used up and they themselves would be waterless.

The place where all our water came from was a series of three big stagnant pools that had collected during the rainy season in natural reservoirs in the rocky bottom of a dried-up river bed. We had had to spend a number of days of very intensive search before finding this supply, and I reckoned that if we rationed the water carefully it would last us until the rains started again.

Of the three pools, one was set aside for washing purposes, and on Sundays any of the men who wanted to wash had to walk ten miles to this pool, wash themselves and their clothes and then come back again to camp. Similarly, our personal servants had to go over once a week to wash our clothes there, as we had forbidden anyone actually to take any water out of this pool. A second pool was set aside to supply water for cooking and drinking. Each day a gang of fifteen men walked over to the pool and came back in the evening, each carrying five gallons of water in a can on his head. Of this 75 gallons a day, a part had to be set aside for the plaster of paris work, and the remainder was divided out among ourselves and our workmen. The third and smallest pool was left as a reserve supply for emergencies.

The feeding of our employees also caused us a good deal of difficulty, for the local natives were quite unable to supply us with all that we needed. As a result, we had to send messengers to districts situated as much as thirty and forty miles away to tell the people that we were prepared to pay cash for all food brought into camp. By this means at first, we were able to obtain a fairly regular supply of maize, millet and cassava, but after a little time fewer and fewer natives came in with food to sell and the position began to grow serious. On investigation, we found that the reason for this lay in the fact that we were only paying the same prices as they could obtain for their products in Lindi. We had considered this quite fair, as by coming to us they saved themselves the walk in to Lindi ; but they pointed out that when they went to Lindi they were able to make use of the opportunity to spend some of the money at the shops, whereas if they came to us they only received cash, and then had to make a special journey to Lindi in order to spend their money. This was, of course, an entirely reasonable argument, but instead of increasing our prices and so making it more profitable to sell to us than to the Indian traders at the coast, we sent for a considerable quantity of cloth and beads, and other things which the natives wished to buy, and announced that in future we were willing to give trade goods as part payment for food supplies to any who preferred this.

Even so we were not always able to purchase all that we needed, and once or twice we had to send some of our men all the way to Lindi to buy extra supplies for our staff.

Another problem in connection with food supply was how to obtain enough meat to be able to give some to every man at least once a week. The Government had given us a special licence entitling us to shoot certain species of animals for food for ourselves and for our men, but in the immediate vicinity of camp game was very scarce owing to the lack of water.

Some twelve miles to the north—much less as the crow flies—was the Mbemkuru river, which, even in the dry season, always has some big pools of water, with the result that most of the game in the district congregated in that region at this time of the year. Every Sunday, therefore, I used to leave camp at about 4.0 a.m., and walk over to the Mbemkuru river to shoot. The animal or animals so obtained were cut up and the meat carried home by a party of the men.

Our special licence had been issued to us at Dar-es-Salaam and it entitled us to shoot "the commonest species of game in the district." When I enquired what the " commonest species " included, I was told that I was to ask for information on this point from the Provincial Commissioner at Lindi. Very much to my surprise I learned that the commonest game here consisted of eland, sable-antelope and greater kudu, so that these were the animals off which we and our men fed. In Kenya all of these three species are considered to be so rare that, at the most, a sportsman may only shoot two males of each in a year ; the idea of being allowed to shoot them regularly for food was, therefore, astounding to me.

Besides these animals, buffalo were fairly common at the Mbemkuru and so were elephant, and on one occasion I narrowly escaped being killed by the latter. I had seen a big covey of guinea fowl and wanted to bag one or two for our own table, so I handed my rifle to the gun-bearer and taking my shot-gun followed after them. Guinea fowl have an unpleasant habit of running away very fast and are consequently very difficult to approach. This covey led me on and on. At last I began to get near them and started crawling along very slowly in some thick bushes. Suddenly I heard a curious rumbling which was presently repeated on the other side of me, and in a minute I realised that I had crawled right into the middle of a herd of elephants. To make matters worse they were cows with young calves, and I had only a shot-gun with me, as I had left my gun-bearer more than half a mile away.

It was an unpleasant moment. With thumping heart I very slowly crawled away again, in terror lest the elephants should catch my wind, in which case they would almost certainly have charged me.

On another occasion my gun-bearer had a very similar experience but he was not so lucky for he was actually charged ; fortunately for him he was near an immense baobab tree with a trunk about eight feet in diameter, and into this he managed to climb. He was then kept treed for several hours, but the tree was so big that although they tried to do so, the elephants were unable to push it over.

During the time that I was at Tendaguru I had two other narrow escapes, one from a snake and the other from a leopard. Let me quote the snake incident as I recorded it in my diary.

" We were on our way home when I saw Salimu (my gun bearer) give a sudden leap aside, and caught sight of a ' maamba ' the most deadly of all African snakes striking at him. Having missed him it darted into the grass, and I followed it at once with my shot-gun at full cock and my eyes skinned to the ground lest it should strike at me. Of course I was a fool, for had I reflected at all I should have remembered that the maamba is a tree snake and loves to strike from above at its victim's neck. As I walked along something made me glance up and only just in time, for there, not a foot from my head, was the maamba up in a little shrub with its head poised to strike. I jumped back and it struck where my neck had been one-fifth of a second before, and then I blew it to a thousand pieces with my shot-gun. Had it got me nothing could have saved me, for one cannot quite put a tourniquet on the neck, and the poison works in about one minute."

The escape from the leopard was very different, for I have no absolute proof that I was in danger, although I think so. We had had a rather severe outbreak of dysentery among our men, and I had been looking after them when I went down with this disease myself, and with malaria simultaneously. I was exceedingly weak, and one night about midnight I suddenly heard footsteps in the living-room that divided my bedroom from Mr. Cutler's. Thinking it was my chief I tried to call out to him to bring me a glass of water, as the fever made me terribly thirsty, but I was so weak that I could hardly raise my voice above a whisper and I received no answer. After a minute or two, the footsteps came towards the door which led to my bedroom and which was open. I then heard deep regular breathing and realised that it was not Mr. Cutler at all but some wild animal. Again I tried to shout but I was too weak to do so. The next minute a leopard leapt on a little pet baboon of mine that was sleeping by my bedside and jumped away with it through the open window.

Later on, the natives brought me another young baboon, a new-born baby. I improvised a feeding-bottle for it from an old quinine bottle with a piece of handkerchief to act as a kind of wick to draw up the milk, as I had no rubber teat available. This baboon, to which I gave the name of " Baby ", used to sleep at first inside my bed for warmth, and after the experience we had had with her predecessor, we took every precaution to see that no leopard could get into the house again at night. Having been brought up on a bottle Baby became completely tame, and during the day was allowed to wander about freely round the camp. Unlike most simian pets she was exceedingly well behaved and seldom got into mischief. After a time I acquired a little black-faced monkey as a companion for her, but he was much older and for a long time had to be kept chained up. In the end he, too, became tame enough to be given his liberty, and although he would sometimes wander away and be missing for hours, he would always come back to camp in the end.

Although our native staff were drawn from a number

of different tribes, and although some of them were Protestant converts, others Roman Catholics, and yet others worshippers after the manner of their own tribes, they all got on exceedingly well together, and quarrels were rare. The few cases of serious trouble that did arise were invariably due to quarrels over the women in camp. A small proportion of the men had brought their wives with them, and one man had brought his sister as well. This girl was the cause of several fights, for she bestowed her favours liberally while telling each admirer that he and he alone was her lover.

When any serious quarrel arose the men had to report the matter to us, and we would hear the evidence of both parties and then arbitrate. In addition to this, the men set up a court of their own, and almost every Sunday, as well as sometimes in the afternoons after work was over for the day, a group of men could be seen sitting under the shade of a big tree holding a court.

African natives are usually exceedingly good orators and they love debating ; they will sometimes even invent a reason for having a civil case with somebody, simply because they want to enjoy the pleasures of a legal debate. Very often, in camp, the cases which were argued out on Sundays before the court which our men had set up for themselves, were not serious at all, but were really in the nature of a game—a means of obtaining experience in the native legal methods of debate, so that if they should ever find themselves engaged in a serious case they would not be at a loss to know how to proceed.

Occasionally I used to go and listen to these debates because they amused me. One example of a case which I attended will serve to show that the matter was often treated as a form of entertainment, in much the same

way that people in this country become members of
debating societies, or hold mock trials.

A man called Pangawassi addressed the meeting and
complained that the cock of a man called Issa had
unlawfully associated with his hen, and he claimed
damages. The president of the meeting then called on
Issa to say if he wished to contest this. He said he
certainly did ; and so Pangawassi was told to state his
case and call his evidence. He then spoke fluently, and
with great oratorical skill, for about half an hour and
after that called witnesses to support him.

Issa then stood up and at equal length proceeded to
show reason why the allegation must be untrue, after
which he argued that even if it was true it was he who
was entitled to claim damages from Pangawassi, because
Pangawassi did not keep a cock himself and yet some of
his hens had recently hatched out broods of chickens.
He counter-claimed, therefore, that if it was true that
his cock had unlawfully associated with the plaintiff's
hens, it had done so with the connivance of the plaintiff
and he, Issa, was entitled to a part of each brood, which
could not have come into existence without his cock.
The assembled audience was then asked if there was
anyone present who wished to make any observations,
and several men thereupon made good speeches, some
in support of the plaintiff and others the defendant.
After hearing all the evidence the senior members of the
assembly retired to deliberate on their verdict and
finally returned to announce that the evidence against
the cock was proved and that he would be fined two
tail feathers. So far as the counter-claim was concerned the evidence was insufficient as there were
other cocks than Issa's in the camp.

The whole proceedings were carried out with as much
formality as if a case had been between a man and a

woman, and when it was over it was held to have been one of the most amusing and entertaining cases of the year.

In addition to holding these " trials " as a means of passing their spare time, our men frequently held dances on Sundays. Many of them also spent a good deal of their spare time in various handicrafts. Several of them were very good wood-carvers, and they made immense numbers of ebony walking-sticks, most of which Mr. Cutler and I bought for sixpence apiece. I brought back to England just over a hundred of these and, as I shall relate presently, they helped to keep me in clothes for my last two years at Cambridge.

Some of the men were expert basket weavers and they made large numbers of baskets which they sold to the various natives who came to camp from time to time selling food.

At the beginning of October most of our men who had come from remote districts announced that they wished to go home again, so as to take part in the work of crop-planting as soon as the rains, which were now almost due, should start. So we paid them off, and after that we were forced to restrict our excavation work very considerably as we were now left with only about thirty local men.

As we had not even had a shower of rain since the middle of May, all the grass and bush in the district was exceedingly dry. For several weeks we had seen big grass fires raging in the distance, and we began to be afraid for the safety of our camp. The wind at this season of the year was very violent, and there was still a very great deal of dry grass and bush on the hillside round our house, although we had cut it back in the immediate vicinity. One afternoon, therefore, when there was a lull in the wind, we decided to fire some of the grass on the hill and so make a more efficient fire-break. Unfortunately, soon after we had started the fire, the wind changed from a gentle breeze to a hurricane and the fire was soon out of control. Several times our buildings were in great danger, and we had to keep constant watch until long after midnight. When at last the fire was out everything in our house was covered in soot and it was days before we were clean again.

Two days later we had our first torrential downpour and in less than five minutes the roof of the house was leaking like a sieve. Although it had originally been waterproof, white ants had been at work for months and had eaten a good deal of the thatch, and in consequence it was very thin in places. Realising that the roof of the store house where our fossils were kept was probably in the same condition, I left the cook and house-boys to do what they could in the house, and rushed down the hill to inspect it. My worst fears were realised, the water was pouring in, and we had to spend a frantic half-hour covering all our specimens with sacking and sheets of waterproof paper.

It was fortunate that on this particular day I happened to be in camp, otherwise most of our specimens might have been seriously damaged. Mr. Cutler and the men were all out at the excavations when the storm broke, and when they returned to camp they looked more like drowned rats than I have ever seen human beings look before or since.

When I joined the expedition it had been agreed that I should leave at the end of October, as by then Mr. Cutler would have acquired local knowledge, as well as a sufficient command of the language, to enable him to continue without my help. But as the time of my departure approached he decided that he would like me to stay on for another season's work, so I wrote to Cambridge to find out what my tutor thought I had better do.

During the second week in October I received a reply to my letter and as a result I decided that I must adhere to my original plan. I accordingly cabled to the Museum authorities declining their offer that I should continue in their employment, and started to make preparations for my return journey.

The *Dumra* was due to leave Lindi for Dar-es-Salaam on November 3rd; I accordingly decided to leave Tendaguru towards the end of October and march to Lindi so as to have a day or two there before I sailed. Mr. Cutler decided to come with me as far as Lindi, and on October 27th I set off on the first stage of my journey home, vainly imagining that this was the last long march I should have to undertake for some time to come.

CHAPTER X

ON REACHING LINDI I found to my dismay that news had just been received that as a result of boiler trouble the *Dumra* would not be coming down to Lindi for some weeks, and no other boat of any kind was due for at least another fortnight. As I had booked my passage from Dar-es-Salaam on a steamer due to leave on November 16th, this was most unpleasant news. After talking the matter over with the Provincial Commissioner and Mr. Cutler I decided that the only thing to do was to walk the two hundred and sixty-nine miles to Dar-es-Salaam. Had I been able to start immediately this would not have been very difficult, but it was not until the evening of November 3rd that I was able to collect enough porters for the journey and so on November 4th I set out with only twelve days left in which to cover this distance. I knew that the two mail runners were in the habit of doing the journey in eight or nine days, but of course I could not hope to travel as fast as they did, as a large party of men always travels more slowly than a small one, and I was taking fourteen porters in addition to my Kikuyu boy, Nahashon, and a headman.

As I wanted to travel as fast as possible I divided up my luggage into much smaller loads than usual, and most of the packages did not weigh more than 30 lbs. In a few cases where a load could not be reduced I took two porters for a single load, so that they could take turns with it and thus keep up with the others.

As I had found considerable difficulty in obtaining

enough porters for the safari, I had decided to leave some of my heavy luggage that I did not want in a hurry to be forwarded later by steamer, and I also dispensed with a tent, and the biggest and most cumbersome load that I had with me was the big cage in which my pet baboon and monkey were travelling. This was slung on a pole and carried by two men on their shoulders.

I got my porters off at 5.0 a.m. on November 4th in charge of the headman. I myself remained behind until eight, as I had forgotten to obtain a licence for the rifle that I was taking with me, and I feared that without a licence I should have difficulty in disposing of it when I reached Dar-es-Salaam.

The track followed the line of the coast, and took me right through the Kikwetu Sisal Estate, so I called in to see my friends Mr. and Mrs. Cooper, and bid them good-bye. They were away, however, but I was given a cup of tea by one of the staff and I learned the news which they had just received, that the Conservatives had won the General Election in England with a majority of about 200. Neither he nor I, nor any of the other Europeans on the estate really believed it.

Shortly after leaving Kikwetu I came across a clean, swiftly running little stream, so I halted, had a meal in the shade of the trees which overhung the banks, and then bathed in one of the pools. Although on arrival at Lindi Mr. Cutler and I had had the exquisite pleasure of washing in a reasonably large quantity of really clean water for the first time since June, I had not been able to have a proper bath, as even there water was short at that time of year ; so this opportunity of a bathe and swim in crystal clear running water was too good to be missed.

Pushing on again, I caught up with my porters resting

beneath the shade of some mango-trees. The fruit was all very unripe but the men were so thirsty that they were sucking the very acid, unripe mangoes to quench their thirst. I let the monkeys out of their cage for a short time and gave them a drink of water—they would not touch the unripe mangoes—and then we started off again. I now took the lead and was soon far ahead of my men.

At 4.0 p.m. I found myself on the outskirts of a little native village called Mchinga, and on enquiring from the inhabitants I learned that there was a small Government rest-house about a mile further on, near the headman's house. So I sent on a note to say that I would be arriving shortly, and intended to spend the night in the rest-house. I requested the headman to have water and food ready which I could buy for my porters and if possible some fresh fruit and a fowl for myself. When I reached the rest-house I found that it was a more elaborate one than any I had seen in the whole Province. It was built of stone and plaster, and had a corrugated iron roof. I learned from the headman that it had been the home of a German trader in pre-war days when this little village had had a European population of five.

As the night was very fine I decided not to sleep in the house, however, but had my bed made up on the white sandy beach under some palm trees. The headman was exceedingly friendly and at once offered to send a messenger on ahead of me with a note to the headman of Kiswere, where I planned to spend the following night. Actually, two men set off together as they hate travelling alone by night, and I gave them one of my lanterns to take with them.

As Kiswere was a long way off, and the sun during the day was very hot, I decided that we would leave at

2.0 a.m. and cover as many miles as possible before the heat of the day. So at 1.0 a.m. we got up, cooked a light meal, and set off in the darkness, guided by a local man who had been detailed for the purpose by the headman.

Just before sunrise I reached a little village called Limbe, having marched without a halt of any kind for three and a half hours. Here I rested on the verandah of the local headman's house, and listened to the plaintive tones of the devout Mohammedans at their prayers in the little mud-built mosque nearby. Presently, having finished their prayers, the headman of the village and his friends arrived and he very kindly gave me some bananas and a cup of tea, while I returned the compliment by presenting him with a packet of cigarettes.

I had reached Limbe far ahead of my porters, and by the time they arrived at 6.30 I was fully rested, so I told them that they could stop for an hour and then follow on, and I started off again hoping to reach Mkoe Sisal Estate in time to have breakfast with an old Cambridge man to whom I had letters of introduction. I got in at about 9.0, and although he had already had his own breakfast, Mr. Pitt very kindly ordered his cook to prepare something for me at once, and I spent a very pleasant morning on the estate. Having made such an early start we were already well on our way to Kiswere, and I decided to let the men rest through the heat of the day. We did not in fact continue our march until three o'clock in the afternoon.

Just as darkness came on, the track along which we were marching faded away and I found myself suddenly floundering in the stinking mud of a mangrove swamp. I wished then that I had not allowed the guide to leave us and go home. However, after a little, we found that the path really continued through the swamp and that beyond it was the open water of the Kiswere estuary.

Beyond the water we could see the fires of a small village so we shouted across and soon a small outrigger canoe came across and after making a number of journeys it eventually landed us and our loads safely on the far bank.

By this time it was nearly 9.0 p.m. We had had a twenty-hour day and were all very tired and very glad to get some sleep. Instead of making an early start next morning I allowed the men to sleep late and we did not set out again until after the worst heat of the day was over at about half-past two. During the morning, while the men were resting, I amused myself by exploring round Kiswere, which had been a German trading centre before the war, and the scene of a great deal of fighting towards the end of the East African campaign. Kiswere had also been the scene of a small naval bombardment and there were still numerous signs of shell holes, as well as a good many old trenches and barbed wire entanglements.

We marched until sunset, then cooked some supper, and having thus rested we started off again at about 9.0 p.m. and eventually reached the little village of Likoma some time after midnight, and camped for the night. We did not, however, sleep long, as I had heard from the local natives, who had been aroused by our arrival, that at Kitandura, about ten miles further on, I should have to take a dhow, or Arab sailing vessel, to get me across an arm of the sea, and they added that the dhow which acted as ferry at this point usually left Kitandura at about 9.0 in the morning.

It was absolutely essential that we should not miss this ferry, as, if we did, we should lose a whole day, so I started off again at 5.0 a.m. after only a few hours sleep and hurried on to Kitandura, leaving my men to come on with the headman as quickly as they could.

I was fortunate in reaching Kitandura before the dhow sailed and I managed to bribe the owner to wait until all my porters arrived, although the last of them did not get in until nearly midday as he was suffering from a slight attack of malaria.

We had almost waited too long, for the tide was rapidly going out and in a few more minutes the dhow would have been too firmly stranded in the mud to move until the tide came in again, but after much pushing and heaving by all the porters as well as the crew we were able to get away, and sailed straight across Kilwa Bay to the island of Kilwa Kiswani, where we landed at 3.30 p.m.

This island is a place of considerable historical interest, and on it there are the ruins of ancient fortifications supposed to date back to the early centuries of the Christian era, when adventurous traders from the Red Sea and the Persian Gulf used to sail down the coast of East Africa. From an ancient Arab record which is called "The Chronicles of Kilwa," we know that in the tenth century the island of Kilwa Kiswani was the headquarters of King Ali, who held sway over much of the neighbouring coast, and who set up his son as King of Mombasa. We also know that when King Ali bought the island, there was already a Muslim settlement and a mosque there. There is every reason to believe that as early as the sixth century there were both Arab and Persian settlements along the coast, and some of the more ancient Kilwa ruins may date back to this time.

Having beached our dhow on the island the crew, and also my men, set to work to cook themselves a meal, while I enjoyed a most interesting walk among the ruins. In addition to these earlier ruins there is the shell of an old Portuguese fort that was set up,

I believe, about 1668, and I very much wished that I could have spared the time to spend several days on the island.

The tide went out and left our dhow high and dry, and it was not until 10 p.m. that we were able to float her again and set off for Horero on the north side of the Bay of Kilwa. We arrived there shortly after midnight, having had a fine breeze to fill our sails, and as soon as we landed we set out to march to Kilwa Kivinji, some twelve miles away.

There is a Government station at Kilwa Kivinji and I knew that I should find a rest-house where I could have a comfortable sleep. I should also be able to buy an adequate supply of food for my porters, who were very hungry, for we had not been able to buy much on Kilwa Island because the people were suffering from a food shortage at the end of the dry season.

I reached the rest-house at 5.0 a.m. and was soon sound asleep, but was awakened an hour later by the arrival of the porters, who had lagged behind. I at once gave them money to go and buy food and told them to eat and sleep and return at 4 p.m.

At about 8.0 a.m., when I was thinking of getting my boy to cook me some breakfast, I received a note from the Police Inspector who had heard of my arrival from one of the sentries on night duty, asking me to come and have breakfast with him. I was exceedingly dirty and very unshaven after the past strenuous days, and did not feel fit to appear in company. However, I did not want to seem rude, so I hastily shaved, put on the least dirty clothing I had with me, and went to his house.

He was extremely kind, and I spent a most enjoyable day with him and did not set off again on my march until six o'clock in the evening. As we had rested all day I intended that we should march most of the night, but we very soon found ourselves stopped by a wide estuary, and although there was a ferry boat there to take passengers across it, the ferry was high and dry owing to the tide being out ; so we were forced to sleep by the bank and were not able to get across until five next morning.

I was very much upset by this delay of eleven hours, and to make matters worse, after we had crossed the estuary we found that the track led through a mangrove swamp which, as the tide was then high, made progress exceedingly slow, and very tiring.

When we reached the next village, Mitega, at 10.0 a.m., my men were all very worn out, so I decided to let them rest during the heat of the day and we did not start off again until after 3.0 p.m. The men were now well rested and we marched almost without pause until 7-30 p.m., when we arrived at Nambuchi, where we slept until 4.0 a.m., and then after a hurried breakfast, started off again. After four and a half hours' march, however, the men complained that they simply could not go on, and I was forced to call a halt for the day at a village called Morendegu.

As there was now an almost full moon, I decided to wait until about midnight, and we then set off again and marched with occasional halts for the next twelve hours and arrived on the banks of the Rufiji river at mid-day on November 11th.

During the afternoon I wandered along the bank of the river with some natives who had begged me to go with them and try to shoot some of the crocodiles that were a constant menace to the people. Several women and children had recently been carried off when they had gone to the river to draw water, and in consequence the natives had built a barricade well out into the river at one place, so that the water could be reached in safety.

In view of the number of crocodiles that infest the
river, and also after what I had heard about the recent
attacks upon the women, I was very surprised to find
a number of men wading well out in the river catching
fish by a most curious method. About fifteen men
walked along the river holding in front of them a very
long reed mat which was weighted at the bottom to
keep it upright. After a time the men at one end of the
line gradually moved round until the mat was in the
form of a semi-circle instead of a straight line and they
then gradually edged the whole mat nearer and nearer
to the bank, in this way enclosing the fish in fairly
shallow water.

A number of men and women then came down,
entered the enclosed space and proceeded to catch the
fish in it with their bare hands and throw them up on
the bank. Judged by the size of the bag which resulted
from a manœuvre lasting only about three quarters of
an hour, this was a very successful method of fishing,
and when they had finished each member of the shore
and the wading parties went off with about five medium-
sized fishes.

I asked the men if they were not afraid of being
attacked by crocodiles while wading in this way, and
they replied by pointing to charms hanging round their
necks which they assured me would keep off any
crocodile. I naturally asked why the women did not
wear similar charms when they went to draw water.
This enquiry produced a roar of laughter, and when
at last they were calm enough to explain, they told me,
quite seriously, that the charm would only work in
connection with fishing activities. The charms were
little bits of bone of a fish-eagle and illustrate one of
the many forms of sympathetic magic which Africans
rely on so largely. They declared that they had not

yet found a charm which would protect women when drawing water.

At this spot, the river was also infested with hippopotami, and these animals had recently begun to attack the canoes used for ferrying passengers across the river, so I was advised not to try and cross until after night-fall when they would be on land, feeding. We planned to start at about 10.0 p.m., but a terrific thunderstorm broke just before that hour and in consequence I waited until 1.0 a.m. when, as the rain showed no sign of abating, I insisted that the ferrymen should take us over. When we reached the other side the storm became worse and I was forced to let the men take shelter so that we did not start off until four in the morning. It was still raining heavily and the men protested strongly, but we had already wasted so much time that I knew that if we did not start now we should certainly not reach Dar-es-Salaam in time to catch my steamer, and, having come so far I was determined to get through.

It rained almost incessantly throughout that day, but I had to make the men go on, and in the end I got all my porters into Kikale after twelve very weary and unpleasant hours. We were all soaked to the skin and terribly cold, in spite of having walked almost continuously, and I was afraid some of my men would go down with malaria, so I dosed them all, as well as myself, with quinine. At Kikale I found there was an excellent Government rest-house, which was occupied at the time by an engineer of the Telegraph Department who was repairing the line which connects Lindi and Dar-es-Salaam.

He very kindly lent me a suit of dry clothes and entertained me right royally that night, not only with good food and drink, but also with very good stories.

During the course of the evening he tapped the line and got into communication with Dar-es-Salaam to enquire whether the date of sailing of my steamer had been altered. I was hoping that it might have been postponed for a day as often happens, and this would have made things much easier for me, but he received the news that she was definitely going to sail on the afternoon of the 16th. That meant I had just four more days. Mr. Scott assured me that it was an easy four days' march and in consequence I decided to let my men have a long night's rest and we did not start again until 7.30 next morning.

The country we had just passed through was absolutely flat and intersected by the many branches of the Rufiji river delta. During the rainy season, which lasts in this region from about January to April, the whole country becomes flooded, and in consequence the natives have devised special houses, or rather shelters built upon piles, to which they retire during this time. I saw a large number of these wet-season houses which were just being put in order again, after having been unoccupied for many months. The rains were nearly due, as the thunderstorms of the last few days had clearly shown.

These pile houses are neither elaborate nor comfortable, but they evidently serve the purpose for which they are devised. Each consists of a small platform, supported by about twenty poles and is some ten feet above the ground. On this square platform a small round hut about ten feet in diameter is built, and the floor of the hut consists simply of the poles which form the platform, with wide cracks in between through which all the rubbish falls into the water below.

Into this hut all the family belongings are taken and there is just room for the family to live. If they want to visit any of their friends they have to go by canoe, and so far as I could make out from the natives I spoke to, when they are marooned in these pile dwellings they spend most of the time making baskets and nets and mats from materials which are collected during the dry season and put on one side for this purpose.

As their dry season huts are certain to be destroyed by the floods every year, the natives of this area do not build such substantial or semi-permanent dwellings as many other East African tribes. The first task when the floods subside is to plant out their fields which have been enriched by a˙ thick covering of silt. Only when the planting is over do they set to work to re-build their dry-season huts, since the pile dwellings are too cramped to live in except when it is absolutely necessary.

It apparently has never occurred to these natives that if they took more trouble and constructed bigger and more comfortable pile dwellings they could live in them all the year round and so save themselves much extra work.

During the next two days' march nothing of special interest occurred. We were passing through a thickly populated area and here the season was much more advanced than it had been in the Lindi region ; among other things the mango trees everywhere were covered with ripe fruit, so we fared sumptuously. Besides mangoes many of the natives were growing beautiful pineapples, but we bought few of these, as we found that there were quantities of wild pineapples in the bush by the side of the track, which could be had for the mere picking. These wild fruit were not so big or so juicy as the cultivated ones, but they were excellent in taste and I myself ate six at a single sitting.

The evening of the second day saw us camped at a little village called Mikere. The natives there warned

me that the next day's march would be very severe as
it was 31 miles to the nearest watering place. Each of
my men was carrying water for drinking, but we were
already too loaded to be able to carry sufficient, and
anyhow, at Mikere water was so short that the villagers
would not spare us very much. We accordingly left
at 2.0 a.m. and reached Kigamba, where there was
supposed to be water, at 11.0 a.m., having covered the
thirty-one miles in nine hours. We were tired out and
meant to camp here and have a good meal and a rest,
but the local inhabitants had barely enough food and
water for themselves and were unwilling to let us have
more than a very little, so we obviously could not
spend the night there, and, after resting until 4.30 p.m.,
we pushed on once more and four hours later reached
Vikindu, eight miles further on, on the evening of
November 15th.

Vikindu is only fifteen miles from Dar-es-Salaam
and it was very pleasant to lie down that night knowing
that we had only five or six more hours of marching
to do, and that the steamer was not due to sail until
late in the afternoon so that we had plenty of time,
provided that she did not leave before schedule.

I was determined, however, to take no risks, and so
we rose at 3.0 a.m. and set off a half an hour later.
Although my feet were very sore and I was tired out,
the fact that the journey was so nearly over put new
life into me, and helped by the fact that the night air
was so cool and fresh I myself covered those fifteen
miles in four hours and arrived at the Burgher Hotel
in Dar-es-Salaam at 7.30 a.m.

Filthy and unshaven as I was, I went straight into
the dining-room and ordered myself a substantial
breakfast, and after that I booked a room and had a
glorious hot bath and a shave and felt a new man.

My porters were very very tired and they did not get in until three hours after I did. Putting down their loads, they took the money which I gave them to buy food with and went away saying they would return later for their pay.

I found on arrival that the steamer had been delayed after all, and was now not due to sail until next morning, so I spent the night in Dar-es-Salaam with Major Noel Davis whom I had met when we were there in April. I had called on him in the afternoon to return some maps which I had borrowed, and when he saw how tired I was, and heard of the forced march I had made, he insisted on my leaving the hotel and spending the night at his house. I was most grateful for this very kind invitation and spent a very enjoyable evening with him.

So ended the most tiring journey I have ever had ; but although I was worn out and foot-sore I had thoroughly enjoyed the experience, and after a few days' rest I felt fitter than I had done for many months.

I disembarked at Mombasa, and took the train up country to pay a short visit to my parents before returning to Cambridge. I took with me my pet baboon and monkey which I could not take back to England, and gave them to my sister at Kabete.

Nahashon, my Kikuyu boy, was overjoyed to be back among his own people once more and for a time was in great demand at all the villages near Kabete, where everyone wanted to hear about his travels, and in particular about the journeys on the steamer. But Nahashon was one of the most silent men I have ever come across, and although he had seen so much that was new, and in spite of the fact that he had kept a diary all the time he was with me, he managed to convey extraordinarily few of his impressions to his friends, and a few years later when I was once more at home I learned from one of his brothers that even his own family had not been able to get much information from him. When I spoke to Nahashon about it and asked why he had not told people more, he replied to the effect that he did not like talking much and anyhow what was the use of telling people things when they kept interrupting him and saying he must be exaggerating !

To Kikuyus who have never travelled away from their own country, much of what they are told by the few who have made long journeys to other countries seems so incredible that they tend to treat all of it as travellers' tales, and I know that both Stefano and Ishmael, the boys whom my father had taken to England in the past, had found the same thing.

To-day things have changed a great deal, for already quite a number of Kikuyu can read English, and so have had their outlook considerably widened by reading books and the newspapers that are published in Nairobi. Some of the Kikuyu boys who have been on my more recent expeditions have had a very different experience from Nahashon's, and in fact when they have told the plain unvarnished truth about their adventures they have often been accused, not of romancing, but of not giving all the facts. That is one of the effects of the advance of civilization.

CHAPTER XI

I RETURNED TO CAMBRIDGE to resume my interrupted studies at the beginning of the Lent term in 1925. I had been away from England for nearly a year, and during that time I had lived almost entirely an out-of-door life. In accordance with my doctor's orders I had not studied at all, but I doubt if the way in which the months had been spent quite conformed to his idea of a rest cure. Although I had hardly opened a book of any kind, I had learned a very great deal, for I had not only acquired the theoretical and practical knowledge of fossil excavation from an acknowledged master, but had also learnt from him a great deal of practical geology, and I had made up my mind to read several geological text books as soon as I was allowed to study once more.

Naturally, I had to devote a great deal of my time from now onward to studying French, for I had only two terms in which to prepare myself for the examination in which I had failed in the summer of 1923. Since that date, owing to unforeseen circumstances, I had forgotten almost all that I had previously learnt, except for French conversation. As far as this was concerned, I had returned from East Africa on a French liner and as there were only a few other English passengers I had had every opportunity to revive my French.

After I had settled down to work again, I concentrated almost all my attention upon French literature, which was the cause of my previous failure.

During the Easter vacation I went over to Boulogne and continued my studies under a Professor Didier, and it was fortunate that my financial circumstances were such that I could now afford to pay for adequate extra teaching. I had saved about £70 as a result of the expedition to Tendaguru, and in addition I had been able to earn some money by lecturing, after my return to England, and by writing articles upon the work of the expedition.

Mr. Cutler had been very unwilling at first that I should do this, but the Museum authorities were anxious that the work of the expedition should be made known, as they wished to raise funds which would enable the excavations to be continued for some years, and I of course was also anxious to do anything which I could to raise funds for my own educational expenses.

By arrangement with the authorities, it was finally agreed that I might give lectures and write articles and that one half of the proceeds were to be given to the Museum towards the expedition fund, while I retained the other half.

To my dying day I shall never forget the first public lecture which I ever gave, for I have seldom been so utterly terrified as I was during the five minutes which preceded it. Plans had been made for me to give a lecture in Cambridge upon the work of the expedition, and for this purpose the Guildhall, which has seating accommodation for, approximately, a thousand people, had been hired. The lecture was to be an illustrated one and I had had a number of slides made ; in addition I had secured a length of film with which to conclude the lecture.

I had seen in the papers that a well-known film company had recently completed the making of a film of Conan Doyle's story *The Lost World*, and I understood that they had succeeded in reproducing some exceedingly life-like Dinosaurs and other early reptiles, so I wrote to the directors of the company and told them of my proposed lecture and asked if I might be allowed to have the use of a reel of film illustrating these giant reptiles alive.

The film had not been released at that time and was not due for its first public exhibition for several weeks after the date of my lecture. However, I pointed out that if they allowed me to show a short section of the film at my lecture it would serve as an excellent advertisement for their film, as the Press would certainly attend the lecture and report it.

After much correspondence they agreed. As the day of the lecture approached I began to see posters eight feet high all over Cambridge advertising the lecture, and announcing that it was to be given by L. S. B. Leakey of St. John's College.

As I was only an undergraduate in my second year, and not yet twenty-two years old, and never having lectured in public before, I grew more and more worried as the day approached. To make matters worse I knew that the Chair was to be taken by the Vice-Chancellor of the University, Professor Seward, and that in addition the Mayor and Dr. Bather of the British Museum, were both to be on the platform.

When the day arrived I spent most of the afternoon in a cold sweat. I had visions of fellow-undergraduates turning up at the hall to boo me, and I was certain that the lecture was going to be a failure. I did not even possess any dress clothes, and had to borrow the tails, white waistcoat, etc., for the occasion from a friend of mine. The fact of being dressed in " borrowed plumage," which did not really fit me, only added to my discomfort.

When I went on to the platform to await the moment when the Vice-Chancellor would call upon me to give my lecture I was so utterly worn out with nervous anxiety that I scarcely knew what I was doing. At last the lights were put out, the first slide had been projected upon the screen, and I had to start. Quite suddenly, all my fear vanished. I forgot the nature of my audience, and found myself describing the way in which I had located Tendaguru Hill and the work we had done and the finds we had made, much as I would have related it to an audience of friends in my own room; and without even referring to my notes.

If only I could have continued in this way all would have been well, but after a short while something momentarily distracted my attention from what I was saying, and in a flash my fear came back and the rest of my lecture was halting and disjointed, and it was with the greatest relief that I was at last able to ask for the film to be put on, and to stop speaking.

After this terrifying opening to my lecturing career the numerous lectures which I gave in various schools during that and the succeeding year were almost child's play, and I soon began to enjoy lecturing instead of hating it, but even now during the last few minutes before I actually start to speak I find myself seized with fear which is a kind of reflection of that awful first lecture at Cambridge.

My tutor, Mr. Benians, was exceedingly kind to me in this matter of lecturing and he was always willing to give me leave of absence for this purpose, and I earned quite a lot of money with which to pay my college bills by lecturing at various public schools.

As far as I knew my head trouble had been completely cured by the year spent in Africa, and when I came back I was able to work for long hours without any sign of a headache, and as the examination was to take place at the end of May I had to work exceedingly hard.

When the Easter vacation came, I went over to Boulogne to work under Professor Didier and I continued to work very hard there, which was not really very wise, as subsequent events proved. One Sunday I decided to knock off work and go for a long country walk with a young English medical student who was also spending his holiday at Boulogne. We had gone some distance when I suddenly developed a splitting headache, and the next thing I knew I was sitting in a tram, halfway back into the town. Apparently I had suddenly said to my companion, " Oh, my head, my head ! " and then collapsed unconscious on the hillside, and he had to carry me as best he could back to the outskirts of the town, where he put me on a tram, and took me back to my lodgings. This was the first recurrence of my headaches and it served to warn me not to work too hard. From then onwards for a number of years I was always liable to collapse unconscious if I overworked.

Although I was giving most of my time to French literature, I was not, of course, neglecting Kikuyu, and I continued to visit Mr. Crabtree regularly and to give him lessons in the language, and at last, in May 1925, I again took my examination in French and Kikuyu.

The papers set me in the Kikuyu part of the examination were more difficult than on the previous occasion, and the most difficult paper of all, was one in which I was given a list of about twenty Kikuyu proverbs which I had to interpret and explain and then give an English equivalent. Although I could interpret them easily, and explain them reasonably well, I found it exceedingly hard to find English equivalents, as my knowledge of English proverbs was exceedingly limited. Some were easy. For instance, one was a Kikuyu proverb which says " When the hyæna goes away the jackals frolic," which is simply their version of " When the cat's away the mice will play." But it was not so easy to find an equivalent for the Kikuyu proverb which says : " The path of the fugitive had dew on it in the heat of the daytime," or for the one which runs : " A foolish bird builds its nest in a ripening banana bunch."

Naturally if one is to find English equivalents for African proverbs, one must first know enough about African conditions and customs.

As an example of this let me explain the two proverbs I have just cited. The network of pathways which lead all over Kikuyu country are narrow, single-file paths and they are often overhung by bush and grass. If one walks along these paths after there has been heavy dew, one is liable to get soaked through, and most Kikuyu try to avoid leaving their homes until the sun has been out sufficiently long to dry the dew. Even a fugitive from justice might reasonably expect to find the pathways free from dew during the heat of the day, and not have this additional trouble during his flight. So the proverb which says that " The path of a fugitive has dew on it even in the heat of the day " means that when you are in difficulties other troubles will surely overtake you. In other words the English equivalent is : " Disasters never come singly," or alternatively, " It never rains but it pours."

Or take the other proverb. Many species of birds find that the top of a bunch of growing bananas provides a most suitable nesting site, and of course, provided that the bird builds its nest in a bunch that is quite unripe, it will have plenty of time to hatch its brood and rear it before the bunch is cut down. A bird that deliberately builds in a bunch that is just ripening cannot expect to rear its brood safely before the bunch is cut. So it is a foolish bird. The proverb therefore is the equivalent of our " Look before you leap."

While I was actually sitting for the examination I had a very strong feeling that some of the questions in my Kikuyu papers had been set by Mr. Crabtree, whom I myself had been instructing in the Kikuyu language for months. This seemed to me rather strange and so when all was over, after I had heard that I had passed with first-class marks, I tried to find out more about it, and so far as I know the story which follows gives a reasonably accurate account of what actually happened.

I had often wondered where the University would procure the two examiners they required, but it had never once occurred to me that when I was teaching Mr. Crabtree I was teaching the man who was to be my second examiner. I had been told that I was to teach him so as to keep myself from forgetting the language, and as my visits to him were ostensibly in lieu of attending lectures in Kikuyu—which of course did not exist—I had had to pay him a supervision fee.

So far as I was able to find out this is what had happened*. When I had applied to the University for permission to take Kikuyu as a modern language they had written to London—to someone connected with the school of Oriental Studies I believe—and had asked if two examiners in Kikuyu could be found. In reply they were informed that two examiners would be available, and in consequence, permission had been given to me to take French and Kikuyu for the Modern and Mediæval Languages Tripos. At a later date the

---

* NOTE.—I believe the version given here is substantially true, but I cannot vouch for all the details. I have recently tried to obtain more detailed information from the School of Oriental Studies and the Cambridge Registrar, but without success. (L.S.B.L., Nov., 1936.)

University authorities had written to ask for the names and the addresses of the proposed examiners, in order to arrange necessary details, and they received a reply to the effect that the proposed examiners were Mr. G. Gordon Dennis, a retired missionary, and Mr. L. S. B. Leakey, in other words myself !

While I was still at school at Weymouth I had seen in *The Times* an advertisement of the School of Oriental Studies to the effect that they were prepared to teach all African languages. I had written to say that if they ever needed someone to teach Kikuyu I would be glad to undertake the work. I had therefore been put down on their list of available teachers of African languages. When they were asked to provide two examiners in Kikuyu they quite naturally never thought that I was the candidate to be examined, and so they had counted upon obtaining my services as one of the examiners.

When the Cambridge authorities found that one of the proposed examiners was none other than the candidate whom they wished to examine, they were in a difficult position, but it was solved by Mr. Crabtree who assured them that he could learn enough of the language from me to become my second examiner.

As may well be imagined, innumerable distorted versions of this somewhat unusual story have since arisen, and it is not uncommon to hear me described as " the man who examined himself in Kikuyu."

As I have already mentioned, ebony trees were very common in the Tendaguru district, and I had brought home with me to England just over a hundred ebony walking-sticks, which I had purchased from our work-men who made them in their spare time. These now came in very usefully as an aid to my exchequer. I took small samples to various Cambridge tailors, and asked them if they could sell them for me at a small commission. To this they agreed, and I fixed prices ranging from ten shillings for the best sticks, to half-a-crown for the less well-carved ones. I arranged with each tailor to credit me with my share of the proceeds, and I was thus able to obtain most of the clothing that I needed during the next year, against this credit, so saving my money for more important things, such as paying my College bills, special coaching, and for my stay in France, as well as purchasing books which I required.

In addition to the ebony sticks I had also brought to England one of the big signalling drums which are used by the Wamwera tribe round Tendaguru. On one occasion this nearly got me into serious trouble with the College authorities.

Some of my friends were in my rooms one evening, and I had been telling them about my experiences in Tendaguru, and happened to mention that the drum could be heard from two to three miles away in open country. One of the men expressed the view that I was exaggerating wildly, so I immediately offered to prove my words. It so happened that my room was one of the attic rooms in Third Court, and some previous occupant had very neatly cut one of the iron bars in the window, so that it could be removed and replaced again at will, without anyone suspecting that it was not intact. By removing this bar it was possible to climb out on to the roof above my room, and in fact this particular window was at that time often used by members of the Roof Climbing Society. I told the various people who were present to go out on their bicycles and proceed to various points at a considerable distance from the college, to listen for the drum, while I would climb on to the roof with it, and after giving them time to get to their posts, would beat out a signal. I warned them that in a town I could not promise that the sound would carry as far as it did at Tendaguru, as the buildings would absorb and obstruct the sound, and in addition there were many other noises from cars and lorries which would somewhat drown the signal from my drum.

Having got the drum ready I climbed out on to the roof, and forgetting all about the effect that the drum was bound to have upon the occupants of the various rooms in the vicinity, I beat out a signal with all the force at my command. The result was shattering. A deafening noise echoed all round the courts of the College, and in a minute I could see heads peering out from windows and hear shouts of " What's that ? " I realised then that the authorities would be on the war path in a few minutes, so I climbed back into my room as quickly as I could.

In my rooms I had a big round wooden tray which had also been made at Tendaguru, and I now took this and put it on the drum—using the drum as a small table—and on the tray I set out coffee things and sat down to read by the fire.

As I had expected, the porters on duty soon came round to all the rooms trying to locate the source of the noise, but they found me hard at work, and never suspected that the tray with its innocent coffee cups was concealing the object of their search.

After a time my friends came back and those of them who had been in suitable positions had heard the drum easily at the distance of a mile, but others who had gone to the centre of the town heard nothing.

As soon as my examinations were over, I visited Dr. Haddon, the Reader in Anthropology, and told him that I planned to take the Anthropological Tripos the next year and asked him what books I should read during the summer vacation. I also bought myself a few books on geology, as I had decided to teach myself as much of this subject as I could, since I knew that it would be useful to me later, and I could not take it for my degree without taking other natural science subjects as well, which I did not wish to do.

When the results of the examination were announced and I was awarded a First Class, the authorities of St. John's College very kindly informed me that they would give me a scholarship for my third year, which meant that in comparison with preceding years I should be comparatively well off, for in addition to the scholarship, I had applied for, and obtained, one of the grants which are made to poor students by the Goldsmiths' Company.

At last all the preliminary obstacles had been surmounted and the way was open to me to train myself in anthropology and archæology. The dreams that I had dreamed as a child after reading Hall's *Days Before History*, were coming true.

CHAPTER XII

THE SUMMER VACATION OF 1925 was, I think, the most enjoyable I had ever spent in England. By passing the examination in Modern Languages I felt as though I had thrown a great load off my shoulders and I was happier than I had been for a very long time. The season that I had spent working for the British Museum had served to intensify my desire to devote my life to scientific investigation, and it was during this summer that I first began to think seriously of making anthropology my profession instead of merely my hobby.

Up till then I had been planning to be a missionary in East Africa, but now I began to realise that I should not really be content treating science as a "part time job."

Knowing how well I understood the Kikuyu people and their problems, and loving them as I did, a part of me was exceedingly keen to go back and devote myself entirely to them and their needs, but another part of me said No. I was not even sure in my own mind if, in the event of my offering myself as a candidate to the Society, I would be accepted, for I had become firmly convinced of the truth of the theory of Evolution as distinct from Creation as described in Genesis, and I had also begun to hold much more liberal views about some native customs than my parents did. I doubted, therefore, if I could satisfy the appointments committee that my views were compatible with missionary work.

And so, after much thought, I decided in favour of being a scientist, although this did not mean that I lost any of my interest in missionary work or in the problems of my African friends, and I made up my mind that I would take every opportunity that came to help them.

Having decided in favour of prehistoric research I began to devote many hours during the vacation to preparing myself for my studies next term. On my motor-bicycle I visited museums in different parts of the country and spent long hours examining the exhibits and making notes, and armed with books and papers describing some of the more important sites where prehistoric discoveries had been made, I visited them and tried to interpret for myself some of the geological sections.

When I had been in North Wales in the summer of 1923, my duties had not allowed me to see much of the country, but I had been very struck with the beauty of some of the mountains and lakes, and I now went back on my motor-bicycle and climbed some of the mountains and explored the country. From Wales I went right across England to the coast of Norfolk, and after spending a little time with my aunt and uncle there I explored some of the famous prehistoric sites of East Anglia and spent long hours in the museums of Norwich and Ipswich, enjoying myself immensely and learning a great deal.

Although I had enjoyed the summer vacation so much I was very glad when at last the four months were over, and I was able to go back to Cambridge again to start the course in anthropology and archæology.

Every Sunday afternoon Dr. Haddon used to be ' at home ' to his students, and although all of the students did not take advantage of this wonderful opportunity, some of us used to go regularly and spend a most interesting time discussing all sorts of subjects in an informal way, and learning almost more than we did from lectures.

In addition, Dr. Haddon allowed us to go into his magnificent anthropological library and borrow any volumes that we liked, while sometimes he would teach us some of the string figures which are so common among primitive peoples.

I imagine that comparatively few people in England realise that the " cat's-cradle " game which they played in their childhood is a very simple form of the fascinating art of making string figures. Nor do they realise that among many of the so-called primitive peoples of the world string figures play a definite part in the social life of the tribe, in one way or another. Dr. Haddon used to tell us that no anthropologist ought to set out to study the life of a primitive people without some knowledge of string figures, as he would find them useful in gaining the confidence of very many tribes.

I myself did not fully appreciate the value of this statement at the time, for the Kikuyu are one of the few East African tribes that do not play any form of the string figure game, but later on I frequently found during my travels in East Africa that what Dr. Haddon said was true, and I have on several occasions since found that a knowledge of string figures was not only useful but invaluable.

Dr. Haddon's daughter, Mrs. Rishbeth, has collected a number of string figures from different parts of the world, and has published a book about them. I set to work to learn to make all these and found it a most fascinating game. Some of the most complicated string figures are those made by the Esquimaux, and in many cases they serve to illustrate simple stories, of which " The Fox and the Whale " and the " Man catching a Salmon " are the most amusing.

Apart from the Esquimaux, string figures are not often used to illustrate stories, but there is one figure, or rather set of figures, from New Guinea which has always fascinated me more than any other.

The first figure is made to represent a typical New Guinea house built on piles, and the story opens as follows : " There once was a man and he lived in a house built on piles out over the water, and the house was open at both ends, and the floor had many cracks in it so that the rubbish could fall through into the water below." At this point the string house is shown and it is pointed out that all the essential features mentioned in the story are represented and are true to life. The tale goes on : " And the man sat in his house one day listening to his pet birds singing ' tweet-tweet-tweet ' in their cage," and, with a deft movement, the figure that was a house is transformed into a very neat representation of a basket-work cage. " As he sat listening to the birds he worked hard making his traps which he was going to set in the water beneath the house to catch crabs and fishes and other things that live in the water." Here, with two more quick movements, the cage is transformed so as to represent a trap. " And he took his trap and put it in the water, and next morning when he went to look he found that he had caught a turtle." Here one quick movement transforms the trap into an extraordinarily good turtle with carapace, head, legs and tail complete. " And he took the turtle from the trap and turned it on its back so that it could not run away." The figure is now taken off the hands, and is laid on the ground and turned over ; " And then he cut off the turtle's head so as to kill it, and he cut off its tail (because ceremonial demanded it) and then as the turtle was dead he turned it back again and cut off its shell." Two more quick movements make the head and tail disappear, and then the figure is turned over and the shell is also removed. " And he took the turtle and he placed it on

the roasting platform to cook, and sat down to watch it."
The figure is now transformed into a representation of a
roasting platform, " and he sat watching the turtle cook
and thinking of his lover who lived on a small island
across a narrow channel of water, and he wished that she
could come and share his feast with him." Here the
figure changes from a roasting platform into two islands
separated by a narrow channel ; " And as he sat thinking, quite suddenly a great tidal wave came and the
islands were swamped." A quick movement and the
islands disappear and the figure resolves itself into the
simple loop of string with which the story began.

Besides learning string figures I spent a good deal of
my spare time in learning to play some of the many
forms of the universal African game which is played
with counters and a number of small holes either carved
in a wooden board or dug out of the ground.

As a child I had learned to play the Kikuyu form of
the game which they call by the name of " Gîuthi," and
I now learnt the variations played by some other tribes.
Several of the other anthropology students used to play
them occasionally with me. This African game which
is variously spoken of in literature dealing with Africa
as African draughts, African chess, Mankalla, Weso, and
simply " Holes in the ground," is often regarded as
having been introduced to Africa from Arabia, where
certain variations of it also occur. I do not, however,
think that this is the correct explanation, for I have found
evidence which suggests that this game was being played
in Africa towards the end of the Stone Age period, and
I am inclined to believe that it was originally an African
game which was later introduced into Arabia and other
parts of Asia by negro slaves ; just as it was also taken
to America and the West Indies through the medium
of the slave traffic.

In Africa this game is so widespread, and there are now such an immense number of variations of it, that it must date back a very long time. The rules of the game vary with almost every tribe, but I have never met or heard of a tribe that did not possess its own particular variation of the game, and within each tribe the rules are strictly adhered to, while the variations played by other tribes are usually unknown.

No one who has travelled in Africa can have failed to see groups of men sitting in village compounds, or by the roadside, resting and playing this game, but comparatively few Europeans have learnt to play even one variation, because at first sight the rules appear to be so complicated that they seldom try to learn them.

The game is, however, one which might well be played in England, for it is quite as fascinating and exciting as many of the other games that Europe has borrowed from the East, as for example chess, mahjong, etc. I will therefore briefly describe the Kikuyu variation in case anyone who reads this book would care to learn to play it for themselves. The Kikuyu do not as a rule have a wooden board as many other tribes do, but dig two parallel rows of six small holes in the ground (six holes a side is the common number but by agreement any number from 5 to 10 holes a side may be played) and into each of these are placed six round solanum berries, or sometimes pebbles.

Each of the two players then sits down behind his row and the game begins.

The following plan shows the position at the start of a game :

(6)	(6)	(6)	(6)	(6)	(6)	= A's side
(6)	(6)	(6)	(6)	(6)	(6)	= B's side

One of the players picks up one pebble or berry and

putting his hands behind his back, juggles a little and then puts both his closed hands forward for the other player to choose which hand he will have. If he chooses the hand with the berry or pebble in it he has first move.

He may then pick up the six counters in any one of the holes on *his own side* and start his move. He may move either to the right or to the left and if he picks up from one of the end holes he may if he wishes start straight across on to his opponent's side. He then drops one pebble into each successive hole (starting from the one next to the one where he picked up all six). He next picks up all the pebbles which are in the hole in which he placed his last pebble and starts to move back. This time he *must* move in the opposite direction from that in which he first moved.

Let us take as an example a first move, with B starting from his right-hand hole, and choosing to move to the left on his own side instead of straight across to A's side and to the left there.

Picking up the six pebbles in his right-hand side hole he places one in each of his other holes as he moves down the line and the sixth in A's right-hand hole (opposite his own left-hand one) so that the position is now as follows :

(7)	(6)	(6)	(6)	(6)	(6)
(7)	(7)	(7)	(7)	(7)	( )

He then picks up the pebbles in the last hole he played into, i.e., the seven in A's right-hand hole, and moves back in the opposite direction to which he came, again putting a pebble in each hole so that the position becomes

( )	(6)	(6)	(6)	(6)	(7)
(8)	(8)	(8)	(8)	(8)	(1)

He now again picks up the pebbles in the last hole he played into (i.e., A's left-hand hole) and moves again in the opposite direction to which he had just come. This time his last pebble will fall into the *empty hole* on the left-hand of A's side, and this means that his move is over, as each move only ends when the last pebble of a hand is put into an empty hole. The position at the end of his move is thus :

(1)	(6)	(6)	(6)	(6)	( )
(9)	(9)	(9)	(9)	(9)	(2)

B's move being over, A has his first move and he too may start it by picking up the pebbles in any one hole on his side, only he may not ever move a single pebble, and of course he may start the move by going either to the left or the right, but once he has started he must always move back in the counter direction, and go on moving until he puts a *last* pebble into an empty hole.

The object of the game is to capture the pebbles of your opponent, and this is done by placing the last pebble of your hand into an empty *hole on your own side*, in which case you capture all the pebbles that are in the hole directly opposite it on your opponent's side.

Let us suppose that A plays with the six pebbles which are in the second hole from his own right and that he moves to the right placing his first pebble in his right-hand hole and then crossing over to B's side. His sixth pebble will be put into the last but one hole on B's right-hand side, making the total there ten, and picking up these ten pebbles he will have to move back in the counter direction, so that this time his last pebble will fall in the empty hole *on his own* left-hand side opposite a hole in which B has two pebbles. He then captures these two pebbles and takes them plus his own single pebble that effected the capture and removes them from the board which is now in the following position :

(3)	(1)	(7)	(7)	(7)	( )
(11)	(11)	(11)	(11)	( )	( )

It is now B's turn again. He may move the pebbles in any of the holes on his own side, and move them in either direction, but if he is wise he will take the eleven pebbles which are next to his two empty holes, and he will move to the left so that the position becomes :

(4)	(2)	(8)	(8)	(8)	(1)
(12)	(12)	(12)	( )	(1)	(1)

the last of the eleven pebbles falling into an empty hole on his own side opposite a hole on A's side which contains eight, which he thus captures.

As the hole on his side next to the one into which he put his last pebble is empty he has also the right to take the pebbles in the opponent's hole opposite to that, so that by this move he has captured two lots of eight pebbles and he removes them and his own pebble that made the capture from the board so that the position that is left is :

(4)	(2)	(8)	( )	( )	(1)
(12)	(12)	(12)	( )	( )	(1)

and it is now A's turn again.

At this point I must explain another rule. If a man moves the pebbles from a hole on *his own side* and his move comes to an end in an empty hole on *his own side without his having had to cross on to his opponent's side*, he has to make a further move for he has not yet raided the enemy's camp.

A can thus now move as follows if he wishes : he can pick up the four pebbles which are in his own right-hand hole and move them to his left so that they end up as follows :

( )	(3)	(9)	(1)	(1)	(1)
(12)	(12)	(12)	( )	( )	( )

As his last pebble went into an empty hole on his own side and he has not crossed over to the opponent's side at all, he has to move again, instead of capturing the pebbles in the hole opposite the one in which he ended (because he had not been over to the opponent's side and so has not made a raid and you cannot capture prisoners without leaving your own territory). This time let us suppose that he moves from the hole with three in it and again starts towards his own left. The last of the three will be put into a hole which already has one in, so he must pick it and the one it joins up and move with these two in the counter direction. This time the second of the two will go into the hole that had nine in at the beginning of the move and it will now have eleven and he must move these to his left again. This will take him all along his own side and all along his opponent's ridge and he will end up this time in an empty hole on his own side opposite one which contains thirteen on B's side, so that he captures those thirteen as well as the thirteen next to them as he has an empty hole on his own side next to the one he put his last pebble into. He thus captures twenty-six of B's men as a result of his move and the board is left as follows :

(1)	( )	( )	(4)	(1)	(2)
(13)	( )	( )	(1)	(1)	(2)

B can now play either with his two or his thirteen, and his best move is to take his two and move across to A's side placing one in the hole with two and one in the hole with one, making it into two. Then taking these two he has to move back placing one in the end hole, which will then have four $(2 + 1 + 1)$ and the other in his own empty end hole, thus capturing the four opposite it.   A now has one in one hole, four in another, and the rest empty, while B has two singletons and a hole with thirteen.

It is now A's turn to play again and he has only the contents of one hole to play with.   These may of course move either to the left or to the right.   His best move is towards his own right so that the last of the four is placed into B's hole.   By this move he ends up in an empty hole on his own side (second from the left) and captures five pieces.   The remainder will then be left in the following positions :

$$( ) \quad ( ) \quad (2) \quad (1) \quad ( ) \quad (4)$$
$$(4) \quad (1) \quad (2) \quad ( ) \quad ( ) \quad ( )$$

and so the game proceeds until all the pieces have been captured by one or other players, or until there are only single pieces left which cannot be moved.   The game is then over and each player counts to see how many he has captured, singles that remain on the board belonging to the player on whose side they are.

Usually it will be found that one or other player is leading, although occasionally each player ends with the identical number that he started with, in which case it is a draw.

If they decide to have a second game, the player who has the fewer pieces has to put them out, and this time instead of having to arrange them symmetrically, i.e., in sixes, he may put his pieces out in any formation that he likes on his own side provided that he leaves no hole without at least one piece in.

When he has arranged them to his liking, his opponent proceeds to put his out in the same order, and the winner of the last game has the opening move of the new game.

The greatest skill is required in arranging the pieces

for a second or later game, as if the pieces are unskilfully arranged the player who arranged them may suffer very badly. Experienced players get to know what are the best formations to put out according to what number of pieces they have when the new game starts, and if skilfully arranged a man may be able not only to recover his losses but to end up the second game ahead of his opponent. There are certain rules governing the putting out of the pieces for second and later games.

If the loser has less than half the original number with which the game started (i.e., if in the game which I have described in which each player started with 6×6 pieces, B found himself with less than eighteen pieces) then he has the right to " cut off " the two end holes on his and his opponent's side and may elect to play with only four holes a side. Similarly if he has less than nine pieces he may elect to reduce the board to three holes a side, and if he has five pieces only or less he may reduce to two holes a side.

The whole game requires considerable calculating ability to be played at its best, but it can be played light-heartedly without worrying to calculate out the result of a move in advance, and I have found it to be as entertaining a game as chess or draughts or bridge.

Although it is meant as a game for two people it can be played by a single player, by taking each side of the board alternately. It is such a fascinating game that one tends to forget all about the time when playing it—as employers of African labour know only too well—and I myself left my writing about three hours ago to go and try out a move that I was describing above on the board and I became so intrigued with problems arising from it, that I forgot all about both my writing and my tea for over two hours.

I am afraid that this rather long description of a

Kikuyu game will bore some of my readers, unless they are sufficiently interested to try it for themselves, but if they do obtain a board and pieces and try to play it themselves I think they will forgive me for having included the detailed description of it.

I have often hoped that this game would one day become a favourite in England, and once I went so far as to write out the rules and offer it as a new game to one of the big firms that sell games in London, but it was refused on the grounds that " it is too difficult for English people," which is obviously fantastic since it is played by quite small Kikuyu boys as well as by adults. Writing about it as I have been doing just now has inspired me to try once more to introduce it seriously to this country, and it is possible that by the time this book is published the game of Gîuthi may be on the market.*

* NOTE.—Negotiations are in progress, but nothing has so far been achieved. (L.S.B.L., 1936.)

CHAPTER XIII

ONE DAY WHEN HE was lecturing to us about the peoples of Africa and their cultures, Dr. Haddon discussed the classification of the different types of bow and arrow that are to be found in that continent, and their distribution. The information which he placed before us was based upon a study by a German scientist, and when I was going over the hasty notes which I had made during the lecture, I found that some of the data which the German scientist had given concerning the areas which I knew personally, were inaccurate. Next day I went to see Dr. Haddon and talked the matter over with him and I suggested that I would like to re-investigate the position and check up the German's statements on other particulars.

At that time I had but the vaguest idea of what I proposed to do, and I simply felt that I wanted to re-examine some of the evidence. Having talked the question over with Dr. Haddon, I started to make my plans, and in a few weeks I decided that I would spend the whole of the Christmas vacation visiting some of the principal museums of Europe where collections of African material existed, and making notes with a view to preparing a new classification of the bow and arrow in Africa.

It was obvious that this plan would involve the expenditure of a certain amount of money and so I went and discussed the matter with my tutor, Mr. E. A. Benians. Although I had not yet taken my degree, and it was therefore perhaps a little premature for me to be embarking upon a piece of definite research, when I ought to have been concentrating upon preparation for my final examination, he was very sympathetic, and he very kindly offered to put my case before the College Council and find out whether they would be willing to make me a small grant towards the cost of the proposed investigation.

The College Council generously made me a grant, and to augment this I sold my motor-bicycle, and with the money from these two sources I started on the work. I went first of all to Hamburg where there was a great deal of African material, and where the collection made by the German scientist whose work I was questioning was housed. It was not until I arrived there that I began to realise the magnitude of the task that I had set myself, and I now found that in this one museum there were over three thousand bows and arrows from Africa, each one of which I had to examine, making detailed notes. Every single feature of each bow, and each arrow, had to be recorded. In the bows I was concerned with the size, the shape of the staff, the way in which the bow string was attached to the bow, and the nature of the string itself. In the arrows I had to note the ways in which the feathers were attached, the way in which the head was fitted to the shaft, the nature of the head itself, and many other minor details. As I was only at the beginning of my investigation I had no idea as to what points were going to prove of any value for classification purposes and what were going to prove useless, so that I had at first to make far more notes than I really needed. In addition, I had to make a careful record of the tribe which used each specimen which I examined and then find out where that tribe lived and mark the place on a map. This at times proved to be very difficult, for some of the tribal names marked on the labels were names I had never heard of, so that I did not know how to begin to locate their geographical position.

By the time I had examined the vast collection at Hamburg I began to feel that I knew something about African bows and arrows, and I went on to Berlin in a much happier frame of mind.

At Hamburg the museum authorities had been exceedingly kind and helpful, and they had not only let me examine and handle all the specimens in the store rooms, but also allowed me access to the specimens in the show cases in the public galleries and had in fact done everything they possibly could for me.

When I reached Berlin I found things to be very different. The museum was officially closed, and the Director was away and at first I was told that I could do nothing there at all.

Fortunately for me, however, I had one or two friends in Berlin, including Dr. Heppe, who had stayed with us at Kabete before the war, and with his help I finally obtained permission to work in the store rooms of the museum, but I had to leave all the exhibited specimens unexamined.

I had long been familiar with the name of Dr. Hans Reck, a German geologist who had done a great deal of work in East Africa before the war, and I took the opportunity when I was in Berlin of making his acquaintance. Dr. Reck had been one of the members of the expedition that had worked at Tendaguru when the Germans had excavated for Dinosaur remains there, and later on he had been in charge of an expedition to the Oldoway Gorge, on the Serengeti plains of what was then German East Africa. While he was at Oldoway he had discovered a complete fossil human skeleton which had caused a great deal of controversy. In addition to this he had found some exceedingly interesting extinct fossil animals, and so from every point of view I was anxious to meet him. My friend, Dr. Heppe, communicated with him and told him that I was in Berlin. I then went to the Natural History Museum, and at last found myself face to face with Dr. Reck. This meeting started a very warm friendship between us.

I had taken with me some of my photographs of the British Museum Expedition to Tendaguru and these I now showed him, and he in turn showed me all of his. We discussed the conditions of life at Tendaguru, and I was able to give him messages from his old native headman Boheti. From Dinosaurs we turned to a discussion of his famous Oldoway human skeleton which I hoped he would show me, but unfortunately it had been sent to Munich so that I did not get an opportunity to see it until several years later.

Dr. Reck then took me down to the public galleries of the Museum and showed me some of the fossils both from Tendaguru and from Oldoway and I told him that I was planning to spend the rest of my life studying the prehistoric problems of East Africa. Half jokingly, half seriously, I said that one day he must come and join me, and that we would visit Oldoway together.

Five years later I was in a position to re-issue the invitation and Dr. Reck came with me on a most enjoyable and exciting safari to Oldoway, but that is a story which must be told in its proper place.

From Berlin I went to Brussels to study the collection of bows and arrows in the special museum there which is devoted entirely to the study of material from the Belgian Congo. The authorities here were very kind and not only gave me every facility to study the specimens in their collection, but also put at my disposal the museum draughtsman to make drawings of any specimens that I wished, and so saved me much time ;

for then, as now, I was very incompetent and slow at making drawings.

The Musée du Congo Belge at Brussels is one of the finest museums I have seen. It has the great advantage of having been built and organised comparatively recently, and has been especially designed to meet the present-day requirements of a big museum, instead of having to be adapted—as older museums have had to be —as new ideas concerning the exhibition of specimens have been developed.

I spent an exceedingly profitable time at Brussels and then went on to Paris, where I found the collection of African bows and arrows very disappointing, and so returned to England just in time for the Lent term at Cambridge.

My next task was to continue my investigations in some of the English museums, and by this time I was able to work very much more rapidly as I had decided which features of the bows and arrows were likely to be useful to me in my comparative study and so I wasted much less time.

Throughout the Lent term at Cambridge I devoted a great deal of time to sorting out my notes and arranging them, and by the end of April I had been able to prepare from them a scientific paper which I entitled " A new classification of the Bow and Arrow in Africa." This paper was in many ways rather revolutionary, as I had decided that previous methods of classification had to be rejected, but it was only a preliminary paper, and I hoped that at some future date I would be able to do more work upon the subject and enlarge it considerably. The opportunity has never come, and so now I can only hope that someone else will take my foundation and build a more complete structure upon it, as I very much doubt if I shall ever do it myself.

I gave a lecture describing the results of my investigation just before the end of the Lent term and spent most of the Easter vacation in preparing the paper for publication, and in particular re-drawing my rough sketches of specimens so as to make them better represent the originals. During the Easter vacation I also started making my plans for an expedition to Kenya Colony to commence the scientific investigation of the history of the country during Stone Age times. I was not planning to leave England until after I had taken my final examinations at the end of the summer term, but I had to start making arrangements a long time in advance in order to raise the necessary funds.

When the Easter vacation was over and I returned to Cambridge for my final term's work, I had already secured a promise from two different shipping companies that they would grant me special reduced passage rates in the event of my taking out a scientific expedition. I had also obtained written permission from the owners of various farms in Kenya to carry out excavations on their land, as well as several provisional promises of financial support. Naturally I could not expect any final decisions on this point until I had taken my examination and had demonstrated that I was, theoretically at any rate, qualified to undertake the research work that I proposed to carry out.

That last summer term was not without its amusing incidents, and three things in particular stand out very clearly in my memory. For exercise during the summer I played a good deal of lawn tennis, and one day I suddenly decided that I hated playing in long white flannel trousers and I decided to introduce the use of white shorts for tennis. In addition to my dislike of long trousers I hated wearing the ordinary white shirts which were customary because I found that they always rucked up round my waist after a few minutes of hard play, and made me feel very hot and uncomfortable. I therefore decided not only to introduce the use of shorts, but also a modification of the East African " Bush shirt." This is a garment made with a fixed collar like an ordinary sports shirt, but it is not worn inside the trousers but outside of them. Instead of having a " tail," like an ordinary shirt, it is of even length all round. It is made to fit very loosely and has a belt round the waist.

In the form in which it is used for everyday wear by farmers in Kenya, the Bush shirt is made of strong khaki and has big pockets in front, and it looks rather like a shirt and coat combined. It has short sleeves. I went to my tailor, taking him one of my khaki Bush shirts as a pattern, and asked him to make me two of white cotton fabric for tennis wear.

The great advantage of the white Bush shirt for tennis wear is that it can be worn quite decently outside the trousers and in this way the wearer not only can keep much cooler, but he also avoids the terrible rucking which is one of the drawbacks of the more conventional garment. I told a number of my fellow students of my plan and persuaded several of them to join me in ordering white shorts and white " Bush shirts," and we then appeared one day upon the courts of St. John's College in this new tennis costume.

Naturally we caused a good deal of comment and were subjected to a certain amount of mild ridicule, but we were quite prepared for that and did not mind. What I was not prepared for was the suggestion that it was indecent to play tennis in shorts, and that the " Bush shirt " added to the indecency ! Yet that is what happened and I was summoned by the Captain of tennis and informed that certain of the Fellows of the College had taken exception to my wearing shorts and " Bush shirt " for tennis because it was indecent, and therefore might cause a slur on the good name of the College, and I was quietly but firmly told that I must desist.

I tried to point out that if shorts were not indecent for Rugby football, for athletics, for hockey and for many other forms of sport which were commonly watched by audiences composed of both sexes, I could not see that they could honestly be described as indecent when worn for tennis. The College authorities were, however, adamant and so I had to abandon my new costume and return to wearing long trousers for tennis.

That was in 1926. During the summer of 1934 I was again in residence at St. John's College, this time with the status of a Fellow, and I was very amused to see that a high proportion of the undergraduates who were playing tennis on the very same courts where I had been forbidden to play in shorts and Bush shirt, were dressed in the former garment, while some dispensed with a shirt altogether.

Towards the end of the term when the date of the examination was rapidly drawing near, the " General Strike " started and the whole life of the country was threatened. At Cambridge a great many undergraduates, certainly most of those whom I knew at all well, were very much in sympathy with the demands of the strikers, but that was a very different thing from being in sympathy with the methods which they decided to employ. That was the big mistake which the Trade Unions made. They probably knew that there was a large body of opinion in the country which sympathised with them and they mistook this for an indication that the general public would not unite to break the strike.

As soon as the strike started, and volunteer workers were called for, the vast majority of the undergraduates volunteered for work of one sort or another. Many of them went to London to work at the docks, others became special constables, and lorry drivers; while a few, like myself, offered their services to the railway companies. At first I was a guard, but after a day or two I was put in charge of a level crossing and signal box on the line from Cambridge to Ely, and while on this duty I had plenty of opportunity to go on studying and so used to take my books with me.

On one occasion when I was travelling back from my signal box to Cambridge in the last train of the day, we suddenly felt the train draw up with a tremendous jerk and a grinding of the brakes. We had heard, only that day, that some of the strikers had threatened to pull up the line, or to put barricades across to prevent the trains from running, and in our minds we half-expected to find that a tree had been felled across the line or that part of the rails were missing. But all we saw as we looked out was the engine driver running down the line towards the rear of the train, and, as he passed, we asked him what was the matter. " My hat," he shouted, " my hat," and went on running. He had been wearing a Trilby hat and looking out incautiously the wind had whisked it from his head. He had therefore applied the brakes and stopped quickly, just as he would have done in similar circumstances when driving a car, and he was now going back along the line to look for it. I only wonder that he did not put the engine into reverse and back the train to save him from having to run !

A few days before the examination started, the strike ended almost as suddenly as it began, and those last few days were spent in a very hurried final study of all my notes. At last the first morning of the examination came, and to my joy I found that I could at least write a good deal in answer to each question. That fact calmed me,

for I had begun to fear that I should find myself with
nothing to write. After the first paper my confidence
returned a little, but I was by no means certain that I had
done as well as I could wish, so that it was a very great
relief when the results were at last announced and I
found that my friends Hugh Stayt, Reginald Hall,
Gregory Bateson and myself had all secured first class
marks.

After the examination results had been announced,
the authorities of St. John's College awarded me a
research studentship, and I also obtained grants towards
the costs of my proposed expedition from the Percy
Sladen Memorial Trustees and from various other
sources, and gradually I was able to get together as much
money as I estimated that I should require.

I did not plan to stay very long in East Africa on this
occasion as my chief object was to make only a preliminary examination of a large number of sites. I did,
however, intend to make a detailed study at one or two
places, with a view to obtaining enough information to
warrant the organisation of much more extensive
operations later on.

The sites that I had decided to investigate in detail
had both been accidentally discovered by settlers in
Kenya, and I knew that at each of them I was bound to
get some sort of results. But in addition I wanted to
re-examine many sites which I had noted as a boy.
These were places where I had picked up stone implements of obsidian on various occasions, and I wanted to
find out whether they were likely to be rich enough in
archæological material to justify extensive excavations.

I had arranged with a fellow student named Newsam
that he should be a member of my expedition, and in
particular he was to be responsible for all plane-tabling
and mapping work. As soon as the examinations were

over he therefore proceeded to take some special training in this work, while I completed the work of collecting funds, and purchased such equipment as was necessary. Actually I bought very little in England apart from cameras and some special excavating equipment—for I knew that I could obtain most of my requirements as cheaply in Kenya. At last, in July, 1926, all our preparations were completed and we sailed for Kenya with the high sounding title of " The East African Archæological Expedition."

CHAPTER XIV

WHEN WE ARRIVED AT Mombasa we went straight up
country to Kabete, where we stayed for several weeks
while I collected the rest of the equipment which we
would need for camping later on. While I was doing
this we also carried out a certain number of investigations in the district round Kabete, where I had made
my first prehistoric discoveries as a child.

In an earlier chapter I have described how I explored
Gibberish Cave by descending the "chimney" and
how in my ignorance I had half expected to find Stone
Age man's implements lying about on the cave floor.
I knew now that if that cave had ever been inhabited
in Stone Age times, the relics that I was looking for
would probably be found buried deep down in the
accumulated cave earth, and so we started a trial
excavation. Newsam and I were assisted in this work
by two elderly Kikuyu workmen, who were not mission
adherents, but after a few weeks' work I realised that
they would not be any use as members of my permanent
staff, and so I paid them off.

As we worked in Gibberish cave, I told these two old
men something of my aims and objects, and as soon
as they realised that I was trying to find the skulls
and skeletons of men who lived long ago, they began
to grow apprehensive, and after a little time told me
that they were afraid that if we did discover any human
bones they would have to leave my employ.

I knew, of course, that by their customs Kikuyu
people may not touch the bones or bodies of dead

people without penalty, but I had hoped that this custom would not apply when the bones concerned were of people who had died thousands of years ago. I put forward this suggestion to these two men, but they did not think that the question of the age of the human bones would make any difference to the taboo. They agreed, however, to consult with some of the other elders of the tribe, and let me know.

The result of this consultation was that the elders-in-council decided that, if my workmen were involved in the digging up of human bones, they would have to go through a ceremony of purification and perform a sacrifice before they could re-enter their homes, or meet their friends. As this would involve them in considerable expense they decided that they would rather not take the risk by continuing to work for me.

This Kikuyu taboo against touching a dead human body or part of a body has resulted in unusual and rather unpleasant customs connected with the disposal of the dead. As no one might touch a dead body without becoming ceremonially unclean, and as it is impossible to bury a body without coming into contact with it, burial rites were only accorded to men and women with an important position in society, and in particular to very old men and women who had been leaders of the village life during their lifetime. Such people were buried by their sons and near relatives, and all who helped in the burial rites had subsequently to undergo extensive purification ceremonies before they could resume their normal occupations and take part in the ordinary social life of the community once more.

Ordinary people were never buried and, moreover, they were not even allowed to die comfortably in their beds. As soon as a sick person was seen to be *in extremis* he or she was carried out of the hut and taken into the bush at some distance from the village, to die. Usually the friends and relations would light a fire and stay by the dying person out in the bush until death actually occurred, or until the invalid showed signs of recovering after all, in which case he or she was carried back to the village again. If the person who was carried out, in accordance with custom, died, the body was abandoned in the bush, and was very soon devoured by hyænas and other scavengers.

Occasionally someone would die suddenly and quite unexpectedly in his hut, and if this happened all the members of the village had to undergo purification ceremonies entailing considerable expense.

As hyænas were known to eat the dead bodies of people who were taken out into the bush to die, hyænas were also considered to be unclean, and under no circumstances would a Kikuyu person touch a hyæna, either dead or alive. Further, if by any chance a hyæna entered a village at night and defæcated in the village, this fact rendered the whole village unclean, and it had to be purified exactly as though a death had occurred there.

Naturally those Kikuyu who have become Christians have abandoned these old ideas and customs, and they are not in the least afraid of touching a corpse or a human skull or skeleton, and this fact has in recent years been the means of providing some of them with a good source of income. The Government has made a law prohibiting the disposal of the dead by leaving the corpses to be eaten by hyænas, and nowadays every Kikuyu who dies must be buried properly. As far as the non-Christian section of the community is concerned, senior people are still buried by their sons, but all ordinary people, who in the past would have been put out in the bush, are now buried by Christians for a fixed fee, and Christian Kikuyus are thus constantly in demand as undertakers.

When my two old Kikuyu men decided that they would not excavate with me any more for fear of our finding human skeletons, I replaced them by Mission men, and among those to whom I gave employment was Ndekei, the boy who was born on the same day as I was, and who had been one of the friends of my childhood. The others were all members of my own age group and one of them was the Christian son of one of the two old men. He joined me at his father's special request, because the old man had become really interested in the work and wanted to keep in touch with it, although he would not go on with it himself.

All the Kikuyu round Kabete were exceedingly interested in our research work, and many of them came out and sat round the entrance to the cave at Gibberish, or else visited me at the Mission, in order to ask me more about it. They were particularly intrigued with the idea that the pieces of obsidian which we were finding in the cave, or which we picked up about the countryside, were the knives and weapons of a prehistoric race. The Kikuyu call all pieces of obsidian which they come across by one of two names —*nyenji cia ngoma* or *nyura-nyura*. The first of these terms means " razors of the spirits " and the second " thunderbolts."

Most of the prehistoric obsidian implements and flakes in the Kikuyu country are buried fairly deeply in the soil and are not normally seen until they are washed out by a heavy thunderstorm. After a very heavy fall of rain pieces of obsidian are particularly noticeable, so it is not surprising that the Kikuyu think that they have come down out of the sky with the rain. As proof of the correctness of this belief they will point out that after a storm they find obsidian flakes in places where they are certain there were none a few hours before.

At first when I told them that, instead of coming out of the sky, the obsidian flakes were being washed out of the soil my Kikuyu friends were frankly incredulous, but when I took them to sites where I knew that flakes were being continually washed out, and dug there for them and produced pieces from deep down in the soil, they began to believe me. When I was further able to demonstrate that some of the obsidian flakes had been trimmed into excellent knife blades and scrapers for scraping skins, their interest was still more stimulated.

After working in the Kabete territory until the middle of October I decided that I had gained as much information there as I wanted for the time being. I was anxious to start detailed work on a site where I knew I should get good results, and so went by train to Nakuru, a hundred miles further to the west, and after spending one night in the hotel we hired a lorry to carry all our equipment to Major MacDonald's farm, about three miles away.

Some years previously Major MacDonald had accidentally discovered a prehistoric site on his farm, and had reported the circumstances of the discovery in the local press. I had got into touch with him at once, and he had very kindly consented to let us carry out a scientific investigation.

When we arrived at Nakuru we called on Major MacDonald, and he took us to see the site, which was against the slopes of a small lava cliff. Piled up against the cliff was a great mass of boulders and stones, which at first sight looked as though possibly they had been placed there to block up the entrance to a cave, but we subsequently discovered that they were actually a rather peculiar form of burial mound.

We pitched our camp near to the site, although there was no water nearby, for I considered it better to be close to the work even if it entailed fetching water from a distance, rather than to camp by water and have to go some distance to and from the work. The nearest water was actually about a mile away, where there was a small irrigation furrow which had been constructed by Major MacDonald, and after the days' work was over Newsam and I and the native workmen used to go over to the furrow, wash ourselves there and then return to camp carrying water for cooking, etc., in four-gallon cans.

By so doing we somewhat scandalised the European settlers in the district, because Newsam and I used to carry water side by side with the boys, and the other Europeans considered that in doing this menial work we were lowering " white man's prestige." One settler was so worried about it that he spoke to me and asked me to stop, but I pointed out that I also worked shoulder to shoulder with my men in the excavation work. He then said that he was prepared to excuse that because it was scientific work and obviously we had to see that no damage was done and had to teach the native workmen how to do the work properly, but he really thought that we ought not to do this water carrying work. I then reminded him that when the day's digging was over the men were just as tired as we were, and I saw no reason why they should be expected to go off and do extra heavy work, like water carrying, alone, while Newsam and I stayed in camp and rested.

My point of view was, of course, one which few

white people in Kenya can appreciate, but, having been
born and bred among the Kikuyu, I had none of that
feeling of inherent superiority due to my skin colour,
which so many Englishmen seem to have. I also
knew that the natives have far more respect for a
man who works side by side with them and shows
himself to be as strong and as fit as they are, than
they have for a man who only likes to give orders and
do " brain-work." Fortunately for me, Newsam was
entirely willing to do as I did, and so we let our neigh-
bours say, and think, what they liked.

I had not brought very many native workmen with
me from Kabete in the first instance, and I soon found
that the task I had undertaken required a bigger staff,
so I asked the Government Officer at Nakuru whether
he could help me to get any local labour in order to
avoid the necessity of sending for more men from
Kabete. He said that there were a number of
unemployed natives in the township and that he
would send some of them out for me to give them
a trial, and in due course three men arrived. They
were all of them Mohammedans, and when I questioned
them they said that they had no fear of touching human
bones if we found any. They all three did one day's
hard work, but at the end of it two of them disappeared
without even waiting for their day's pay. The third
man, Juma Gitau, stayed on, and he has been in my
employ ever since and has proved himself to be a
born scientist. Had Juma had the advantages of a
European education and a scientific training I believe
that he would have been a really great man.

When I asked Juma where his two companions had
gone, he said that they had found the work to be much
too strenuous for their liking, and so had run away
for fear that I should insist on their staying a full

month. As my attempt to enlist local labour had proved so unsatisfactory, I sent to Kabete for some more men from the Mission, and in the end I had a working staff of twelve, most of whom proved to be excellent workers who have remained with me ever since.

Juma was a very much older man than any of the rest, and he had been through the war as an officer's servant in German East Africa. He had picked up a good deal of military vocabulary, and loved to get hold of my rifle and show us how to " present arms," " slope arms," etc., calling out the orders to himself in quaint English as he did so. He was a member of the Kikuyu tribe who had been converted to the Mohammedan religion during the war. He told us that before the war he had been married and that his first wife and a daughter were somewhere in Kikuyu country, but that he had lost trace of them both. At the time that he came to me at Nakuru Juma had with him a woman married by Islamic law, and so instead of making him reside in camp with the rest of my native staff, I obtained permission for him and his wife to live in an empty hut near the water furrow.

At first I was not very keen to retain him in my service, because I feared that the difference between his age and religion and that of my other men might cause friction, as indeed it has done on a very great number of occasions. But after a few weeks Juma made himself so invaluable to me as a worker, that I decided to keep him in my employ at all costs.

After we had been working at the Nakuru site for some time I decided that we must have some sort of conveyance of our own, and so I bought a very old 'T model' Ford car, and with this we visited a number of places in the district studying the geology of the country and trying to find evidence relating to the climate and geography of the district in prehistoric times.

In the course of our excavations we had discovered a number of fish bones, showing that the prehistoric men who had lived at this Nakuru site had been in the habit of catching and eating fish, and this gave us the first definite clue to the fact that the climate had been very different in Stone Age times.

The shore of Lake Nakuru was about three miles from the site, and to-day its waters are so alkaline that it contains no fish at all, yet it was clear that there had been fish in the lake in Stone Age times. Another thing was that the water furrow where we got our water supply from was due to the energy of Major MacDonald who had made it to bring water to his farm from a range of hills many miles away. The only other water in the district was the lake which, however, was quite undrinkable owing to its high soda content.

From these facts we were led to the conclusion that at the time that this prehistoric settlement had been inhabited the lake water must have been sufficiently fresh to be both drinkable and to support fish life. After a time we found traces of an ancient beach 145 feet above the present level of the lake, and when the lake stood at this level its waters would have been only half a mile from the prehistoric settlement, and would probably have been fresh.

This was only the beginning of our discoveries concerning the climate of Stone Age times, but it led us to make investigations in the right direction, and finally to the discovery of a great deal of information concerning past climatic changes and changes in the geography of the country.

Some years previously I had heard of another site in this region. It had been discovered by a Mr.

Ulyate, who had a farm at the south end of Lake Nakuru, in what is known as the Elmenteita district. Mr. Ulyate had been cutting away a part of a low cliff in order to make a water furrow, when he had exposed a number of human skulls and other bones, which were obviously of considerable age, and he had sent a small sample of his finds to the Museum in Nairobi in 1918.

In 1926 Mr. Ulyate was no longer living in the district but I had been in communication with his brother-in-law, Mr. Gamble, and one day, while we were still at work on the Nakuru site, we went over to Mr. Gamble's farm in our old Ford. Mr. Gamble then very kindly took us to see the site where Mr. Ulyate had found the skulls.

I did not really expect that this site would prove to be worth detailed excavation as I imagined that the whole of it had been disturbed and destroyed when the water furrow was originally made, but as soon as we arrived at the place and I started looking round, I found a more or less complete skull projecting from a pocket of silt that was filling a hole in the cliff face. This discovery was so important that I immediately decided that we would move camp to Elmenteita as soon as we could conveniently do so, and we therefore speeded up the work at Nakuru, and at the same time I started making plans for our move to Elmenteita.

When Mr. Ulyate left the district his farm had passed into the hands of a Mr. Ross Munroe, who lived in London, but who had appointed an agent in Nakuru, and the farm was at that time unoccupied. At the first opportunity I went to see Mr. Munroe's agent and from him obtained permission to work the site and to camp on the farm.

On January 4th, 1927, I went over to Elmenteita again and after a little digging I discovered a second skull in perfect condition. This further discovery made me still more anxious to start work there as soon as possible, and a week later we moved camp.

The old farm house at Elmenteita, although unoccupied, was not put at my disposal (as I admit I had secretly hoped it would be) and we consequently decided to make our camp in a very large and airy outbuilding that had formerly been a pigsty. This building had a more or less rain-proof thatched roof and a slightly sloping concrete floor, and it was roughly divided into five " rooms." The partition walls, as well as the outside walls, were made of upright poles. spaced about two inches apart, and as these spaces were not filled in any way, our quarters were decidedly airy. But they were much less cramped, and therefore much more comfortable than tents, and so for the rest of the time that we were in the district we lived in this old pigsty.

Newsam and I each had one room as a bedroom, a third was turned into a living room, while the fourth and fifth were respectively the kitchen and store-room.

The Makalia river, a stream coming down from the high forested hills that lay to the west of us, near our camp, provided an excellent water supply, and as there was a track from the camp to the stream, all our water was carried in the old Ford car, thus saving us a great deal of labour.

The actual site we were excavating was only a few yards from the bank of the stream, and this too was very convenient, because we could bathe and refresh ourselves when the day's work was over, before returning to camp.

Our work at this site was exceedingly successful, and we recovered a very large number of human skulls and parts of skeletons belonging to a Stone Age people, who had buried their dead along the edge of a little cliff by the river. At some later date owing to a change of climate the level of Lake Nakuru had risen very considerably and the valley of the Makalia had been swamped, and had become an arm of the lake, with the result that the old burial site had been covered up by lake silts. As these silts were rich in mineral salts the bones had become fossilised and so were well preserved.

In addition to the human bones we found a quantity of obsidian implements as well as hundreds of fragments of pottery and one complete pot, showing that the site did not belong to the very early part of the Stone Age, but to a time when the art of making pots was already known.

At the same time there were various indications that we were here faced with the remains of a people who had lived at an earlier period than those who had occupied the Nakuru site. Moreover the evidence from the two sites could be linked, and so used as a basis upon which to start reconstructing a picture of the past history of the area.

There were a number of Kikuyu families living in the district as squatters upon the farms of the settlers, and they very soon discovered that we kept a medicine chest in camp, with the result that we had a fairly regular stream of patients requiring our medical aid, as well as of visitors who were anxious to speak with the first white man they had ever come across who spoke their language as fluently as they did themselves.

During our stay at Elmenteita the time for the annual initiation ceremonies of the tribe came round, and I found it very interesting to see how this little colony of Kikuyu people, miles away from their own homes, maintained the traditional ceremonial under distinctly difficult circumstances. It was particularly interesting to note the various modifications of ceremonial that had been introduced locally, for a variety of reasons, as this threw considerable light upon the way in which people's customs can be changed by circumstance.

In the ordinary course of events in the Kikuyu country a part of the initiation ceremony has to take place near a sacred fig tree of a particular species. But there were no fig trees of the right kind at Elmenteita, so the local elders had decided that a fig tree of a different species (and which had no sacred significance for the people) should be used, but for the purposes of the ceremony it was called by the name of the other species of tree, Mugumo.

Then again, fronds of young sugar-cane play a definite part in the initiation ceremonial in Kikuyu country, but at Elmenteita no young sugar-cane fronds were available and so young maize plants were substituted, but were spoken of by the word for young sugar-cane fronds.

A still more curious change in the ceremonial, and one which was not dictated by necessity, was the use of horn-rimmed spectacles with dark glass by the young male candidates for initiation, as a substitute for rings of black paint round the eyes. When I remarked upon this to some of the elders they laughed and said that the young men had wished it and that they did not think it really mattered what the dark ring round the eyes was made with, so long as it was there during the ceremony, and that dark glasses were probably just as effective as the traditional rings of black paint for preventing the effects of the " evil eye."

Some weeks after the initiation ceremony was over, and after the candidates had recovered from the operation of circumcision, the young men and girls who had been initiated, and who were now novices, started touring the district performing the dance known as Nguro, and they came and danced near our camp on several occasions. An incident on one of these visits taught me something which was new to me and which I might never have discovered otherwise.

After initiation and during their novice stage, the young men are for a time treated as though they are women, and they have temporarily to observe many women's taboos. As a symbol of this state they wear during their novitiate small leather aprons which are a characteristic feature of Kikuyu women's and girls' dress.

It so happened that while we were staying at Kabete Mission Newsam had somehow acquired one of these women's leather aprons as a curio, and, seeing the novices wearing them, he went into his room and brought this apron out to show that he too possessed one, and he tried to hand it to one of the natives who was standing by watching the dance. In a moment there was a panic and every male, including my Mission workmen, rushed away from Newsam in horror and almost in terror. In this way I discovered that it is taboo for any full grown man to touch one of these garments,. and that the penalty for breaking this taboo is ostracism by the rest of the community. A man who had been so ostracised could only gain re-admission to the community by undergoing a lengthy and expensive purification ceremony. The fear which the men exhibited is, therefore, hardly surprising.

In the forests of the Mau Hills to the west of us there lived a few families of that small and curious hunting tribe known as Wanderobo. A good many of the people who are to-day spoken of as Wanderobo in Kenya are not real Wanderobo at all, but are social outcasts from other tribes such as the Kikuyu and the Masai, who have taken up a wandering, hunting life after the manner of the true Wanderobo. But these families in the Mau were genuine Wanderobo with a language of their own, and only one or two of them could understand any other language. There was one who spoke a little Kikuyu and another who knew a few words of Masai and of Kiswahili, and both of them had acquired the little linguistic knowledge that they had while serving short sentences in prison for some offence against the laws of the white men.

After a little while these Wanderobo found that we were very friendly, and they began to come to camp frequently in the hope of obtaining presents of meat, of which we often had a good supply, as we were shooting fairly regularly for food and often had a surplus. The Wanderobo live by hunting with the bow and arrow, by trapping birds and small game, and by taking honey from the nests of wild bees which are plentiful in holes in the forest trees. This latter source of food supply often brings them into conflict with the government authorities, for they tend to set fire to trees and to start serious forest fires as a result, especially during the dry season.

The Wanderobo always have a pack of dogs with them—curious, cock-eared, long-tailed, tawny beasts, which are excellent hunters—and they regard their dogs as their most valued possession. Whereas in many other African tribes a young man before marriage has to hand over a certain number of goats and sheep to his future parents-in-law as a guarantee of good faith, among the genuine Wanderobo I found that the prospective husband has to hand over a number of hunting dogs, and this reflects the great value which their owners place upon them.

The Wanderobo who visited our camp were skilled bowmen, and on several occasions they gave us a demonstration of their marksmanship, shooting their iron-tipped bows at a target which we made for them. Although they know how to prepare a number of different poisons with which to smear their arrow tips they do not by any means rely upon poison for killing the animals they shoot at, and I have once seen a Wanderobo man stalk up to within thirty yards of a zebra and shoot it with an unpoisoned arrow. The zebra ran away at great speed and fell down dead about forty yards away; and when I examined it I found that the head of the arrow had penetrated to the heart.

While we were encamped in our pigsty at Elmenteita we visited most of the European farmers in the neighbourhood, and were often invited out to tennis on Saturday afternoons. One day when we were playing at the Gambles' house, Mr. Gamble told me of some caves on his farm and asked me if I would like to look at them. As we had nearly completed our work at the site on the Makalia river, I very gladly accepted his invitation, and went to see them. The two caves, or rather, rock shelters, were situated half way up the side of a steep hill, and I saw at once that they must have been ideal places for prehistoric man to live in, and so I decided that when we had finished at the Makalia site we would make a trial excavation in these rock shelters, and accordingly on April 4th we started work there.

As we were now very comfortably settled in our shed on Mr. Munroe's farm, we decided not to move camp, and so we used to motor over to Mr. Gamble's house in the old Ford and leave the car there and walk over to the caves for the day's work and return to camp again in the evening.

These two rock shelters on Mr. Gamble's farm proved to be very rich sites and we continued to excavate there until the middle of July when our funds were exhausted and we had to pack up ready to return to England. The work on the caves was, however, really only just begun, and it was obvious that many more months' work remained to be done, before all the secrets hidden in the deposits of the cave were revealed to us; and so I told Mr. Gamble that if possible I would make plans for a second expedition soon after my return to England, and that if I succeeded I would come back and continue the work.

During June we had the good fortune to be visited by Dr. Erik Nilsson, a Swedish geologist who was then in Kenya studying some of the problems concerning changes of climate in prehistoric times, and I invited him to stay with us for a time so that I could show him some of the evidence that I had already found which indicated that in Stone Age times there had been several very marked fluctuations in the level of Lake Nakuru, fluctuations which I interpreted as indicating important changes of climate.

Dr. Nilsson stayed with us for about six weeks, and he very kindly gave us the benefit of his great geological experience, and we spent many long hours discussing the problems that our discoveries were creating for us, and when he left we felt that we really had begun to find a solution. A great deal depended upon whether the evidence which we had obtained from the Nakuru lake basin was confirmed elsewhere, and so Dr. Nilsson, after leaving us, went on to the Naivasha lake basin to check up our results. When he came back from there he was able to tell us that the new evidence which he had obtained confirmed our preliminary work, although it had also raised certain new problems. In view of this I decided that if I did succeed in raising the necessary funds for a second expedition I would spend a part of the time in the Naivasha area investigating these new problems.

It was with mixed feelings that we packed up all our specimens at Elmenteita camp and prepared to leave. I was sorry that my first archæological expedition had come to an end and that I must now return to England, for I did not know what the future might hold in store for me. I was determined, if possible, that I would come back to continue the work, and in my more optimistic moments I felt certain that the results that we had already achieved would convince the experts at home that there was more work to be done, and that I should be allowed to do it. But at other times I could not help wondering whether I had not been over-estimating the value of our discoveries, in which case I might never be able to obtain the funds necessary for continuing my work.

But although one part of me was sad and worried another part of me was full of happiness. Whatever the future held in store for me, I had achieved far more than I had dared to hope for when I left England a year before.

Newsam and I had between us discovered a number of prehistoric skulls and skeletons in circumstances which made it possible to date them in relation to the changes of climate and geography which had taken place in Stone Age times, and we had laid a foundation upon which the fuller solution of these problems of climatic change could be built. We had proved beyond doubt that Kenya Colony was a really rich field for all branches of prehistoric research. The ambitions of my childhood were gradually being realised.

CHAPTER XV

WHEN WE HAD FINISHED packing at Elmenteita we went down to Kabete to get ready for the journey to England.

During the course of the year's work we had collected altogether one hundred and six cases of specimens, and the next few days were spent in packing these into large strong crates, each of which contained four of the cases. Many of our specimens were very fragile, and if they were to be broken in transit to England they would be irreplaceable, and so I decided to take every possible precaution to ensure that they were carefully handled.

First of all I visited the manager of the railway and obtained his permission to load the crates on to the train at Nairobi with my own trained native staff. I further arranged to take some of my own men down to Mombasa, three hundred miles away, to offload there, and to put the crates on to the steamer that was to convey them to London. Having seen something of the way in which freight is handled by native dock labour, I was unwilling to let my specimens be so treated, but it was not without considerable difficulty that I obtained permission from the harbour authorities to handle the consignment with my own staff at the docks.

The Union Castle Steamship Company had very kindly agreed to convey these scientific specimens for half the usual rates, and they have generously made this same concession on each occasion since when I had specimens to be shipped to England. The individual officers, too, have always been most helpful to me. On this occasion Newsam and I were returning to England on a French steamer to Marseilles, as we had return tickets by the French line, and although we were not due to sail until a day or two after the English ship, I knew that we should be in London first, as we would be travelling overland from Marseilles.

As I was not going to travel on the same boat as my specimens I went and saw the Chief Officer and the Purser and told them the nature of the cargo which I had just put on board. They showed great interest and promised that they would not allow the crates to be handled at the docks in London until I was there to supervise the offloading.

None of my Kikuyu workmen had ever been to the coast before, and the biggest stretch of water they had seen previously was Lake Naivasha, which is about twelve miles wide, so that the sight of the sea was a thrilling experience for them. When the French boat that we were to sail on came into port I obtained permission to take my men aboard and show them over her, and they could hardly believe their eyes when they saw the rows and rows of cabins, the dining saloons and music rooms, and everything else that was so new and strange. And yet it was none of those things that struck them most, but rather the fact that a high percentage of the crew were Africans like themselves. The Messageries Maritimes Shipping Company employ a good many negroes from Madagascar on their steamers, and two of my boys immediately decided that at some future date they would come to the coast again and offer their services as sailors, in order that they might be able to visit Europe without expense to themselves.

When we said good-bye I assured my workmen that if I possibly could I would come back in about a year's time to continue our work, and they in their turn promised to keep a lookout for any sites round Kabete where we might be. able to excavate with satisfactory results on some future occasion.

All my men except Juma were going back to their homes at Kabete, but I had obtained special permission for Juma to go on living at our camp on Mr. Munroe's farm at Elmenteita. As a Mahommedan he had no home of his own to go to in the Reserve, and if I had not arranged for him to stay at Elmenteita, he would probably have spent the time till I came back wandering about the country. In one of my more optimistic moments I had told Mr. Munroe's representative at Nakuru that I hoped to return before long, to continue my excavations at Gamble's Caves, and he had consented to allow Juma to live in one of the outbuildings of the farm until I either returned or wrote to say that I would not be coming.

By the time the first season was over Juma had acquired a great deal of knowledge of how to excavate scientifically, and so I left him a certain amount of shellac and plaster of paris and the other necessary equipment, and told him that if, while I was away, he found any fossils in a position where they were in danger of damage by the weather, he was to excavate them and then report the matter to me by letter.

I did not really expect that he would do very much, but one day I received a letter saying that he had found a complete prehistoric human skeleton and that he had recovered it intact, and to prove his facts he sent some excellent photographs which he had persuaded some-one to take for him. Moreover when I returned to Elmenteita in 1928 I found this skull and skeleton in perfect condition ; in fact he had done the work every bit as well as I would have done myself.

When I reached England I immediately had to make arrangements for the distribution of my cases of specimens which were due to arrive in a few days. I had hoped that Sir Arthur Keith, the Conservator of the Royal College of Surgeons would be willing to study and describe the human remains, and so I approached him about it. He, however, said that he could not undertake to do the work himself, but that he would gladly put a room at my disposal to work in and would advise me and help me in any way that he could, provided that I would do the main work. So the cases containing the skulls and skeletons went to the Royal College of Surgeons.

The animal bones which we had found in association with the human skeletons and stone implements, were sent to the British Museum of Natural History at South Kensington to be studied by Dr. A. T. Hopwood, whom I thus met for the first time. Since then he has continually helped me in connection with this aspect of our East African investigations, and on one occasion has worked with me in the field.

The stone implements, pottery, stone bowls, and other Stone Age artefacts which comprised the rest of the collection, I took with me to Cambridge, where the authorities of St. John's College very kindly provided me with a commodious set of rooms in College. I at once turned one of the rooms into a laboratory, as this was much more convenient for me than having to work on my collection in one of the rooms in the building of the Anthropological Department. By having my specimens in my own rooms in College I was able to work as late into the night as I cared to.

For the next three terms I was exceedingly busy,

dividing my time between Cambridge and London where I had to learn a very great deal from Sir Arthur Keith before I could start work on the skeleton material which I had brought home. At first I planned to prepare an account of the work of the first expedition for publication at once, but when the prospects of a second expedition became brighter, I was advised to withhold publication until the second season was over and I had a still more complete story to put forward.

My contact with Sir Arthur Keith at this time was exceedingly helpful to me. Although the course which I had taken at Cambridge included a brief study of skull structure, I really knew very little about skulls and skeletons, and a more helpful and kind teacher than Sir Arthur I could not have found. He not only helped me a great deal in my actual work, but he also encouraged me from the outset to make plans for a second expedition, and he and Dr. Haddon between them were almost entirely responsible for the fact that I obtained all the grants that I needed for my second season's work, and I can never thank them enough.

I had for a long time been interested in the famous Oldoway skull which Professor Reck had found in 1913 in what was then German East Africa, and I had hoped to see it when I was in Berlin in 1926, but had not been able to do so. In view of my own discoveries I was now still more keen to see this famous find, and so during the winter of 1927 I went over to Munich to see it.

For years there had been a controversy over this skull and many British scientists were of the opinion that it was not of prehistoric age at all, but represented the remains of a modern Masai native. From the photographs and from the descriptions of it that Professor Reck gave me in 1926, I was by now fairly certain that this skull was very similar indeed to some of those from Nakuru and Elmenteita (which were certainly of Stone Age date) and so I wanted to investigate the facts for myself.

I went, first of all, to Berlin to see Professor Reck again, and tell him in person of my discoveries, as I knew they would be of interest to him, because of the support which they gave to his own find. From Berlin I went on to Munich, taking with me a letter from Professor Reck to Professor Mollison who was engaged upon a study of the Oldoway skull at that time. Unfortunately, owing to a misunderstanding about dates, when I arrived at Munich I found that Professor Mollison was away on a holiday, but his assistant at the Institute of Anthropology very kindly showed me the skeleton and gave me every facility to examine it carefully. I came away more firmly convinced than ever that the Oldoway skull and skeleton represented a race of prehistoric men very closely allied to that represented by the skulls from Elmenteita.

When I had returned to Cambridge from Kenya I had decided to submit my name as a candidate for a Research Fellowship at St. John's College and so now, although I had for the time being abandoned the idea of publishing my first season's finds in detail, I was very busy preparing a manuscript report which I could submit as a Thesis for the Fellowship, together with my published paper on the classification of the bow and arrow in Africa.

In the course of my work I met a good many of the leading British anthropologists, and they were all of them so sympathetic towards my plans for further research in East Africa that I no longer had any doubts that I should be able to obtain the necessary funds.

Accordingly I began to make my plans early in 1928

with a view to sailing towards the end of July. I had made up my mind that I must have a fully qualified geologist as a member of the expedition, because the first season's work had clearly shown that a great many purely geological problems would have to be solved if we were to achieve a proper understanding of the prehistoric climatic conditions.

At St. John's College there was a young geologist, Neville George, with whom I was friendly, and I invited him to be a member of my party. He welcomed the suggestion, but in the end he was unable to come with us, as he was offered a salaried appointment and he could not afford to miss this opportunity of starting his career. If he had accompanied my expedition he would have had all his expenses paid but would not have received a salary, as I could not possibly raise sufficient funds.

This fact has always been one of the biggest handicaps to my work in East Africa. The ideal plan would be to have a fully qualified and experienced geologist to co-operate with me in all my work, but such men cannot usually afford to devote their time to unpaid research, nor is it reasonable to expect them to do so.

One day when I was working in my rooms at Cambridge I received a visit from a young undergraduate of Trinity College who had found some skulls and other human bones of Saxon or Roman date near Cambridge. He brought these to me for my advice on how to preserve them. One of these skulls was in a very broken condition, and I told him how I would set to work to put the pieces together, and he went to see what he could do himself. When I saw the result a few days later I was so struck by the skill with which the work had been done that I immediately invited Donald MacInnes to become a member of my next expedition, and he consented. He accompanied me on my expeditions both in 1928 and 1931, and proved to be a most valuable colleague.

MacInnes is extraordinarily clever with his hands, and has a greater gift for reconstruction of fragmentary fossils than anyone else I have ever met. This gift is due to a combination of great patience and natural ability, to which he has added a sound knowledge of vertebrate anatomy. A more useful member of an expedition I have never had. He also shared with me a very deep interest in ornithology, which added to our friendship.

Partly in order to add to my income, and partly because I have always been very fond of teaching, I undertook a certain amount of coaching for the Anthropological Tripos during the year that I was in residence at Cambridge. In this way I met most of the students who were taking the course that year, and I decided that I would offer to take two students with me on the next expedition, provided they paid their own expenses. I knew how very valuable the experience that I had gained on the British Museum Expedition in 1924 had been to me, and I wanted to extend an opportunity of gaining experience to fresh students in their turn.

Among those who were studying Prehistory that year were two women, Mrs. Creasy and Miss Kitson, and in the end they were the two who joined my next expedition. As I was engaged to be married and, as I planned to marry before I sailed and to take my wife with me on the expedition, there was no reason why Mrs. Creasy and Miss Kitson should not come too.

My proposed party for the next season had thus risen to six, George, MacInnes, Mrs. Creasy, Miss Kitson, my wife and myself, but I still wanted a surveyor, and so I asked my brother, who was then at Cambridge taking the course in Geography and Surveying, if he would care to undertake that side of the work. He was at first doubtful about doing so, as it would involve absenting himself from Cambridge for at least a year before he had taken his degree, but in the end he decided to ask for special permission from the authorities, as a year's practical work in surveying was certain to be useful to him when the time came for him to look for an appointment.

I did not in the least intend to increase the number of my party any further, but one day another undergraduate of Trinity College, Mr. T. Powys Cobb, came to see me and asked if I would have him on the expedition if he paid all his expenses. He explained that his father was a settler in Kenya and that he himself expected to settle in that country later on. As he was interested in things prehistoric, he felt that he would like to gain a little knowledge and experience before he settled down to farming, so that if he ever came across things of interest he would be able to recognise them. As he had no qualifications for this work I was at first reluctant to accede to his request, but in the end, as he undertook to pay any additional expenses that his membership of the expedition involved, I consented, so that our total was now raised to eight.

In June, 1928, I heard that I had been awarded an "1851" Senior Studentship, which meant a grant of £400 a year for two years. Although I had not yet obtained all the funds which I estimated I would need if I was to carry out the full programme which I had planned, I decided that with this I now had enough to start on, and so I booked the necessary passages to East Africa and made final plans.

I had been in touch with Mr. Ross Munroe in

London, and he had very kindly agreed to allow the expedition to make use of the unoccupied farm house on his estate at Elmenteita during the forthcoming season, instead of using the pigsty and tents. As I knew that these buildings would require some repairs, I asked my brother to sail in advance so as to get the place ready for our use.

In August, my wife, MacInnes and I sailed, and I arranged that Mrs. Creasy, Miss Kitson and Powys Cobb should follow a little later, as I wanted to get the work started and everything properly organised before the party reached full strength. Neville George had unfortunately to abandon the idea of joining the expedition, and, as I had not yet obtained all the funds I needed, I had to leave the question of a geologist temporarily unsolved. I had made several applications for funds to scientific societies which had not at that time announced their awards of grants for the year, and I very much hoped that my applications would be favourably considered, in which case I should be in a position to negotiate for a geologist later on.

And so, after an interlude of about a year, I returned to Kenya to continue the investigation of the pre-historic deposits of Gamble's Caves in particular, and of other sites in the Nakuru–Naivasha region in general.

CHAPTER XVI

DURING THE FEW DAYS that I had spent at Mombasa at
the end of the first season's work, I had lectured on
the Stone Age discoveries that we had made, and I had
told my audience that although I had found one or
two specimens on the island which shewed that prehistoric man had been in the district, I had never found
any real sites, and I suggested that there was a splendid
opportunity for some of the local inhabitants to do a
little investigation themselves.

No sooner had we disembarked in 1928 than I was
informed that a Mr. Rickman would like me to call on
him as he had made a big collection of local archæological material and he wanted to have my opinion on
it. I found that Mr. Rickman was a former member
of St. John's College and a surveyor by profession and
he had made excellent use of his spare time ever since
my lecture. He had found a very large number of
stone implements at different places on Mombasa Island
and the adjoining mainland, and after he had showed
me his collection he very kindly took me to see some
of the richer sites.

Mombasa is a coral island and I had formerly believed
it had existed more or less in its present form long before
the time when man first appeared upon the scene, but as
soon as I saw some of Mr. Rickman's sites I began to
realise that we were faced with evidence which could
not be reconciled with this view.

At one site in particular there was a very thick deposit
of marine sands overlying an old land surface upon

which there were quantities of rough flakes chipped by man, suggesting that at some period after it had been occupied by Stone Age man the island had been submerged again below the ocean. In other words, here was evidence that there had been fluctuations in the relative land and sea level during the Stone Age.

This was not an entirely new discovery, for it had long been known that round the coast of England and France there are high level marine beaches which can be shown to date back to a time when prehistoric man was living in Europe. But I had frankly not expected to find similar evidence on the coast of East Africa, and I was able to tell Mr. Rickman that he had made a discovery of very great importance to us in the interpretation of the past history of the country.

We could not stay long at Mombasa on this occasion, and so I urged him to continue his investigations and make a map showing the position of his sites, promising to come back at a later date, and spend more time upon this problem.

We then went up to Kabete, collected the equipment that I had stored there, and proceeded as quickly as possible to Elmenteita, where my brother had already repaired the thatch on the roof of the farm house and made the place habitable. The house was a magnificent one from our point of view, although it was a little dilapidated and would not have been at all comfortable as a permanent home. There were two big rooms with wooden floors, and the biggest of these we made into the dining and living room for the whole party, while the other became a bedroom for my wife and myself. Then there were three small rooms which had earth floors but whose wooden doors were still intact. One of these was allotted to MacInnes, and the other two were set aside for Mrs. Creasy and Miss Kitson when they arrived. Between these rooms and our bedroom there was a bathroom with a big concrete bath in it and a cement floor. The bath itself was no longer usable, but we installed a large zinc bath and felt that we had achieved unheard of luxury for a camp.

Near the dining room was a very small room that I imagine had once served as storeroom and larder, and this became my brother's bedroom, while Powys Cobb had a tent of his own to complete the sleeping accommodation.

As soon as we arrived at Elmenteita I went with Juma to see the site where he had excavated the human skeleton while I was in England, and I found that he had, in fact, located a small prehistoric cemetery and living site, and so I decided that we would excavate at this new site while at the same time continuing the work at Gamble's Caves.

This new site was named Makalia Burial site, and after I had initiated the work there I put Powys Cobb in charge, while my wife and I worked at Gamble's Cave and MacInnes prospected for fossils in the various exposures of ancient lake deposits in the neighbourhood.

My brother started work at once to make a map of the new site, and when he had finished that, he began the really important part of his work, which was to find the levels of all the main prehistoric lake beaches which we had located.

Soon after we arrived at Elmenteita I heard from England that the additional funds which I had asked for had been granted, and, as this meant that I could now afford to have a geologist, I cabled first to Neville George to see if he could by any chance come out ; and, when I heard that he could not do so, I sent a further cable asking Dr. Haddon at Cambridge to try to find me a geologist, and send him out at once, as many new and urgent geological problems were coming to light.

During his search for fossils in the old lakebeds MacInnes had found a site where there were quantities of animal bones projecting from the side of a small cliff, and among them were one or two human bones, and it was very important to fix the geological age of the deposits forming this cliff. I was fairly certain in my own mind that they were of the same age as the deposits which had filled up the old valley of the Makalia and buried the skulls and skeletons at the site which we had excavated in 1927, but it was essential to have a geologist's verdict on the point.

Meanwhile the site was so promising that I temporarily suspended all work at Gamble's Cave and started to make an extensive excavation in order to recover these bones from the cliff face.

I had given Juma a roving commission to wander about hunting for signs of prehistoric relics, and one day he came in with some finds which raised a still more acute geological problem, so that it was with great pleasure that I at last heard from Dr. Haddon that a geologist was sailing immediately to join us. Near the camp was a fairly high cliff which I had briefly examined with Dr. Nilsson in 1927 and we had come to the conclusion that the deposits exposed in it were part of a series which had been studied and described by a very eminent geologist, Professor J. W. Gregory, and that their age was Miocene. This meant that they belonged to a period which long antedated the appearance of man in the world, and in view of this I had paid no further attention to this particular series of strata, as I was only concerned with deposits which might be expected to yield evidence of the Stone Age.

Juma, of course, knew nothing about geological

matters, and his ignorance proved to be a great blessing, for, as he did not know that these deposits were sup-posedly of Miocene age he had no reason for not trying to find stone implements in them. One afternoon, he came into camp with a rather beautiful specimen of an obsidian implement, and when I asked him where it came from he told me that he had dug it out from the side of a cliff, and pointed to the cliff of alleged Miocene deposits.

I had never known Juma to be anything but scrupu-lously honest ; as far as our scientific work was concerned, and I regret to have to record that I at once told him that he must be lying and that I knew that what he said was impossible. Juma was rightly very indignant at the suggestion that he was not telling the truth, and replied that if I would go with him at once I could see the truth for myself, as he had left several specimens sticking out from the cliff for me to see. Although I was still very sceptical, I abandoned my tea, and accompanied by all the others, rushed off to see. Sure enough, there were several more obsidian flakes and tools of undoubted human origin projecting from the cliff face. I was staggered. There seemed to be only two alternatives. Either the eminent geologist was wrong and this series of deposits was not of Miocene age at all, or else Juma had made a most remarkable discovery which would revolutionise all ideas about the origin of man. Anyhow, a full geological investigation was essential.

As far as this particular site was concerned, we eventually discovered that the deposits exposed in the cliff did not belong at all to the series of strata that had been described by Professor Gregory as of Miocene age, but at the same time the discovery led us to examine critically all deposits which were supposed to be of that age, and in the end we found that many of them were in fact laid down in human times ; but that is a story that must be told in its own place.

The work at the cliff where MacInnes had found the fossil bones was continued, and after a time we located a part of a human skull, and I decided to leave this in position until it could be examined *in situ* by a geologist, and so we applied preservative to it as it lay and then protected it with boards and temporarily left it. The position was somewhat precarious, and I was afraid that the cliff would not stand for very long as we had been forced to undermine it a little in recovering some fossil animal skulls, so I wrote and invited Mr. Wayland, the Director of the Geological Survey of Uganda to come and visit us and examine the evidence and be a witness to the excavation of this skull.

He replied that he would come in November, and so we left the site carefully protected, and resumed work at Gamble's Cave, where we very soon reached an exceedingly rich horizon which yielded us thousands of most perfect obsidian knife blades and scrapers.

So rich was this particular deposit that we were obtaining literally hundreds of perfect implements, as well as thousands of flakes, each day, as the following figures from my report book for four days show :

Oct. 23 .. 140 implements.
" 24 .. 533 implements.
" 25 .. 715 implements.
" 26 .. 339 implements.

On November 19th Mr. Wayland arrived, and he accompanied us to the site where the skull was, and after he had made detailed notes concerning its position in the deposit, MacInnes and I set to work to extricate it. It was in a very difficult place to get at, and we had to lie on our sides and work with small knives and slowly cut away the surrounding rock. Above us was the cliff of silt and clays, which we had found too solid to dig away, and which we dared not remove by blasting for fear of damaging the specimen beneath.

At last, after about half an hour's work, we got the skull safely out and I carried it a little way from the cliff to show it to Mr. Wayland, leaving MacInnes still lying under the cliff to dig a little further into the rock and make sure there were no associated bones there. Powys Cobb took my place by his side, and I called out to them to be careful and not to dig in too far, for fear of bringing the cliff down. Almost as I spoke there was a horrible crashing sound, and part of the cliff collapsed, and both MacInnes and Powys Cobb were covered in the fallen rock.

It was a sickening moment, and I cursed myself for having let them go on once the skull was safely out. I imagined that they must both be dead, and in feverish haste and with leaden hearts Wayland, my wife and I, together with my native workmen, set to work to remove the fallen rock debris and uncover the victims. Fortune had been on our side, however, and the very undercutting which had caused the disaster had also saved their lives. Both of them had been lying with their heads and bodies right in under the cliff in a sort of little cave that we had made in the course of digging out the bones, and when the rock collapsed the debris missed their heads and the upper part of their backs, and only fell on their posteriors and legs. They were not seriously hurt, and we were exceedingly thankful that they had escaped with nothing more than serious bruises and some deep jagged wounds where sharp rock fragments had cut into them.

Of course, the Kikuyu workmen all said that the accident was caused by the spirit of the man whose skull we had just taken from its resting place, and I imagine that there are a good many English men and women who would also subscribe to that view ; but I knew that no spirit was responsible for the catastrophe and that I had only my own self to blame for what might have proved a fatal accident.

Rather than run the risk of damaging an important scientific specimen, I had been willing to take certain risks myself, but I ought not to have allowed MacInnes and Powys Cobb to remain in the danger zone once the skull was safely out. By good fortune the consequence of my foolishness was not too serious, but I learned a lesson that I have never forgotten.

After Mr. Wayland had left us to return to Uganda, I motored down to Nairobi to see the Governor of the Colony. We had discovered so many new sites in the Elmenteita district, and Gamble's Cave was also proving to be so much richer than I had anticipated that I had begun to realize that we should have to spend much longer on the work than I had estimated, and this of course meant that I should need additional funds, and so I decided to approach the local Government for a grant-in-aid.

The Governor—Sir Edward Grigg—was very sympathetic, and promised to see if anything could be done, although he would not commit himself to any promises. After some discussion I agreed to the principle that, in the event of a Government grant being made, I would return a proportion of the scientific specimens obtained with it to the Government for disposal by them in the Nairobi Museum or elsewhere at their discretion. Eventually after further negotiations I was given a grant of £1,000 towards the work.

On the following day, Sunday, Mrs. Creasy and Miss Kitson were due to arrive in Nairobi, so I waited in town to meet them, and intended taking them up to Elmenteita by car next day. When they arrived, however, they

announced that they must spend at least a day in Nairobi
to do shopping before coming to camp, and so I arranged
for them to travel up by train to Elmenteita next day,
where I promised to meet them, and I went back by car
that afternoon.

Before I left them I had gathered from their conversation that they were expecting all sorts of excitements in
camp. In actual fact—apart from the scientific work—
life at our Elmenteita camp was almost as humdrum as
it might be in a suburb of London, and so when I told
the rest of our party that our new members were expecting a wild and dangerous life we decided to stage something especially for them.

The Elmenteita station was about eight miles from our
camp, and the road from it was little more than a track,
first across a flat, treeless plain and then through some
fairly dense bush on the edge of one of the farms. The
train from Nairobi was due to arrive after dark, so that
there would be every opportunity to arrange " an
incident " which would have been almost impossible in
daylight.

It so happened that about a mile from camp there was
a place where there were two alternative tracks, both
leading eventually to Mr. Munroe's farm, and so we
agreed to stage a lion incident at this point. I was to go
in one car to meet Mrs. Creasy and Miss Kitson, and as
soon as those in camp saw the headlights in the distance
(about three miles away) they were to take the second
car and go quickly to the place where the road forked and
hide in the bushes nearby and then roar like lions at the
appropriate moment.

As we drove from the station I told my passengers that
if they were lucky they might hear lions roaring, and then
as we approached the place where the two alternative
tracks met I told them that this was what we called " lion

corner," because we so often heard or met lions there. They were duly impressed, and then suddenly we heard a thunderous roaring which no one who had ever heard a real wild lion could possibly have thought to be genuine, but which served admirable for the purpose for which it was intended. " By jove," I said, " they are closer than usual to-night," and I stamped on the accelerator and turned up the left hand track as hard as I could go, and did not slow down again until I was two or three hundred yards away. Then, with the excuse that the track here was very rough and irregular I slowed right down so as to give the others time to start their car again and get back to camp before us.

When we arrived my wife and the others all trooped out of the house to meet us, and they were given a highly interesting account of how near the " lions " had been, and so we sat down to supper.

In the middle of supper there was a shout from one of the Kikuyu workmen outside, and then another, and in a trice my brother, young Powys Cobb and MacInnes rushed out of the room, calling to me to " look after the women " and shouting that it was a raid by the Masai. This was followed by the sound of shots and more shouting. I had not been warned of this second " show " that was to be staged for the benefit of the newcomers, but I guessed at once what it was, and so played my part, but I was afraid that Mrs. Creasy and Miss Kitson might become too seriously alarmed, so later on in the evening we told them that the " Masai raid " was a " hoax," but for some weeks more they still firmly believed the lion story.

The climax to the evening came in a most unexpected manner. My wife had gone across to show Mrs. Creasy and Miss Kitson their rooms, when I suddenly heard a shout of " Snake, snake ! " from my wife. At first I suspected that this was just one more practical joke, but the tone of voice sounded rather too genuine, so I rushed across, and, sure enough, wriggling across the bathroom floor was a big, black, and very much alive snake, which I quickly killed. When my wife first noticed it, it had been lying quite still, and she too had for a moment thought it was one more trick, and, thinking that this was really going too far, she stepped forward to pick it up, when suddenly it moved.

Actually, snakes were almost the only dangerous creatures in the district, and only a few weeks later, on the very day that John Solomon, the new geologist arrived, he very nearly trod on a large puff-adder. I think I saw more snakes during the second season at Elmenteita than in all my previous years in the country.

During the month of December we concentrated chiefly upon Gamble's Cave, but several other minor sites were examined and some exceedingly interesting results were obtained at them, but everything else was eclipsed by the discovery of a more or less complete human skull and skeleton at Gamble's Cave on December 18th.

We were working at a level which was about 14 feet below the floor of the cave. At this level we had already found several very fragmentary skulls in such a poor state of preservation that they would be of very little scientific value, and I had almost given up hope of getting a well preserved specimen in this deposit when the discovery was made.

At the point where we were working the deposits had been more or less consolidated by the percolation of water with some form of lime in it, so that the skull and skeleton were embedded in a relatively hard matrix, and I very quickly decided not to try and take out each bone of the skeleton separately, but to dig out the whole block in which it was embedded, as a single piece, and take to England to be developed there.

The task was a very slow and arduous one, and a good deal of the work of chipping away the matrix near the actual bones had to be done with small dental picks, as we did not want to risk damaging the skeleton in any way. This work had a very amusing sequel some time later. News of our discovery became widely known, and one day I had a visit in camp from the local representative of one of the English illustrated daily newspapers. I described to him how the block with the skeleton in it, which was then on view, had been partly cut away from the surrounding rock with dental picks, and I believe that in his own mind he was quite clear that the dental picks had been used *by me*. I don't know exactly how he worded the message which he cabled to England, but he must have used ambiguous English, for the newspaper concerned announced the discovery to its readers in the following words, so far as I can remember : " Mr. Leakey discovers the first dentist ! Fossil man found with dental picks ! "*

By the time the block containing the skeleton had been cut free and had been encased in a protecting cover of plaster of paris and hessian, it weighed about three hundredweight, and the task of getting it from the cave to camp was a very difficult one. The ordinary path from the cave to the river level below was very steep and we had to spend some time in clearing a graded pathway. We then made a strong stretcher attached to two long bamboo poles and with eight of us manning the poles, and eight others accompanying us and ready to take turns, we slowly and gradually carried the precious load to the bottom of the valley and a little way up the other side, where a lorry was waiting.

* I have unfortunately lost this cutting.

The skeleton from Gamble's Cave belonged to a much earlier date than any of the human remains which we had found previously in Kenya, and it was of comparable age to many of the well-known fossil skulls from France, such as the oft-mentioned Cromagnon skull.

After we had brought the entire block safely to camp I had it placed on view for a long time, and we had over two hundred visitors to camp to see it. Most of the visitors came at the week-ends, and this we did not mind very much, but sometimes they would arrive on a week-day afternoon when we were tired out and hungry, and then it required a good deal of patience to answer all their questions and explain about how the age of the various discoveries was worked out in relation to other things.

Some of the visitors were really interested in the problems that we were investigating, while others came simply out of idle curiosity, and some of those in the latter category were responsible for the most astounding comments and remarks, which caused us intense amusement at the time. Unfortunately, I cannot accurately remember the best stories, but this one will give an idea of their nature. A small party of people, derived from the commercial community of Nakuru, had been shown the skeleton and some of the stone tools, and I had started to explain about the old high level beaches round Lake Nakuru, and pointed out that there must have been some general tilting of the earth's crust in this region since one of the beaches had been formed, as it was considerably higher above the present lake level at the north end than it was at the south.

" But," said one of the party, " I don't see that that follows at all. Why should not the water have stood higher at one end of the basin than at the other ? "

I cannot help thinking that this must have been the man who was responsible a year or two later for the following paragraph that appeared in one of the local newspapers :

"The rains have been particularly heavy round Nakuru and the lake has risen three feet near the town, while at the south end it is nine feet above normal level."

Towards the end of January we at last reached rock bottom at Gamble's Cave, after we had extended the excavations to a depth of twenty-nine feet below the floor. The whole of the last ten feet we had been digging through had been almost solid with obsidian flakes and implements, and we had obtained an average of eighty-four finished and perfect tools from each cubic foot, in addition to hundreds of untrimmed flakes and bone fragments.

Although there was still a good deal of work to be done at this site, I decided that we no longer needed a large gang of workers—for, having reached rock bottom we could estimate better how much more remained to be cleared—and so I arranged to set up a subsidiary camp about fifteen miles away, near another rock shelter on the side of a hill known as Lion Hill. By this time MacInnes, Mrs. Creasy and Miss Kitson had gained a good deal of practical experience in excavation, and I therefore decided that they should be stationed at the new camp and work Lion Hill cave, while I completed the work at Gamble's Cave with my wife and Powys Cobb to help me.

Solomon was still working hard on geological problems and my brother was co-operating with him in mapping and levelling, and they hoped to finish their work in the Nakuru basin soon and move to Naivasha. Unfortunately there was no water at all within miles of the Lion Hill cave, and so every drop of water for the use of that camp had either to be brought by lorry when I came over to inspect the work from time to time, or fetched from Nakuru town, nine miles away, if the lorry happened to be going in for provisions.

The tents were pitched among some trees about a mile from the cave, but even so it was very hot and rather unpleasant. The deposits in the cave were unusually dusty and the dust, combining with the sweat on the workers' bodies made them filthy, and my Kikuyu boys promptly named the place " Kampi ya Giko," or the Dirty Camp. Owing to the shortage of water, washing had to be reduced to a minimum just when it was most necessary.

At Elmenteita camp our water supply was also getting precarious, and, after a time, the Makalia stream dried up altogether, and we had to start fetching our supply from the stream near Gamble's Cave. Then that too ceased to flow in its lower stretches, and by the end of February we were having to spend a good many hours every third day fetching water for camp. There was, unfortunately, no way of getting the lorry upstream to where there were still pools, and we had to walk long distances and bring the water down in cans.

With water so short at Elmenteita we could no longer supply Lion Hill camp with it, and at intervals I had to send the lorry into Nakuru to fetch water for them. It is a curious thing that again and again in connection with our prehistoric excavation work in East Africa we have been troubled by water shortage, and in fact the troubles that we had here at Elmenteita, although we thought them very serious at the time, were quite eclipsed by the water problems that confronted us a year or two later, when we were working in the Oldoway region, and I am still looking forward to the day when I shall discover a really rich prehistoric site that is near a good and plentiful water supply.

In the course of our study of the old lake beaches in the Nakuru basin we had frequently wondered what was the present depth of the lake. I had made many enquiries in Nakuru, but no one seemed to be able to give me any reliable information. One man said that he had been out in a boat and had let down a weighted line one hundred yards long and that he had not touched bottom, and another assured us that he knew that it was very deep indeed, probably unfathomable. These statements did not at all agree with our general views, and I imagined that a maximum depth of 30 or 40 feet was more likely.

Enquiries from local natives were no more helpful, and all the information they could give us was that " the lake must be very very deep because it has a great monster living in it that is as big as a very big house, and the waters are deep enough to hide it completely."

After a time I decided that the best thing to do was to find out the facts for ourselves, and so I started making enquiries for a boat, and in the end the Public Works Department very kindly put a large, flat-bottomed, very heavy punt at my disposal. The paddles which were supplied with it were rather like glorified ping-pong bats. They consisted of a round blade about the size of a dinner plate fixed to the end of a long pole. I was very doubtful of their efficiency as a means of propelling the punt but we could not know until they were tried out.

We brought this " boat " to the south end of the lake, but when we tried to launch it we found that the mud along the shore was several feet deep, making it impossible to get out to the open water. The Public Works Department, however, gallantly came to our aid, and one of the engineers was detailed to help us build a small pier across the mud, and after a long and very hard day's work, we managed to complete the construction

and the " boat " was launched. We soon found, however, that the paddles were hopelessly inadequate for
such a heavy boat, but we had the good fortune to be
able to borrow a small outboard motor and with the help
of this the " boat " could be made to travel about three
miles an hour.

My brother then started making a detailed chart of the
lake depths. He was accompanied on his " voyages " by
Miss P. M. Jenkin, a Cambridge zoologist who was
temporarily attached to my expedition. She was engaged
upon a study of the aquatic fauna of some of the East
African lakes, and this sounding work on Lake Nakuru
gave her an excellent opportunity to acquire specimens.

Evening by evening the party returned from the lake
and reported depths of 9 feet, 9 feet 2 inches, 8 feet, and
so on, and we kept telling ourselves that presently they
would come to the deeper part of the basin. But in the
end, after the whole area had been sounded, we found
that the deepest point anywhere of this " bottomless
lake " was 9 feet 3 inches. The next lake to be similarly
studied was Lake Elmenteita which was also alleged to be
" very deep," and here the greatest depth proved to be
only just over 6 feet.

Among the many results which emerged from this
work was the conclusion that this part of East Africa was
very rapidly drying up. We knew from our prehistoric
work that about 2,000 years ago the beaches of Lake
Nakuru had stood at 145 feet above its present level, and
we further found that since 1906, when the lake had been
properly mapped for the first time, the mean level had
decreased by a further 5 feet. This news was far from
satisfactory for the local farming population, but it seems
to be true, and similar evidence of progressive desiccation
can be found all over the country.

Towards the end of April I decided to make a brief

visit to the basin of Lake Baringo, which lies to the north of Lake Nakuru on the southern fringe of the northern frontier semi-desert belt. On May 1st six of us set off with a car and lorry. Solomon and Powys Cobb were to remain at Baringo for a fortnight and they travelled in the box body car with all the equipment which they needed for their stay, while I drove a newly acquired lorry and was accompanied by my wife, Miss Kitson and Miss Jenkin.

The rainy season had just started and I was not at all sure that the lorry would be able to get through to Baringo, and as I wanted Solomon and Powys Cobb to go there anyhow to examine certain geological problems, it seemed better that they should be self-contained, so that if the lorry stuck in the mud they could go on without us.

We had a most difficult journey and the lorry sank into mud up to her axles on several occasions, but eventually we all reached Marigat, a little trading station to the south of the lake, and looked for a place to camp. Just below Marigat was a river bed with a moderate stream flowing in it, and, as we saw an Indian trade lorry ford it comparatively easily, I decided to cross over in our vehicles and camp under some trees on the far bank.

The body of the lorry which we were using had been specially built for a journey which I proposed to make shortly to Johannesburg, and I had decided to try it out on this Baringo trip. On either side of the lorry were detachable canvas awnings that could be fitted up into a sort of tent, and the idea was that Miss Kitson and Miss Jenkin were each to sleep in one of these two " tents," while my wife and I slept in the lorry. We had therefore only brought ordinary camping equipment for Solomon and Powys Cobb.

Having got the vehicles safely across the ford we

pitched their tent, and then started to make the lorry
ready for the four of us to sleep in, as planned. But the
awnings as we then had them proved to be quite inadequate to keep out the rain which started to come down in
torrents as it grew dark, and in the end we all four had
to sleep on the floor of the lorry packed like sardines.

By the time we had finally decided to abandon any
further attempt to make the side tents of the lorry rain-
proof, we were all more or less soaked to the skin, so that
there could be no question of just lying down to sleep in
our day clothes. We therefore had to undress and get
into dry pyjamas as best we could. We did not want to
soak our bedding and so did not undress in the back of
the lorry, but in the semi-shelter of the abandoned side
tents. I undressed first in one side tent and crawled
into the back of the lorry, and one of the funniest things
I have ever seen was the procession of pyjama-clad female
figures, with their rain-soaked hair falling over their
faces, climbing up over the edge of the lorry and coming
into bed head foremost.

Had we not all been able to see the funny side of the
situation and laugh heartily it would have been a really
miserable night ; even as it was, I don't suppose any of
us will ever forget it.

Throughout the night it rained, not only locally, but
up-country towards the sources of the stream, and by the
morning there was a raging torrent which had risen well
above the level of the banks, so that there was about
three or four inches of water over all our camping ground.
I would gladly have taken the lorry and car back to the
high ground by Marigat trading village at once, had that
been possible, but the river was now quite unfordable,
and all we could do was to hope that it would not rise
further and flood us right out. During the preceding
weeks we had been suffering from a severe water shortage,

and it was rather ironical to be now suffering from too much water, and yet to have none to wash in or cook with, for the flood waters were so heavily laden with sediment that it was the colour and consistency of a thick cup of cocoa. By putting it into cans and letting it stand for a time we were able, after a while, to get enough clear water to make some tea, and later in the day the floods subsided a little and the water became cleaner again. But the stream did not show any signs of returning to its normal level and we had very considerable difficulty in getting the lorry across to the Marigat side again two days later.

We left Solomon and Powys Cobb at Baringo until May 14th, but owing to the very bad weather they were unable to do very much exploring and no important discoveries were made. Meanwhile the work at Gamble's Cave was still going on, and the rich occupation deposit which formed the lowest horizon in the cave was found to extend over a far greater area than I had expected. We had already obtained far more obsidian implements from the site than we needed, and I would have ceased work long before had it not been for the fact that there was still a chance of finding a human skeleton somewhere in this lowest deposit, and I very much wanted to do so.

We had already found another well-preserved skeleton at the same level as the one we had taken out in a solid block, but I was anxious to get human remains from the considerably older deposits which we were now excavating, and all that we had so far found were three isolated human teeth. In this particular quest we were destined to have no success, but in the course of our work, long after we had acquired enough obsidian implements from that horizon to satisfy all scientific needs, we found a small piece of pottery which was of the greatest scientific value, and which amply repaid us for the time and money spent on the additional work.

We were at this time working in a deposit which had been accumulated during what is known as the Aurignacian stage of culture, and, according to what was previously known, there should have been no pottery present at all as early as this. On the other hand, it was obvious that the discovery of the value of clay was not impossible for a people who had reached such a high degree of manual skill as was represented by the tools and implements of this horizon. Once or twice already we had found very small fragments of pottery which *appeared* to be derived from this particular deposit, but we had not been able to prove it, and then at last one day I found a fairly large piece myself, under conditions which made its relation to the culture of the horizon unquestionable.

I was very pleased with this discovery, for I had often put forward the view that if we were to account satisfactorily for the highly developed pottery of the somewhat later culture which we had found at the site near the Makalia river during the previous season, we must postulate that the first use of clay dated back to at least the time of the Aurignacian culture, and here at last was the proof.

But the discovery was not at all well received when I reported it to various authorities on Prehistory in Europe ; and in fact I was informed quite bluntly by one or two people to whom I wrote that I must have made a mistake and that I had better withdraw such a foolish claim at once. However, I knew that there was no mistake, and before the season came to an end I was able to gain support for my claim from various authorities, but that was not until after my return from Johannesburg where my wife and John Solomon and Elizabeth Kitson and myself attended the South African meeting of the British Association.

We were due to leave by lorry for South Africa about the middle of June, and so towards the end of May we began to pack up everything as the camp was to be closed for the time being. Mrs. Creasy had left the expedition and gone up to the Kavirondo country to investigate the tribal customs of a section of Luo tribe. MacInnes had been very unwell and had to go to England for health reasons, and my brother was due to return to Cambridge to resume his interrupted studies, while Powys Cobb had decided to join a Zoological Expedition that was going to the Congo. The personnel of my expedition had thus been drastically reduced, and the only thing to do was to close down camp until we returned from the south.

I intended taking down a large representative series of our finds to exhibit at the scientific meeting at Johannesburg, and I was bitterly disappointed that we had not, as yet, found any site where the so-called hand-axe culture occurred under conditions where it would be satisfactorily dated. It was therefore particularly satisfactory when one day John Solomon and Miss Kitson discovered a site which yielded the evidence we needed so much, and thus almost on the eve of our departure for the south we were able to add one more chapter to the story of the gradual evolution of the Stone Age cultures of East Africa.

The deposits in which Solomon and Miss Kitson found these hand-axes were part of a series of ancient lake beds which had been cut through by the faults of the Great Rift Valley. In other words, these implements represented a culture which had been in existence before that great crack had appeared in its present form.

The discovery was, therefore, of the very greatest importance, as it threw entirely new light upon the age of the great Great Rift Valley, and led us to initiate a whole series of fresh investigations.

CHAPTER XVII

FOR SEVERAL YEARS I HAD been hoping for an opportunity
to visit South Africa, as I wanted to see something of
the prehistoric discoveries that had been made there, and
the meeting of the British Association for the Advancement of Science, which was due to be held in South
Africa in 1929, provided me with an excellent excuse, as
it had been suggested that I should read a paper before
the Anthropological section of the Association describing
some of the discoveries we had made in Kenya. At first
I thought of travelling south by steamer, but after further
consideration decided that it would be more satisfactory
to travel overland in our own lorry. By doing so, we
would not only save money, but would also be able to
visit many sites of outstanding prehistoric interest
en route.

The rainy season was only just drawing to its close in
May, and the roads were likely to be in a very bad
condition so that I had to allow rather a long time for the
journey, especially as I wanted to stop for a few days at
Broken Hill in Northern Rhodesia, and elsewhere. We
therefore started off from Nairobi on June 13th, although
we were not due at Johannesburg until the last week in
July.

The lorry that we were to travel in was the $1\frac{1}{2}$-ton
Chevrolet that had taken us to Baringo, and I had had the
side tents, which had failed us so badly on that occasion,
altered and modified, and they now provided two
excellent " rooms," one on either side of the lorry.

For ordinary short runs we often had three people sitting in the front seat of the lorry, but this meant that the driver was somewhat cramped, and so for this long journey I arranged to have two canvas chairs in the back of the lorry so that two of us could sit there while the driver only had one person next to him. All four of us, Miss Kitson, John Solomon, my wife and myself were licensed to drive, and we arranged to take turns at the wheel, and changed over approximately every fifty miles.

We had a fairly heavy load on board, as we were each taking a trunk with tidy clothes to wear in Johannesburg, and in addition we had all our bedding, a good deal of spare petrol and water, a big range of spare parts in case of breakdowns, and a heavy case containing stone implements to be exhibited at the scientific meeting.

All of my Kikuyu boys clamoured to be allowed to accompany us, but I refused to take more than one, and selected Jannai Kigamba, because he knew more about cars than the others, and so would be more useful if we had to change a broken spring or mend a puncture. Before he could go on this journey he had to be provided with a British passport. He was exceedingly proud of this possession when he found that it was exactly like ours in every detail, and before we left he exhibited it gleefully to all his friends.

The journey started most inauspiciously—a superstitious person would have said it was because of the date —for we had gone barely 13 miles on the 13th of June before the lorry developed engine trouble, and so, having limped into the little Government station of Ngong, I had to telephone to a garage in Nairobi to send out a mechanic to repair it. Had we been further from our starting point Jannai and I could probably have effected the repairs ourselves, but as the garage had just overhauled the engine and guaranteed her to be in good order for the journey I considered that they ought to put the lorry right themselves.

This mishap held us up for an hour or two, and we passed the time very pleasantly watching some Masai men play their variation of the universal African game of Weso, but I did not have time to learn all the rules. When the lorry was once more running smoothly we started off again, but we did not go very far, as I usually make it a rule that the first night of a long safari shall be spent fairly near to the starting point so that if anything is found to have been forgotten, when camp is prepared for the night, we can go back and get it.

On this occasion everything proved to be entirely satisfactory, and we had a very comfortable night by the road side, and next morning travelled on towards the Tanganyika border, where we found the road in a most appalling condition, and consequently had to travel very slowly indeed. The soil was very light and the " road " consisted simply of a track made by passing traffic prior to the rainy season. Wherever there was a slight slope the rain water had run in rivers down the depressions made by the wheel tracks of the past, and had transformed them into gullies two or even three feet wide and over a foot deep. Dust lay so deep in these gullies that it was very hard to detect them until one was in them, and several times we came to an involuntary standstill owing to the axles of the lorry being jammed against one of the ridges between the ruts.

In 1929 this particular section of the road on either side of the Kenya-Tanganyika boundary was probably the worst anywhere between Nairobi and Capetown, but since then it has received a good deal of attention and when I travelled over it again in 1935 I found that one could easily proceed at 25 instead of 5 miles an hour.

We only stopped at Arusha—the centre of the farming

area in north-east Tanganyika—for a very short time
while we purchased petrol and stores. We had decided
that we would only spend a night in an hotel on very
rare occasions when we felt that we simply must have a
bath and a few creature comforts, so we camped some
miles beyond Arusha in a region which I now know is
infested with lions, but we neither saw nor heard any.

Although I had lived so many years in Kenya I had
seen very few lions, while none of my companions had
ever seen or heard a wild lion, so we all hoped that in
the course of our journey south we should come across
the king of beasts, as we would be passing through some
of the finest lion country in Africa. But we neither saw
nor heard a lion until the last day of our return journey
when we were just outside Nairobi once more. We then
had an encounter with twelve of them, which I will
describe presently.

We experienced a certain amount of difficulty in
crossing the Mbugwe flats, near Lake Manyara, and in
fact ours was one of the first vehicles to succeed in getting
through from Arusha to Dodoma that season. During
and just after the rainy season the flats tend to become
quite impassable, and I have known of unfortunate
travellers who were stuck in the mud there for a fortnight. As with the section of the road from Nairobi to
Arusha, so too here, conditions have very much altered
since 1929, and by 1936 a new road had been constructed
in such a way as to by-pass the Mbugwe flats, and it is now
possible to make the journey from Arusha to Dodoma
all the year round.

After we had safely negotiated this treacherous piece of
road, we temporarily abandoned the Great North road
of Africa—which, theoretically, runs from the Cape to
Cairo—and made a detour so as to visit a Mr. Nash who
had discovered some interesting rock paintings which

were presumably of prehistoric date and which I was therefore very anxious to see.

Mr. Nash was in charge of the Kikori Research Station where he was investigating the problem of the tsetse fly, the dreaded carrier of both sleeping sickness and a fatal cattle disease, and we spent a most interesting afternoon hearing about his work and seeing some of his experiments. He had a number of cages containing tsetse fly which were being used for experimental purposes, and these flies had to be fed at regular intervals. At mealtimes a sheep or goat was held against the wire of the cage so that the flies could settle on the poor beast's skin and stick their proboscies into it and suck the blood. Mr. Nash, and also some of the natives whose duty it was to feed these flies, every now and again would deliberately let the flies feed off their own arms, saying that it was less tiring than holding the sheep against the wire. There was no danger involved in doing this as these flies were not infected with sleeping sickness, but it must nevertheless have been extraordinarily painful. We had ourselves passed through a fly belt the day before and had found that the prick of just one fly in search of a meal was enough to make one very irritable. But Mr. Nash explained that after a time you become accustomed to it and that then it did not hurt so much. I still think that I would have preferred to hold the sheep against the cage, rather than provide the flies with a meal from myself.

Just at that time Mr. Nash was trying to discover whether these little insects detected their prey by sight, by sound, or by smell, and in order to do so, he was daily catching large numbers of flies for an experiment. At the time of our visit the question of the eyesight of the tsetse fly was being investigated, and so each day vast numbers of captive flies had their eyes painted over and were then liberated. The following day native boys would be sent out in pairs, one to act as a moving bait to attract the flies, and the other to catch the flies so attracted. If a sufficient number of blinded flies had been liberated, and if they could locate their prey unhelped by sight, then a proportion of them were bound to be attracted by the boys and so would be caught.

Another problem which was being investigated was how far the flies could travel, and numbers of specially marked flies were liberated at certain points, and if any of them were caught again later careful note was kept of the distance from the place where they had been set free.

The whole of the work at Kikori was fascinating and I would have liked to spend several days at Mr. Nash's laboratory, but we could not afford the time to do so.

Before we left, Mr. Nash gave us sketch maps of various places where he had found rock paintings, and he took us to see one of the best sites at Cheke, about ten miles from his house. I was immediately struck by the close resemblance of the style of some of these paintings to many of those from South Africa that I had seen illustrated, and when I had seen these Tanganyika paintings I became all the more eager to see the Rhodesian and South African sites.

From the look of the country round Cheke, I was convinced that there must be many other sites in the neighbourhood, and I made a resolution to come back and make a more detailed study of the area later on. I did not, however, get an opportunity to do so until 1935, and then I could only spare ten days, but I hope to return to the district in the not too distant future. I have recently published illustrations of some of these Cheke paintings in my book *Stone Age Africa*.

After leaving the Kikori district we made our way back to the Great North Road once more, visiting one or two other sites on the way, and then resumed our journey southward, and after a few days reached Iringa, which is the counterpart of Arusha in the Southern Tanganyika Highlands. The country round Iringa was only just beginning to be opened up for white settlement. There were a good many people who had moved there from Kenya, and we met a number of acquaintances. Although the country was fertile enough and the climate good, the outlook for the farmers did not appear to me to be too good, as the Iringa district was nearly two hundred miles from the nearest railway, which meant that all produce intended for export would have to be transported to Dodoma by lorry, which would inevitably be a very costly procedure owing to the high cost of petrol and oil. The settlers were all hoping that a branch railway would be constructed, in fact many of them were counting upon this, but so far their hope has not been fulfilled, and I do not imagine that it will be for many years to come.

At Iringa we stopped at a hotel for one night and enjoyed hot baths which by then we badly needed, and after a day's rest we drove on towards the Northern Rhodesia boundary. The road became exceedingly bad, and once I thought that we should be forced to unload the lorry in order to negotiate a very steep hill up which this road ascended. Instead of being graded in any way, the track was laid up a slope of 1 in 3, and the surface was very loose and uneven.

However, our lorry was fitted with an extra low gear intended for use in just such a circumstance, but hitherto I had never had any real opportunity to test its powers, so I did not know what it was capable of doing. Our brakes were by this time a little worn, and I had unpleasant visions of stalling the engine half way up, and then rolling down the hill to crash at the bottom. To avoid such a disaster I made Jannai and Solomon get out and follow the lorry, each carrying a large boulder which they were to jam in behind the back wheels if the engine stopped and the brakes failed to hold. But all was well; the extra low gear did its work magnificently, and with a sigh of relief we reached the top with nothing worse than the water in our radiator boiling most furiously.

On our map Abercorn was marked in big letters, and in our ignorance we imagined that it was a small township like Arusha or Iringa, and so, although it grew dark when we were still about twenty miles away, we did not camp, but decided to go right on, promising ourselves the luxury of baths, comfortable beds and a hot meal ready cooked for us at the Abercorn hotel. After a while we reached a signpost which proclaimed that Abercorn was only two miles away, and from then on we kept a sharp look out for the lights of the town. We were getting very hungry and the night was cold, and we began to talk of the joys of sitting by a warm fire in the hotel lounge. Presently we saw one dim, flickering light on our right. "On the outskirts now," we said to each other, and we felt that we soon would be warm and well fed, but at the end of another two miles the town was still nowhere to be seen. After consultation we decided to return in our tracks and go to that single light we had seen and make enquiries.

There was a narrow avenue leading off the main track and up this we drove, pulling up outside a bungalow. The sound of our engine had been heard by the occupants and an Englishwoman came out on to the verandah, so one of us got out and went and asked to be directed to Abercorn.

"This is Abercorn," said the lady. This was somewhat of a shock, so the next request was to be directed to the hotel.

" Hotel ? There is no hotel, and never has been ! "

The bungalow turned out to be the residence of the Government Officer, and attached to it were a few round huts with concrete floors that were occasionally used as guest-houses when visitors came, and when the Commissioner's wife realised our plight she very kindly offered to let us camp in these huts, and with gratitude we accepted her offer.

She pressed us to come in and have a meal, but as it was very late and she had already had her dinner we declined, as we did not want to cause too much trouble. We accepted the offer of a drink, however, while Jannai got a fire lighted and put on some food to cook, and then we busied ourselves getting our bedding into the huts and making ready for the night.

It was a sad ending after all our plans for hot baths and comfortable armchairs by the fire in the hotel lounge, and I have never since seen the word Abercorn without a feeling of anger at the way we were cheated. My resentment, illogically, is against the place and the name, but the people who really deserve all the blame are those who were responsible for marking Abercorn on the map in large bold letters as though it were a township.

We had not only planned to sleep in the hypothetical hotel but also to buy petrol at one of the garages which we imagined we should find, and I had a very restless night, trying to work out whether the little petrol we had left would get us to the next place marked on the map.

In the morning, however, I found that my worries had been unnecessary, for there was a small shop kept by a Scotsman, and he did stock petrol for the use of the few planters living in the district round about. The petrol was, however, terribly expensive (six shillings a gallon as far as I can remember), for it had to be taken by rail from Dar-es-Salaam right across Tanganyika Territory to Kigoma on the shores of the lake from which the country takes its name, and then brought by steamer to the extreme south end of the lake, where there is a small port about twelve miles from Abercorn.

There was not enough petrol for us in stock at the shop, and we had to go down to the lake in our lorry to get what we required from the godown there. The road was not good, but I was very glad that we had to make this journey for it resulted in our finding two old high-level lake beaches, in one of which we discovered a prehistoric stone implement, while on the shore itself we located several shell mounds, which marked the encampments of a comparatively recent Stone Age people whose diet had consisted almost exclusively of mollusca. We had no time for a detailed investigation, but made a very small trial excavation in one of the mounds, which showed us that these old rubbish heaps of the past would very well repay a full investigation.

From Abercorn the Great North Road runs for nearly five hundred miles through the most dreary country I have ever seen in Africa. For almost the whole distance there is thick bush on each side of the track, so that nothing can be seen, and the monotony is only broken by an occasional river which has to be crossed on a ferry.

Here and there, especially near the rivers, there were small clearings in the bush where a few natives had made a settlement, and whenever we came to one of these we stopped and tried to buy eggs and a fowl for supper. We could not speak the local language and on several occasions the natives were at first most unfriendly and refused to sell us anything, and it was then that for the first time I made use of string figures as a means of establishing contact and friendship. It was really rather amazing to see the difference in the attitude of the people as soon as one of us pulled out our string-figure string and started to make some of the figures of other tribes. The sour, angry looks of the villagers promptly changed and their faces beamed, and in a minute one or other of the onlookers would take the string from us and proceed to show us some of their figures, and the whole audience would laugh heartily as we tried to learn these new ones. After that we were friends, and very often some member of the village who had previously shown no under-standing of English would start to speak to us in broken, halting English, and ask us what we would like, and even invite us to spend the night with them.

At last we reached Broken Hill, the mining town where in 1921 an exceedingly interesting fossil human skull had been found, and here we broke our journey and stayed for several days, camped in the garden of one of the residents. I cannot remember his name, or how it was that he came to invite us to turn his garden into a camp-ing ground, but I know that he was exceedingly kind, and that we had a most enjoyable rest.

I was very anxious to obtain more details about the discovery of the famous skull at Broken Hill and I was fortunate enough to find that the Swiss miner Zwiglar, who had actually found it, was still employed at the mine, and from him I obtained some very interesting information. We also found that a large proportion of the ancient cave deposits which had been cut into during mining operations was still lying in enormous dumps just where it had been tipped as it was dug out, and we spent a good many hours hunting over these for fossil bones and stone implements, and recovered two cases full. They were of little scientific value, however, for there was of course no record of their exact position in the original cave deposits, but we worked in the hope that we might possibly find some human bone fragments that would fit on to the specimens that were now in London. In this, however, we had no success.

From Broken Hill we went to the Victoria Falls, where we camped for two days while we searched the district for Stone Age relics which abound in the old river gravels that were deposited long before the Gorge below the Falls had been cut back to its present position. The Falls themselves were of almost staggering beauty, but I must confess that we devoted much less time to admiring their grandeur than to collecting stone implements.

The road southwards to Bulawayo was very trying, and we soon began to realise why people whom we had met at the Victoria Falls had advised us to put our lorry on the railway for this section of the journey. Except where it crossed a range of granite hills the actual surface of the road was comparatively good, but at intervals was crossed by deep V-shaped gullies which were exceedingly hard to negotiate with a long-bodied, heavily loaded lorry. If you tried to drive across these gullies fast you were liable to smash the rear springs, and even the back axle, while if you drove too slowly the wheels of the lorry would become embedded in the soft sand at the bottom of the V, so that you could not proceed until the lorry had been jacked up and branches put under the wheels to give a grip. On one stretch of the road in particular, these gullies were very numerous, and we had to negotiate about thirty in a single day, and in the end we completely smashed a back spring.

By that time we were almost at Wankie, a little coal-mining town, and so, having replaced the broken spring by a spare one, we decided to spend a day at Wankie while the broken one was repaired in case we had similar troubles ahead of us.

We took the opportunity of this stop at Wankie to visit the colliery, which is a rather remarkable place. The coal seam is only about a hundred feet below the surface, with the result that there is no coal gas and open lamps can be used with complete safety. But that is not all ; the seam is so thick (in places there is a forty-foot thickness of solid coal) that it is worked by blasting and not by hand picking methods at all. Owing to the absence of gas, blasting is, of course, quite safe. The coal is taken out in such a way as to leave solid coal pillars at regular intervals to hold up the roof, and as you walk about in the dark mine between these avenues of vast coal pillars the light from your open lamp is reflected in an eerie way ; you have a feeling of complete unreality and ghostliness.

I asked the manager how much coal he reckoned was available in the Wankie area, because I had often heard it said that the coal supplies of the British Empire were limited and that we must look to the day when they might be exhausted. His reply, as far as I remember it, was that the mine's experts, estimated that there was enough coal in the district to yield three times the present annual consumption of the world for at least six thousand years ! He added that owing to the nature of the mine it could be produced at pithead for about 3s. a ton.

In other words, the real trouble at the moment is the question of transport, and I believe that in this, as in other things, it is the cost of transport over long distances more than anything else that is going to hold up the economic development of the African continent.

My Kikuyu native Jannai accompanied us down the mine, but he was not nearly as struck by it as I had imagined he would be. This was chiefly due to the fact that his mind was still full of something that he con- sidered to be far more amazing. At Wankie, for the first time in our journey, we found gold currency in use, and after I had changed a traveller's cheque for some sovereigns I took Jannai with me on a shopping expedition. As I bought the various provisions that we needed, I handed them to him to put in a basket, and soon the basket was nearly full with bread and butter and cheese and fruit and other necessities. He then saw me hand over a small and rather insignificant coin to the shop-keeper, and remarked *sotto voce* to me in Kikuyu, that I had not given enough. (He thought that I had absent-mindedly given a shilling when I ought to have given at least a half-a-crown.) When he saw the shopkeeper not only accept my coin but give me back a considerable amount of silver and copper as change, he nearly dropped the basket in his amazement.

I then explained to him that this little coin was the " pound " of which he had heard in school but which he had never seen or even visualised, and, after that, nothing would satisfy him until he had been paid some of his wages in sovereigns. Although it meant keeping twenty whole shillings locked up and unusable, he retained one of these sovereigns as a memento until his unfortunate death a year later. When he was met at Kabete after our trip was over he never wearied of telling his Kikuyu friends the story of how I had paid for a whole basket full of provisions with one such coin *and had been given back a quantity of silver change !*

After leaving Wankie we passed through a stretch of country that was said to be infested with lions and we were all eagerly on the look out for them when suddenly I thought I saw seven. We stopped the lorry at once, and all grabbed at the one pair of field glasses that we had with us, in order to see the magnificent beasts better. They were some little distance away and were moving about in fairly long grass so that they could only be seen for a moment at a time, and then not too clearly. At last one of them moved to a patch of short grass where it could be very clearly seen and we then perceived that our supposed lions were domestic donkeys. I have seldom felt more like one myself.

To mistake donkeys for lions is idiotic but not dangerous, but a friend of mine in Kenya once confused these two animals the other way round, and as a result had the fright of his life. He was pushing his cycle along a narrow footpath through very tall grass, when he thought he saw the ears of a donkey moving along a path that was converging to meet the one he was on. He took little notice and went on his way when suddenly he came to the meeting of the ways and found himself face to face with a lion. I do not know which of the two was the more surprised, and for a moment they looked at each other silently. Then my friend pulled on the handle bars until the bicycle was standing on end with its front wheel free in the air. With great presence of mind he then waggled it about violently, ringing the bell hard at the same time. The lion was so taken aback by this strange and noisy apparition that it turned tail and fled, and my friend very promptly did the same—only in the opposite direction.

We arrived at Bulawayo fairly early one afternoon, very tired and extremely dirty, in old and slightly torn khaki clothes. As I had a letter of introduction to the parents of a student whom I had coached in Anthropology at Cambridge, we went straight to the house, quite frankly hoping for some tea, and hoping, too, that our untidiness and dirty clothes would be pardoned in view of the nature of our journey.

After we had driven up to the front door and could not possibly get away without being seen, we discovered to our horror that there were a number of very rich looking saloon cars also drawn up there, and in a minute we found ourselves in the middle of a very elite tea and tennis party, at which the Chief Justice of the town was entertaining his friends. I had not realised at all that my student's father was Judge Russel, one of the most important men in the country, and the situation was exceedingly difficult. But Judge Russel and his wife were charming people, and somehow they managed to put us entirely at our ease, and before long we had been given baths and tea, and I had actually been lent a pair of white trousers and some shoes and was engaged in a game of tennis !

Before leaving Kenya I had written to the Reverend Neville Jones, a keen archæologist who was also a missionary, telling him that I was planning to pass through Bulawayo on my way to Johannesburg, and he had invited us to come and camp at the Mission and see his collection. At Wankie I had despatched a telegram to tell him the date of our expected arrival, and so that evening—as his Mission station was only about ten miles from Bulawayo—we drove on and arrived at Hope Fountain about 7.30, only to find that he had not had my wire and was not expecting us at all.

However, as we had arrived, he very kindly proceeded to arrange things for us, although it put him to considerable inconvenience, and before long we were happily camped on a patch of grass near the house.

Having reached Bulawayo we were now only a few days' journey from Johannesburg, and as we had a good deal of time to spare we decided to see some of the very interesting prehistoric sites of Southern Rhodesia.

A friend of mine from England, Mr. A. L. Armstrong, was at that time engaged upon an excavation at Bambata Cave, in the Matopo Hills to the south of Bulawayo, and we first of all went there and spent a few days in camp with him. The walls of the Bambata Cave were all decorated with wonderful friezes painted at different periods by Stone Age man, and it was particularly interesting to see how some of the painting styles compared with those in Tanganyika Territory.

Moreover Mr. Armstrong's excavation work had revealed a sequence of Stone Age cultures very similar to that which we had discovered in Kenya, and we spent long hours comparing notes and discussing our common problems.

I was fascinated by the Matopo Hills district, which must abound in prehistoric sites, and should have liked to stay longer, but another friend of mine, Miss G. Caton Thompson was excavating on behalf of the British Association at the famous Zimbabwe Ruins to the east, and as we wanted to see these ruins we had to say good-bye to Mr. Armstrong and proceed to Zimbabwe.

For many years a violent controversy had centred round the extensive ruins of Southern Rhodesia. There was one school of thought that held that these ruins represented temples and fortresses built by the Phœnicians, or some other ancient civilised people, who had come to Rhodesia in search of gold and ivory, while another school of thought, basing its ideas upon the excavation work carried out by Dr. Randal MacIver in 1905, argued that the ruins were of mediæval date and were probably the work of an African tribe.

In order to obtain further accurate information about the ruins, the British Association for the Advancement of Science had asked Miss Caton Thompson to carry out further detailed investigation and to report at the meeting to be held in Johannesburg. By the time we arrived there she and her assistants had already obtained a great deal of information which supported the idea of a mediæval age for the ruins. We spent a few very interesting days at Zimbabwe, being shown the evidence, and viewing the so-called " Elliptical Temple," the Acropolis, and the Valley Ruins.

Although the scientific evidence, which Miss Caton

Thompson has published in her admirable book *The Zimbabwe Culture*, clearly indicates that these great stone enclosures which are now in ruins were constructed by an African race in comparatively recent times, many of the European inhabitants of Rhodesia and the Union of South Africa refuse to believe that it is so, and they still cling to the idea of " Phœnicians " and of " King Solomon's Mines," although there is apparently no satisfactory evidence to support such views.

They seem to be afraid that if it is generally accepted that Zimbabwe and the other similar ruins were the work of a negro people they will cease to be of any interest to *tourists*, and, since tourists mean money, they naturally want tourists to come. My own opinion is that Zimbabwe becomes infinitely more impressive and interesting, when viewed in the light of the new evidence, than it ever was before, and I am sure that my view is shared by many others in England.

From Zimbabwe we made our way by easy stages to Johannesburg, camping each night by the roadside, and when we were just a little north of Pretoria, Jannai experienced what was in his opinion the second most amazing thing on the whole journey. When he had finished washing up the plates after supper and clearing up everything, he did not, for some reason or other, tip away the water in the washing-up basin, and early next morning I was awakened by him calling me to come quickly, because the water was bewitched. There had been a hard frost in the night, and the basin was filled with a solid block of ice, which he had never before seen, although he had often heard of it.

This incident revealed to me, once more, how impossible it is to teach anyone anything simply by means of words and that a visual impression is almost an essential. It has helped to convince me of the potential value of such modern devices as the cinema for educational purposes.

The scientific meeting at Johannesburg was exceedingly interesting and very well worth the long journey that we had made in order to attend it, and when it was over we were looking forward to spending a few weeks visiting some of the local sites of prehistoric interest that we had heard so much about. But that proved to be impossible, for I discovered that a big body of the British scientists who were attending the meeting had made arrangements to return to England by the East coast route, and that many of them were going to break their journey at Mombasa and travel inland to see something of Kenya. Moreover, about seventy members of this party were particularly anxious to see Gamble's Cave and some of the other sites where we had made our discoveries. There was therefore only one course for us to pursue, and that was to return overland as fast as we could travel, in order that we might arrive ahead of the visitors, re-open camp and get everything ready for them to see.

We had taken nearly six weeks coming to Johannesburg, and we now had a bare fifteen days in which to return to Nairobi, 3,000 miles away. This meant that we must keep up an average of 200 miles a day. It would have been tiring enough to do this in a well-sprung car on good roads, and doing so in a lorry over bad roads was very like hard labour. To make matters worse I had developed a bad abscess on my leg and had had to undergo a minor operation at Johannesburg so that I could not drive, while Miss Kitson was leaving us to go to Capetown, so that it meant that the whole burden of driving must be shared by Solomon and my wife.

Fortunately, the roads were by this time much drier and in addition we now knew the way, and in the end we did succeed in getting back in exactly fifteen days.

On the very last day, after having travelled 6,000 miles through Africa without once seeing a lion, we encountered thirteen of them. In the morning, soon after we started we came across a solitary maned lion and congratulated ourselves on our good luck. We little dreamed that before the day was out we should have to leave the road and drive furiously across country in order to avoid an attack !

When we were about fifteen miles from Nairobi we met a car which signalled us to stop, and the occupants informed us that there was a pride of lions on the road ahead of us and that they were in an angry mood and liable to attack. I did not take this news very seriously for I had never heard of lions attacking a car, and it is usually held that so long as you remain in a car or lorry you can safely approach quite close to lions. In fact, that is the way in which some of the finest photographs of wild lions have been obtained.

We wanted some lion photographs, and so, on hearing the news, we got our cameras ready and drove on, elated with the idea of a chance to get some good pictures. Quite suddenly, about sixty yards ahead of us, we saw four lionesses lying on the road facing us, and as we drew nearer we saw others on both sides in the long grass, and counted twelve in all. We were just about to stop in order to use our cameras when I noticed that the behaviour of the lionesses on the road was rather menacing. They had started to advance slowly to meet us, crouching low to the ground with their tails switching slowly and angrily. They looked for all the world like enormous tame cats stalking a bird or a mouse, and it was our lorry that they were thus stalking and I am convinced that they meant to spring. Solomon was at the wheel and I called to him not to stop but to accelerate quickly and turn off to the left (luckily there was open

country on that side) and, as he did so, the lion jumped
forward and started to chase after us. We banged empty
cans and shouted loudly, and before long they abandoned
the chase, and very glad we were to see the last of them.

Only a short while before we reached these twelve
lions we had passed a solitary native driving two
bullocks along the road, and I have wondered ever since
what happened to him and his charges that evening.

CHAPTER XVIII

WE ARRIVED BACK ON the evening of August 21st and I had to spend the next day in Nairobi making purchases of stores and seeing the secretary of the local committee that was making arrangements for the visit of the British Association scientists, of whom some three hundred were expected.

I was, of course, only concerned with the parties that were to visit my camp and see something of our work, but I had to find out what arrangements were going to be made to feed them and transport them to and from the sites. I found that elaborate plans had been made to provide every visitor with hospitality as well as with free transport on the railway, and the parties that were to visit Gamble's Cave were going to be accommodated by various settlers and officials in and around Nakuru, and that they would be brought out to my camp, 28 miles away, by car. The committee asked me, however, to make arrangements for giving each party lunch, the cost of which would be paid for by the Entertainment Committee from funds which had been collected for the purpose.

I promised to see what could be arranged, and then purchased a supply of suitable stores, and next morning we went off to Elmenteita to get everything ready.

Before we started for South Africa, a great many of our best specimens had been packed ready for shipment to England, and I had to unpack a number of cases in order to have a reasonably good display of specimens to exhibit. Also I had boarded up the cave in order to prevent unauthorised persons from hunting for " curios " during my absence, for the Gamble's Cave had become well known, and was frequently visited at week-ends.

We had exactly two days in which to get everything ready, and then the first party of sixteen arrived. My wife and I had enlisted the help of Mrs. Gamble over the question of providing food for the visitors, and she most kindly offered to arrange luncheon for the whole party on her verandah, so we took over all our crockery and cutlery to supplement hers. Several other local residents also helped in the same way, and thanks to Mrs. Gamble's excellent organisation everything was most satisfactory.

As soon as the party arrived they were taken up to Gamble's Cave where I explained the details of the section that was exposed, and also dug a small portion of the deposit in order to show the visitors how exceedingly rich the lowest occupational level was. As we had already obtained thousands of perfect specimens from this deposit I allowed the visitors to take the specimens that we found while they were there as mementoes. One man, a Professor of Agriculture, acquired in this way an excellent obsidian knife-blade, which he insisted on using at luncheon. It served admirably, and caused a good deal of amusement, and he was delighted when I told him that it had been made at least 20,000 years ago.

After luncheon at Mrs. Gamble's house the party was taken to our camp where they saw the skeleton which had been found earlier in the year (and which I had unpacked again especially for their benefit), and also many of the other more important finds of the season, and then they returned to Nakuru.

The evening of the same day Professor Fleure, whom I had invited to spend a few days in camp, arrived, and the next two days were devoted to showing him our work in greater detail, as he was an archæologist himself and keenly interested in all the new problems that our work had created. In particular, there was the problem of the very early pottery found in association with the Aurignacian culture, and we had the good fortune to recover another excellent fragment actually *in situ* when I was digging a part of the deposit in his presence. Thus I obtained an independent expert as a witness.

On the third day a second party of scientists visited the camp, and this time the party was very much larger —thirty people—and it strained our luncheon organisation very seriously. But once again Mrs. Gamble's perfect organisation made everything run as smoothly as might be under the circumstances.

The following day I motored Professor Fleure to Nairobi, showing him various sites in the Naivasha area en route, and after a day in Nairobi, where we lunched with the Governor, I returned to camp for a few days' routine work before the third party of scientists arrived a week later.

This time only fifteen came and our organisation was by now well tried, so that their visit was much less tiring. This was fortunate, for as soon as they had left I had to get into my car and motor the hundred miles to Nairobi, as the Governor had made arrangements for me to interview the Director of Education and put before him my views on the question of whether English or Kiswahili should be made the official language for higher education in the native schools.

The Education Department were at that time anxious to make it compulsory for a native school-boy to learn Kiswahili after he had learned to read and write in his own vernacular, and they wanted to limit very considerably the number of pupils who were to be allowed to learn English.

I felt very strongly indeed (as I do still), that it would be very much to the advantage of both the natives of Kenya and the European immigrants if every encouragement was given to the Africans to learn English rather than Kiswahili. Englishmen are not as a rule good linguists and this is especially true of those who try to learn a foreign language after they are grown up. Very few Englishmen in Kenya ever learn one of the up-country vernacular languages, because they are very complex in their grammatical structure, and the normal procedure in Kenya has always been for the European to converse with the African through the medium of Kiswahili. In other words, both the Europeans and the natives of all the up-country tribes, if they want to be able to talk to each other, have to learn a language which is foreign *to both of them*. Very often neither the whiteman nor the up-country native acquires a really adequate knowledge of Kiswahili, and so all kinds of misunderstandings arise. No one in their senses would dream of asking both the English and the French to learn Russian in order to talk to each other, and I argued that the position in Kenya was similar, and that it would be better to give instruction in English to as many Africans as possible.

I regret to say that I failed to convince the Director of Education, and soon afterwards the teaching of English was restricted to the very few pupils who could spare enough years at school to reach the advanced classes.

In fairness to the Education authorities I must give the chief argument which they used in support of this action. They held that there were not enough teachers who were capable of teaching the English language properly, and they were afraid that if my ideas were carried out many of the pupils would learn English in a very inadequate manner and that their pronunciation would be appalling. To some extent I agree, but (and it is a very big but) I know that even if a native cannot learn English in school he will certainly try to learn all he can in other ways, and I fear that the consequence of their picking up English untaught will be the spread of a kind of pigeon English like that which is to be found on the West Coast of Africa. I would rather hear reasonably accurate and grammatical English, badly pronounced, than the atrocious parody of our language on which " a beef " has come to mean anything from a fly to an elephant !

Having failed in my mission I returned to camp and a day or two later we had the pleasure of a visit from the Governor, Sir Edward Grigg, who had heard so much about our finds that he wanted to see them for himself. His visit was entirely informal, and after he had gone I had considerable difficulty in making my Kikuyu workmen believe that our visitor that day had been His Majesty's representative in Kenya.

The very next day I had to motor back to Nairobi again to meet a party of archæologists and geologists whom I had invited to come and spend a night in camp. The party consisted of Professor J. L. Myers, Professor Balfour, Professor P. G. H. Boswell, Professor Cox and Mr. Double, and I wanted them to see the evidence upon which I was basing my conclusions as to the change of climate in Stone Age times, and the sequence of cultures that was connected with them.

After the British Association meeting in Johannesburg was over, they remained in South Africa for a few weeks in order to visit various sites there, and they now had only two days to spend in the Highlands of Kenya, while their boat was loading a cargo at Mombasa. Their visit was therefore a very hurried one.

Their train arrived in Nairobi at about 9.30 a.m.,

and Solomon and I were there to meet them with the
expedition car and a hired one, and we immediately
rushed them off to Elmenteita, stopping to show them
one or two sites of interest en route. We reached camp
about teatime, and after a short rest and a meal, rushed
them to Gamble's Cave so that they could see the
sections there before sunset.

The evening was spent examining some of our best
specimens by lamplight, and next morning we started
back to Nairobi as they had to be at the station again
at 4.0 p.m.

On the way we stopped at some of our more important
sites in the Nakuru and Naivasha Lake basins, and we
planned to give them lunch comfortably at a hotel in
Naivasha and then motor them on to Nairobi just in
time for their train. But even the best plans go wrong
and as we drew into Naivasha the expedition car
suddenly developed engine trouble, and although I
worked hard to put it right, it was of no avail and in the
end we had to squeeze all five of our visitors and their
luggage into the hired car, which had an excellent Masai
driver, and thus heavily loaded the car just managed to
reach Nairobi before the train left. Our visitors had had
the most strenuous thirty-six hours imaginable, and
I doubt if any of them will forget their visit.

As soon as we had succeeded in putting our car into
running order again we returned to camp in the hope
of spending the next two months peacefully completing
our work at Gamble's Cave and at the site on the
Kariandusi River, where Solomon and Miss Kitson had
located the deposits containing the hand-axes just before
we started for South Africa. But our hope was not to
be fulfilled, for we had only been back in camp two days
when a telegram arrived from the Governor asking me
to come to Nairobi at once and spend the night at

Government House, as he wished to see me urgently.

John Solomon had just taken the expedition car and gone away on a six weeks' prospecting trip, and the only vehicle I had in camp was the lorry. By the time the telegram reached us it was already past noon, and with the lorry we had only just time to travel the hundred miles to Nairobi if we started at once. So without waiting to change into tidy clothes or get ourselves clean my wife and I merely put a few things, including evening dress, into a suit case, and started off.

We drew up our rather ramshackle lorry before the main entrance to Government House just as it was growing dark, and the sentries on duty nearly had a fit, when, having demanded my business, I informed them that we had come to spend the night at the invitation of His Excellency. However, at that moment, the A.D.C. appeared and recognised me, and very soon we were parking our lorry alongside some of the Government House limousines.

Feeling very dirty and out of place, my wife and I were then conducted upstairs and shown into a most palatial suite of rooms which we were to occupy for the night. We were told that dinner would be at 7.45, and were left to make ourselves presentable. I had a horrid feeling of desecrating a holy place as I wallowed in a glorious porcelain bath, and made the whole place very filthy, and then I leisurely started to dress myself while my wife went to the bathroom. When I was nearly ready there came a knock on the door, and the aide-de-camp came in and announced, " I just came in to say that His Excellency has decided that it is to be dinner jackets and not tails to-night, and no decorations." I thanked him and gave a sigh of relief as he went out, for dinner jacket was the only form of evening dress that I possessed.

I found that our fellow guests were the Chief Native Commissioner and the Provincial Commissioner of the Kikuyu Province, and after dinner His Excellency told us the reason for this hasty summons. He had decided to appoint a Special Committee to investigate and report upon the Kikuyu system of land tenure and he wished me to be a member of it. The Committee was to start its work a week later, so I had to go back to camp and make all the necessary arrangements for my native staff to do work that did not need my personal supervision, as I was likely to be away for three weeks or more.

The Chairman of the Committee was the Hon. G. V. Maxwell, the Chief Native Commissioner, and the only other member besides myself was Mr. S. H. Fazan, a District Officer who had already shown very great interest in land tenure problems. The greater part of the evidence which we took was from Kikuyu elders, and as I alone of the Committee could speak Kikuyu I acted as interpreter throughout.

Our report, which was not as detailed as I could have wished, was published in November, 1929, under the title of *Native Land Tenure in the Kikuyu Province*, and is available to anyone who is sufficiently interested to ask for it from the Colonial Office, or buy it through the Crown agents for the Colonies, so I will not discuss the details of the Kikuyu land tenure system here, but confine myself to general observations.

Very many people in England hold the erroneous belief that all African tribal land is held on a communal basis, and that any member of a tribe has the right to occupy and cultivate any land that is at the time uncultivated. It was this type of misunderstanding, for instance, that influenced the Government of Kenya in the early days of white settlement to allow settlers to occupy a part of the Kikuyu country with quite inadequate safeguards and compensation. The Government erroneously believed that the Kikuyu families thus dispossessed were not really being caused any serious hardship as all they had to do was to move away and take possession of some of the uncultivated portions of the Kikuyu country elsewhere.

Nothing could have been further from the truth, and the innumerable problems that have arisen from this mistake still await a satisfactory solution.

Among the Kikuyu, and also many of the other agricultural tribes of East Africa, there is a very definite system of land ownership, which is often controlled by very complicated rules and regulations. The native laws governing land tenure are, however, seldom known to Europeans because agricultural Africans are so jealous of their land that they are commonly afraid to divulge information about it to white men for fear that the knowledge should be used against them, as the following incident will show.

A few years before this Committee was appointed by the Governor, I one day received from the Chief Native Commissioner a typescript copy of a report on Kikuyu land tenure, with a request for my comments. This report had been drawn up by a Government officer after a very painstaking enquiry which he had made—he even took the trouble to quote verbatim a great deal of the information which he had been given, together with the names of his informants.

I was quite frankly astounded by this report in which there were innumerable statements that were the exact reverse of the true facts as I knew them. And what was still more surprising was that most of these inaccurate statements were actually quoted as the verbatim answers to questions which had been put to some of the best Kikuyu legal authorities on the subject !

I happened to be at Kabete when I received this report to comment upon, and immediately went to interview some of the people mentioned as having supplied the information in the report, as I wanted to find out exactly what had happened.

I discovered that the officer in question had summoned a meeting of the Kikuyu elders and legal authorities and had told them that he was anxious to draw up a report upon their system of land tenure, but he had not adequately explained the reason why he required the information. Before replying to his questions, the assembled elders had asked leave to withdraw and hold a short private consultation, and, permission having been granted, they hastily discussed what they should do. Some of the more enlightened men present had been in favour of giving a truthful reply, but the overwhelming majority had decided that such procedure might be dangerous, and so it was agreed that incorrect information should be given.

I enquired why they had come to this decision and was promptly told that they were afraid that the Government might be planning to use the knowledge which they were seeking as a means of taking more of their land from them in order to give it to white settlers. In other words, their conduct was dictated by fear, and was, incidentally, entirely in keeping with an age-long Kikuyu rule which is (or used to be) instilled into every child. The rule was : " If you are asked a question by a stranger, lie to him first of all ; if later you find that he is a friend and not an enemy, you can always give him the truth in due course."

This rule was of course made at a period in the tribe's history when any stranger was a potential enemy or a spy who might later lead a raiding party, but it is a rule which is so deeply inculcated in the minds of the older generation of Kikuyu that they adhere to it almost unconsciously.

Often in the Elmenteita district, when I first went there and was not well known to the local Kikuyu, I have had an incident like the following one happen to me. I would be motoring to Nakuru and pass one or two Kikuyu walking along the road obviously making for the same destination as myself. Seeing them I would stop with the intention of offering them a lift. Having exchanged the usual greetings I would say : " Are you going to Nakuru ? " and the Kikuyu would say, " No." Then I would say, " That is a pity, I was going to offer to take you there by car," and the Kikuyu would then say, " Oh, but I am going to Nakuru really. May I come in your car ? "

To the European who does not understand African psychology and who does not know Kikuyu customs, this kind of thing is aggravating in the extreme, and he cannot see why the native could not have told the truth in the first instance. In the native's mind, however, on being asked the question, his thoughts probably were : " Now, I wonder what he wants to know if I am going to Nakuru for ? Probably he has some load in that car of his which he wants to have taken there, and if I say ' yes ' he will make me carry it, in order to save himself the trouble of going all that way," and, not wishing to run the risk of being made to carry a load to Nakuru, he says " No, I'm not going there " ; then, when he finds that this stranger's intentions are kindly, he gives the truth.

One of the chief reasons why I was made a member of the Government Committee to investigate the Kikuyu system of land tenure was that I was not a stranger to the tribe and moreover they knew I was a staunch friend. I believe that as a Committee we did succeed in obtaining a truthful account of the Kikuyu land tenure system, although on one or two occasions I myself very nearly came to be regarded by the people as a renegade and an enemy simply because I was associated with a Government Committee that was enquiring into their land customs. At a few of the outlying parts of the country it took all the persuasive powers of some of the influential Kikuyu who knew me personally to persuade the assembled elders that I was really a friend who could be trusted.

Needless to say, the object of the Government in setting up this enquiry into Kikuyu land tenure was emphatically not in order to take more land from them, but rather to help the Government officers to administer justice more fairly and to safeguard Kikuyu interests. Otherwise I should not have consented to be a member.

One of the difficulties with which we had to deal in preparing our report was that the system of land tenure in Kikuyu country varied in each of the five main districts, since the laws governing land ownership had been altered or modified in each district according to the particular local requirements. The biggest differences of all were in matters connected with the transfer of land from one family, or individual member of a family, to anyone else.

Throughout Kikuyu country all the land is divided up into family estates which range in size from several square miles to as little as a hundred acres, and these family estates are the absolute property of the male adult living members of the family *as a whole*, while each individual male is the owner of certain portions of the whole estate. But whereas in the four northern districts no member of an owning family can ever sell his share of the estate outright, in the southern district outright sale is allowed under certain conditions. The chief reason why land is regarded as saleable in this southern district, is that in this area most of the land was obtained by the original Kikuyu individuals (from whom the various families are descended) by direct purchase from the previous owners who were members of the Wanderobo hunting tribe.

When the Kikuyu occupied and turned it into arable land, the trans-Chania area had been forested country belonging to the Wanderobo, and each Wanderobo family had its own section of the forest with fixed known boundaries, in which it exercised the sole hunting rights. As the Kikuyu tribe increased in numbers in their country north of the Chania river, some of them crossed over in search of new land, and, finding the forest already owned and occupied, they proceeded to purchase it from the Wanderobo.

It may be wondered why they should have gone to the trouble and expense of buying the land, when with their numerical superiority and better weapons they could very easily have driven out the Wanderobo and simply taken the land by force. The answer lies in the fact that the Kikuyu, like so many other African tribes, had a very real belief in the powers of the spirits of departed people to exercise a harmful influence against the living. They believed that if they took the land from the Wanderobo by force, the departed spirits of dead Wanderobo would combine to render their cultivation unprofitable, to cause their flocks to die, and even to kill the invaders themselves by supernatural means.

Another very interesting fact in connection with this purchase of land from the Wanderobo is that before any transaction between a would-be Kikuyu purchaser and a Wanderobo seller was completed, the two parties would go through a very binding ceremony of blood brother-hood, which amounted to each one adopting the other for life as a member of his family and clan. This was done as a kind of a guarantee that both parties intended to behave absolutely honourably in their dealings with each other, for both of them believed that anyone who failed to behave with scrupulous fairness to a blood-brother would certainly die a prompt and supernatural death.

Having thus instituted the custom of direct and outright purchase in their original acquisition of the land south of the Chania, it was only natural that the Kikuyu in this district should have modified the tribal laws governing land tenure in such a way as to allow outright sales of land between individuals. In other districts the earlier laws, which only allowed for the temporary transfer of land ownership in return for a loan of cattle or sheep, were retained.

Incidentally, in connection with these transfers of land for a loan we have a most interesting example of the innumerable differences between European and African logic, differences which frequently cause serious misunderstandings, and even grave miscarriages of justice when an official who is not fully conversant with native law and custom tries to settle land disputes.

Supposing that a Kikuyu in one of the northern districts wished to raise a loan of twenty sheep and goats, he had the right to offer the lender of the stock his portion of the family estate, on the understanding that it could be redeemed at any time provided that due notice was given. Now, if the man who thus acquired the temporary ownership of that land cleared it, cultivated it and improved it in every way, when the redemption was made he would only receive the same number of goats and sheep as he had originally lent. If, on the other hand, he left the land as it was when he received it and neither grew crops on it nor used it in any other way, so that even the cultivated parts of it reverted to bush, then when the loan was redeemed he would have to be given not only the original number of goats and sheep, but in addition a further number equivalent to all their computed natural increase during the intervening years.

To the white man this seems wholly unreasonable. An Englishman would argue in exactly the reverse way, and maintain that if the land had been greatly improved in value by cultivation while it was in the lender's hands, then he ought to receive more than the amount that he had originally lent, while if he had allowed it to deterio- rate he could not expect any interest.

But the Kikuyu looks at it differently. He argues that if the man who took over the land cleared it and cultiva- ted it, then he must have derived considerable profit from it and so, as he has had interest from the land in the form of crops, the borrower is entitled to the interest—in the form of the offspring—of the original goats and sheep borrowed, and vice versa. I must say I entirely support this point of view.

Very seldom, if ever, was any Kikuyu family estate put entirely under cultivation, and a proportion of it, often a very big proportion, was kept as bush and grassland. This fact, coupled with the fallacious idea that land was held communally by the tribe, caused very grave misunder- standings and led to eviction of many families from the land which they owned, as it was required for white settlement. The families evicted had either to buy land elsewhere, or take up the unsatisfactory position of being tenants on someone else's property, instead of owners of their own. It is, therefore, not unnatural that they still nurse a serious grievance against the Government and the settlers.

In connection with the Kikuyu land that was alienated to Europeans it is frequently argued by Englishmen that much of it was virgin bush (although part of it was culti- vated) and that no injustice was done by taking this. It is even now not realised that the uncultivated parts were just as much private property as the fields of corn, etc., nor is it understood that the possession of bush-land is just as essential to a Kikuyu family as his crop land. But that is actually the case. Our European sheep like short grass for grazing, but the Kikuyu goats as well as the sheep infinitely prefer grazing in bush, as they eat the leaves of very many of the bush plants, and so bush-land is to the Kikuyu what grazing fields are to European stock owners.

In addition to that, the Kikuyu depended on their bush land for the supply of most of their building materials, such as grass, bracken for thatching, withies for constructing granaries and doors, and the bark of various plants for making cord and string which until recently was their sole substitute for nails.

After the Committee had spent three weeks taking evidence all over the Kikuyu country, I returned to my Elmenteita camp for a short time to see how my native staff were getting on and at the same time to draft those sections of the report for which I was responsible, and then I had to go back to Nairobi for further meetings of the Committee before we finally agreed on the form of our recommendations.

By the time the work of the Committee was completed, I was feeling so completely worn out that it was all I could do to finish off the excavations that we actually had in hand at Elmenteita, and then pack up and take our specimens down to Mombasa for shipment to England. I was therefore unable to carry out the more detailed excavations that I had planned to make at the Kariandusi River site, and I had to leave that piece of work to be done during my next season—if I succeeded in raising funds for yet another expedition, as I hoped to do.

CHAPTER XIX

DURING MY ABSENCE IN Kenya in 1929 I had been fortunate enough to be elected to a Research Fellowship at St. John's College, so that, although my research studentship had now expired, I was again able to make Cambridge my headquarters while in England studying the material we had collected. What was still more important for me, was that I again had the three rooms in College at my disposal to work in.

The vast collection accumulated during the 1926–27 season was still in my rooms at St. John's, and to this I now added a further 60 cases of specimens, while the remainder—the human bones and the animal remains— were sent as before to the Royal College of Surgeons and the British Museum of Natural History, respectively. With all this additional collection to unpack and sort out I required all the space that my three rooms in College gave me, and, as I was married, I no longer lived in College but rented a small but very delightful cottage some miles out of the town.

In order to make more room in which to work I transformed both the bedroom and the sitting room into workrooms with long trestle tables and numerous shelves, and I moved the bed into the small " gyp room " (as the kitchen sculleries of College sets at Cambridge are called), and on several nights a week I slept in the gyp room after working until 2 or 3 o'clock in the morning.

Almost as soon as I was back in England I started making plans for a third season in East Africa, this time with the Oldoway Gorge as my main objective, and as I very much wanted to publish the results of the work at Elmenteita and Nakuru before I went abroad again, I had to work very hard. At first I planned to publish two books more or less simultaneously, one dealing with the Stone Age cultures and the other with the human remains, but in the end only the former was published before the third season started, and the other book was held over until a later date.

But although the human remains book was not published until much later, I spent a great deal of time working on them in London, and in the difficult task of taking the skeleton which we had found at Gamble's Cave from its matrix and then reconstructing it, I was very ably assisted by MacInnes. He had by now recovered from the malaria which had made it necessary for him to come to England before the season was over, and he was living in London and studying vertebrate-zoology at London University.

This work proved to be much more difficult than I had anticipated, because the bone was in a much softer state than the surrounding matrix, but after weeks of work we succeeded in getting the skull and jaw and some of the limb bones free without damaging them seriously. In some ways this skull and skeleton was even more like the Oldoway skull than those found during the first season, and as I wanted to include some reference to the Oldoway skull in the book which I was preparing, I went over to Germany again, and this time I made sure that Professor Mollison would be at Munich at the time of my visit, so that I could discuss the whole matter with him.

Professor Reck had for years claimed a much greater antiquity for the Oldoway skull than could possibly be ascribed to the Gamble's Cave skeleton, and after I had been to Munich and noted not only the resemblances between the two skulls, but also the very similar way in which both skeletons had been buried in a crouched position, I formed the opinion that Professor Reck's estimate of the age of the Oldoway skull was not correct, and I went to Berlin to discuss the question with him, and at the same time to invite him to be a member of my next expedition which had the Oldoway Gorge as its chief objective.

After a long and very interesting discussion, I told Professor Reck that I was now certain in my own mind that the greater part of the Oldoway fossiliferous deposit was probably of the same age as the beds at the Kariandusi River where Solomon and Miss Kitson had located the hand-axe culture, and I expressed the opinion that we should find implements of this culture at Oldoway. Professor Reck did not agree. He assured me that while he was at Oldoway he had searched diligently for Stone Age implements and although he was anxious to go with me to Oldoway he warned me that I had better give up the idea of going there altogether if I wanted to find prehistoric implements, as all we would find would be the bones of fossil animals.

I was very anxious to see the actual site where he had found the Oldoway human skeleton, and I also wanted a collection of the Oldoway fossils for the British Museum, so I told him that I considered that on these grounds alone a new expedition to the Gorge would be justified, but I also made a small bet that I would find Stone Age implements at Oldoway within 24 hours of arriving there. I was convinced that if there had been a lake there in prehistoric times—as Professor Reck's fossil collection amply proved—and if man had also been present—as the human skeleton testified—then there must also be Stone Age implements. And so it was arranged that Professor

Reck should be a member of the next expedition, and we each quite amicably looked forward to proving the other wrong in due course.

Ever since I had been a member of the British Museum Expedition in 1924 there had been tentative suggestions about a joint expedition to the Oldoway fossil beds, and I now informed the Director of the Museum that I was planning to go to the Gorge in 1931, and invited the co-operation of the British Museum authorities. After a certain amount of discussion it was agreed that they would send out a palæontologist and that the Museum would share in the expenses of that part of the season's work that was to be carried out at Oldoway. My friend, Dr. A. T. Hopwood, was appointed British Museum representative on the expedition. It was further arranged that while he was in East Africa he was to take the opportunity of visiting some Miocene fossil beds which had been discovered at Koru, and I promised to do everything I could to help in this work.

I was very anxious, if possible, that the world-famous French prehistorian, l'Abbé H. Breuil, should see something of our work in East Africa, and I went over to Paris partly to discuss some of my problems with him and partly to invite him to come out during the forthcoming season, but unfortunately I found that he had arranged to go to China, where very important new prehistoric discoveries were being made by a band of workers under the guidance of the late Dr. Davidson Black, and so that plan had to be abandoned.

After visiting Paris I took the opportunity while in France of going to the Dordogne district in the south and seeing some of the famous caves which are decorated with paintings and engravings made by prehistoric man some twenty thousand or more years ago. I was accompanied on this trip by my wife, Donald MacInnes and

Miss Joan Beales. Miss Beales was the daughter of a Kenya settler who had become so deeply interested in the Stone Age that she had come to England for a year's study under Professor Fleure.

We had a most enjoyable time, and I shall never forget the thrill of seeing the actual originals of all this prehistoric art which I knew so well from illustrations in books and scientific papers. At the time when the discovery of the paintings on the walls of caves was made, access to them was exceedingly difficult, and the early explorers often had to crawl for long distances on their knees along dark passages, with only dim candle light for illumination, but to-day the French Government has fitted electric light in most of the caverns (personally I think this is a pity), so that visitors can see and examine the earliest known art at their ease.

Very many French people visit these sites each year, and I have often wondered why English tourists display so little interest in the Stone Age art. Possibly it is that they have never even heard of it, or do not realise how easily it can be seen. At any rate, I can assure anyone who decides to go to the Dordogne and see the engravings and paintings of reindeer and mammoths and cave bear, etc., that they will not go in vain.

Slowly and gradually the plans for my third season were completed and the necessary funds were obtained. Once again the Royal Society and the Percy Sladen Memorial Trustees made exceedingly generous grants towards our work and at last in June, 1931, I was able to sail for Kenya to complete the arrangements necessary for taking a big expedition to Oldoway.

I was going out alone and the other members of the expedition were all to join me later, and I travelled, as I usually do, overland to Marseilles and thence by French steamer. As I got off the train at Marseilles, I noticed a young English girl looking exceedingly worried and quite obviously unable to understand a word of French, so I went up and asked if I could do anything to help her. It turned out that she was travelling to East Africa by the same steamer as myself, and that she now could not find her luggage which she had registered through from Victoria to Marseilles. Our boat was due to sail at four o'clock that afternoon and she had just been informed in broken English that her luggage had not come on the train with her and that it could not now arrive until to-morrow morning.

She was naturally most terribly upset by this news, as all she had brought with her in the carriage was a small dressing case, and it now looked as though she must either travel to East Africa without her luggage or miss her boat and wait for the next one in a fortnight's time. Neither prospect was very attractive, and she asked me to see if I could find out what had happened to her luggage and do something to help her.

Having taken her to the station hotel and left her to rest, I set about making enquiries and discovered that her registered luggage had certainly reached the Gare du Nord at Paris, and that there was just a chance that it would arrive at Marseilles at 3.0 p.m., but that it was more likely that it would not come until next morning. This was not very good news, but I promised her that if it did come on the three o'clock train I would somehow get it through the Customs and on board our steamer before she sailed at four o'clock. As it was most unlikely that it would come, we made arrangements with an agent to have it forwarded in a fortnight's time, and meanwhile Miss P—— decided that she simply must purchase some dresses, underwear and toilet necessities before she embarked, in case she had to travel with nothing but what was in her dressing case.

It was impossible to leave this shopping expedition until after the train came in at 3 o'clock, as there would then be no time to spare, and so I went off with her on one of the most curious errands I have ever undertaken. I had only met Miss P—— a few hours before, and now I found myself acting as her interpreter as she went from one shop to another purchasing all sorts of intimate feminine requisites. In spite of many notices announcing that " English is spoken here," each of which raised my hopes of being spared an embarrassing situation, we did not find a single shop assistant who understood a word of English, and as Miss P—— spoke no word of French, I had to interpret everything for her.

Fortunately we both appreciated the humorous side of the situation and were able to laugh heartily.

In the afternoon, having taken Miss P—— down to the ship and put my own luggage on board, I interviewed the Captain and told him that I might not be able to get to the docks by four o'clock, and begged him to postpone departure for at least half an hour if I was not there. I then went back to the station to meet the three o'clock train, which exasperatingly came in nearly a quarter of an hour late, but which fortunately had the missing luggage in the van. I had already spoken to the Customs authorities on the station and made arrangements for them to pass the luggage if it did arrive, with the minimum of delay. In the end I got the luggage on board just as the bell was being sounded to warn all visitors to leave the ship as the gangway was about to be pulled up. When Miss P—— saw her lost cases arrive she was immensely relieved, for they contained not only things which she needed for the voyage, but the whole of her trousseau, for she was going out to be married.

On previous occasions I had always gone from Mombasa to Nairobi by train, but I had discovered that the

Mombasa prices of cars were at least £10 less than in Nairobi, and so I bought a box-body Chevrolet as soon as I landed, and set out next morning to do the journey by road. By so doing I not only saved the extra cost, £10, on the car, but I also found that the cost of the petrol and oil consumed during the journey was considerably less than the price of a second-class train ticket. The only serious disadvantage was the fact that the road was so bad that I arrived in Nairobi completely tired out, but that was chiefly due to the fact that I had no one with me to take turns at the wheel.

Both in 1926 and 1928 I had been able to use the house at Kabete as a base camp for my expedition, but this year I could not do so, as my parents had retired and the station was in charge of a new young Missionary. My father had bought a small plot of land at Limuru, some eighteen miles from Nairobi, and he had given me permission to build myself a small house there to serve as a base camp and as a home for my wife and baby daughter who were coming out a few months later.

My first task on arrival, therefore, was housebuilding, and with the help of eight of my Kikuyu workmen who had been on my last expedition and who had re-entered my employment, I started to build a three-roomed bungalow with mud and wattle walls, a corrugated iron roof lined inside with banana bark to reduce the heat of the sun, and with proper doors and windows which I bought second-hand in Nairobi.

I had to interrupt the work a good many times and it was not completed until six weeks later, but the total cost was only £36. Some of my less kind friends say, " It looks like that," but at least it served its purpose, and I could not afford to spend more on it.

On the last day of July, Dr. Hopwood arrived in Nairobi, and after a few days spent in getting the neces-

sary camp equipment together for him, I motored him up
to Koru, where he was to work on the Miocene fossil beds
until we were ready to start for Oldoway.   At the end of
the previous season I had stored the lorry which we had
used on the journey to and from South Africa, and as
soon as I had arrived in Nairobi I had it overhauled so
that it was now in perfect running order.   I now put it
at Dr. Hopwood's disposal, for although I had arranged
to take him up to Koru and get a camp fixed up for him,
I could not spare the time to remain with him for more
than a few days, as I had to complete the arrangements
for the journey to Oldoway.   As he could not speak
Kiswahili and also did not wish to drive the lorry himself, I obtained for him an English-speaking driver who
could act as interpreter as well.   This man was one of
the very few educated members of the Masai tribe that I
have come across, and like the others he showed that the
Masai were perfectly capable of benefiting by education
if only they would consent to do so.   He was a good
mechanic and driver, and he not only spoke English
tolerably well, but could also speak Hindustani and four
other native languages in addition to his own.   He was
well worth the wage of £5 a month which he asked.

I did not stay long at Koru, but during the next six
weeks I went up at intervals and helped Dr. Hopwood,
and in the meantime completed the building at Limuru
and also undertook some excavations at the Kariandusi
River site which I had had to leave unworked at the end
of the previous season.   This site proved to be extraordinarily rich, and in about ten days I and my Kikuyu
men excavated over two thousand hand-axes from what
proved to be an old factory site.

Professor Reck, who was coming to join us for the
expedition to Oldoway was due to arrive in Mombasa on
August 27th.   I had promised to meet him there and

lend him some camp equipment as he wanted to go on to Tanga (a little port on the northern part of the Tanganyika coast), to do some independent geological work there before we went to Oldoway, and so I went on to Mombasa by train, taking with me the things he wanted.

I had decided that we would need two more lorries for the journey to Oldoway, and had ordered a new one with a specially constructed body to be prepared for me at Mombasa so as to save another £10, and after I had met Professor Reck and given him the equipment and fixed up with him the date on which he would arrive at the base camp at Limuru, I drove it up to Nairobi.

I had arranged my plans in such a way as to start from Mombasa with the new lorry on August 30th, for six months previously I had promised that I would be at Voi station, which is about half-way between the coast and Nairobi, on the evening of that date, to meet a friend of mine, Mr. I. L. Evans.

Mr. Evans, who was also a Fellow of St. John's College, Cambridge, had travelled by steamer to West Africa and then overland right across the continent to Tanganyika Territory, and if he had kept to his schedule, he was due to arrive by train at Voi in order to visit Kenya Colony. I had heard nothing from him since he started for West Africa, but as I had promised to be at Voi station to meet the train on August 30th, I kept the appointment, knowing that Mr. Evans would certainly also keep it if he could. As the train from Arusha drew into the station, I was waiting on the platform and we met just as though we had made an appointment by telephone the day before.

Mr. Evans was engaged in a study of some of the problems of Colonial administration in British Africa, and I had promised to spend a day or two with him in the Kikuyu country, and together we visited various Kikuyu villages and had tea with Chief Koinange whom Mr. Evans had entertained at Cambridge during the Spring of 1931. Chief Koinange had come to England with several other East African natives to give evidence before the Joint Committee of the two Houses of Parliament that was considering the question of " Closer Union " between Kenya, Uganda and Tanganyika Territory.

I had been the official interpreter when Chief Koinange gave his evidence, and I had also interpreted for him on his visit to Cambridge as well as on the occasion of his interview with the then Secretary of State for the Colonies, Lord Passfield. The Kenya natives very strongly opposed the idea of " Closer Union " on the grounds that one of the reasons why the European element wanted it was that it would be a step towards responsible self-government by the settlers, and they felt that if this ever came to pass they would be more likely to have more of their land taken from them than they would under the existing Crown Colony conditions.

The natives of Tanganyika and Uganda had also been in opposition to the scheme, their objections being due to the fact that they were afraid that in the event of " Closer Union " some of the Kenya laws, such as the Natives' Registration Ordinance would be imposed upon them as well. In the end, after hearing the native evidence as well as the views of all sections of the European community, the Committee had decided against it. They had also recommended an enquiry into the Kenya natives' grievances about their land, and this had caused great satisfaction to the Kikuyu tribe in particular, as they hoped that at last their troubles would be settled and that they would receive more adequate compensation for the losses which they had sustained.

After Mr. Evans had spent a few days with me, I left

him to continue his investigations and I returned to the task of preparing for the expedition to Oldoway.

As we were going into a region where lions and rhinoceroses were very plentiful and sometimes dangerous, I did not want to have the sole responsibility for the safety of the members of the expedition, and so I engaged a Captain J. H. Hewlett, an experienced hunter, who had accompanied the Prince of Wales on some of his hunting trips, and I now arranged for Captain Hewlett to take his lorry and prospect for a practicable route to Oldoway. There was a road for the first 110 miles and a rough track for the next 100 miles, but after that it was a question of finding the best way for the lorries across the Serengeti plains in the direction in which we wanted to go. The chief obstacles were likely to be deep gullies and patches of dense thorn scrub, and the late Mr. Priddle, who was at that time District Officer in charge of Loliondo, the Government station nearest to Oldoway, had promised me to give Captain Hewlett every possible assistance and also a sketch map, as he had been to Oldoway on foot and knew what the most likely route for our lorries would be.

Having sent Captain Hewlett off I went up to Koru on September 8th and worked with Dr. Hopwood for nine days and then on the 28th we both returned to the base camp at Limuru in order to be there when Captain Hewlett returned and Professor Reck arrived. They were both now due—and my plan was to start for Oldoway on September 22nd.

We found Captain Hewlett already in camp, and Professor Reck arrived two days later, and the last few days were spent in a final overhauling of our lorries and car, in checking all stores and equipment, preparatory to going off to a place 200 miles from the nearest Post Office, garage, or shop, other than little Indian trade stores.

CHAPTER XX

WHEN WE LEFT THE base camp at Limuru just before noon on September 22nd, 1931, the party consisted of Professor Reck, Dr. Hopwood, Captain Hewlett and myself. We had, in all, eighteen Africans with us, of whom two were lorry drivers. Our convoy consisted of three Chevrolet 1½-ton lorries and one Chevrolet car, and into these vehicles we packed all our camp equipment, food supplies, petrol and oil, spare parts for the lorries and car, and excavating tools.

I had reduced our equipment to the absolute minimum and had even refused to allow Professor Reck to take all his boxes of books with him, but, even so, we could not carry all the stores and petrol that we needed. This, however, did not matter very much as I knew that I should have to send a lorry back very soon to fetch Donald MacInnes—who was due to arrive from England soon—and V. E. Fuchs, a young geologist who had been working with another expedition up in the Northern Frontier Province of Kenya and who was now going to join us.

According to my usual practice we only travelled a short distance on the first day, and camped at the foot of the Kikuyu Escarpment at the point where the main road from Nairobi to Uganda reaches the floor of the Great Rift Valley after a long and dangerous descent. It was at this very spot that, in 1893, Professor J. W. Gregory had camped during his first journey to investigate the geology of the Great Rift Valley, and it was near here, too, that he had picked up some of the first obsidian implements ever to be found by a scientist in Kenya. Since then I had located a very rich prehistoric site near the camping place, and after I had made sure that everything was in order and that we had forgotten nothing we needed for our journey to Oldoway, I took Professor Reck and Dr. Hopwood to see it.

Next morning we moved on once more, but our progress was slow as the lorries were very heavily loaded and the road was very dusty. It took us the whole day to do a little over a hundred miles, and we camped about thirty miles from the Kenya-Tanganyika boundary. For about the first eighty miles we had been on what is usually classed in Kenya as a " second class " road, but what would not be called a road at all in England. After that we had travelled along a track which was occasionally used by Indian lorries trading for hides with the Masai, but which was not even marked as a " third class " road on the local map. We found it in an appalling condition and often it was necessary to slow down to about five miles per hour ; even then the lorry and car springs were seriously strained. The place that we camped at that night was a little trading village called Barikitabu, where there were two little Indian trade stores where sugar, flour, beads and brass wire were given to the Masai natives in exchange for sheep and goats and ox-hides. There was a little stream nearby which provided the only permanent water for many miles, and we found a very nice camping site under the shade of some thorn trees.

Professor Reck, whose work in East Africa had been done in the days before cars and lorries were being utilised, had told me that he was quite certain that we could not reach Oldoway by motor, and that evening he again expressed this view, pointing out that the track we had travelled on for the last thirty miles was as smooth as a billiard table in comparison to the country round Oldoway. He even hinted that he was doubtful whether Captain Hewlett had really reached Oldoway Gorge on his reconnaissance trip, and thought that possibly he had found his way to some new and unknown but more accessible gorge. To reassure him, I rashly told him that there was practically nowhere that a car or lorry could not be taken, and before the next three months were over Professor Reck had much greater faith in what a car could do than I had, and he sometimes wanted us to take him by motor to places that really were inaccessible unless actual road-making was undertaken.

We crossed the border next morning and by lunch time had reached Loliondo, where we were welcomed by Mr. Priddle, the Government officer, who had improved on his promise to help Captain Hewlett with directions and had actually accompanied him to Oldoway when he had reconnoitred the way there. Mr. Priddle wanted us to spend the night with him for he seldom had anyone to talk to, but I was anxious to get to Oldoway as soon as possible, so after we had had lunch with him we went on again and camped at the foot of a granite hill called Len Lemoru.

Here there was a very small and rather dirty waterhole, and we were very thankful that we had filled all our water cans at the stream at Loliondo and so did not have to use this somewhat odorous liquid. But the time was to come when the Len Lemoru waterhole became synonymous with the " nearest place where there is really drinkable water," but that is a story that will be told in its right place.

From Len Lemoru we moved south and I hoped that we should be able to cover the seventy odd miles to Oldoway Gorge before nightfall, but that proved to be impossible. With the lorries as heavily loaded as they

were and no road or even track to follow we were unable
to travel more than an average of five miles an hour.
This was partly because our actual pace was very slow
indeed, and partly because we had to halt so frequently
to allow our engines to cool. It was absolutely impossible for the lorries to be driven in top gear over the
very rough ground and in both second and low gear
the water in the radiators very soon reached boiling point.
We were actually using about four gallons of water for
each lorry for every fifteen miles travelled. This was a
serious drain upon our water supply, and so we stopped
at a little hill which we named Apis Rock. Here there
was a pool which contained a liquid consisting of
rain-water diluted with baboons' urine. It was quite
undrinkable, but it was usable in the radiators and it saved
us from the necessity of using up all our good water.

That evening we were still 30 miles from Oldoway
Gorge, but by starting very early next morning we
managed to get there by 10.0 a.m.

As we drew near, Professor Reck could hardly hide the
emotion he was feeling at once more returning to the
scene of his very great scientific discoveries. Just when
the war broke out in 1914 he was on his way back to
Oldoway for a second season's work there, and after
German East Africa had become a Mandated Territory
under British rule, and the German economic collapse
had made expensive scientific expeditions an im-
possibility, he had resigned himself to his fate and made
up his mind that he would never be able to complete the
geological study of the Gorge. Now that he was
practically within sight of the Gorge once more, and, as
the geologist of the expedition, was about to have every
opportunity to complete his work, he was visibly moved,
so I made him change places with Dr. Hopwood (who
was travelling in the car with me while Professor Reck

was in one of the lorries with Captain Hewlett), and I took him on ahead so that he might have the honour of being the first of our party to set foot on the banks of the Gorge.

In 1913 Professor Reck had had about a hundred native porters with him, and there had been ample water for them at a pool in the Gorge, and although Captain Hewlett had reported that he could find no water at Oldoway, Professor Reck had assured me that he knew just where the pool was and that he would be able to locate it once we got there. As soon as we had all arrived, he and Captain Hewlett went down into the Gorge to find the waterhole while Dr. Hopwood and I started looking for a good place to pitch the camp.

Professor Reck found the place where the waterhole had been all right, but he had not taken into account the fact that progressive desiccation is affecting large parts of East Africa. There was now no water at all, and so immediate steps had to be taken to find some other water supply for our camp.

In addition to the waterhole in the Gorge from which the native porters had obtained their supply in 1913, Professor Reck had utilised the water of a small spring some thirteen miles away on the slopes of the Ngorongoro Mountains, because the water from this spring was very pure and he preferred it for his own use to the water in the Gorge which had been rather " tasty." He now suggested that, if he could have one of the native drivers and the use of the car, he would go across immediately to see if he could locate this spring while I pitched camp. Dr. Hopwood said he would like to go too and so the two of them set off. Professor Reck assured me that they would be back long before nightfall and as I was very busy I forgot to enquire exactly where they were going to.

I was rather worried about the water situation, and I

was afraid that this Langavata spring might also have been affected by the prevailing desiccation, and so I immediately despatched one of the lorries with the second native driver and some of the workmen to a rock pool which we had passed about twenty miles back that morning. They took with them every available empty can, and I told them to bring as much water as they possibly could. This rock pool was at a place called Mugurigine, and it had been shown to Captain Hewlett by Mr. Priddle when they came down together. Mr. Priddle had camped by it on various occasions when visiting the nomadic Masai herdsmen who live in this part of the country.

After the two water parties had gone off, Captain Hewlett and I set to work to pitch camp, and we soon found that the site that we had selected under the shade of some thorn trees was impracticable because the surface soil was too loose to hold the tent pegs, and immediately beneath there was a thick bed of limestone into which we could not possibly drive the wooden pegs. We found, however, that a little way away from the trees the soil was more consolidated by grass roots and so we had to pitch the tents there, out in the blazing sun.

When we had got everything straight Captain Hewlett and I went down to the site of the old waterhole at the bottom of the gorge once more and dug a little in the sand to see if there was any trace of water deeper down. But although we did find a slight dampness which encouraged me to put some workmen to dig still deeper next day, there was no water worth speaking of there, and all we ever got was a few pailfuls of rather green fluid which we used occasionally for the lorry radiators.

On the way down to the waterhole we were keeping a sharp lookout for any sign of Stone Age implements, and one of my Kikuyus picked up a very beautiful hand-axe of late Acheulean type, which gave me very great pleasure and filled me with hopes of finding other specimens *in situ* before long.

By sunset, at 6.0 p.m., there was no sign of the car with Professor Reck and Dr. Hopwood, and I began to be rather worried, but I decided not to institute a search yet, as it was possible that nothing worse than a puncture was delaying them.   At 7.0 they had still not arrived and so we lit some big fires thinking that perhaps they had lost their way in the darkness and hoping thereby to give them a landmark to make for.   At 8.0, as there was still no sign of them, Captain Hewlett and I took one of the lorries and some lamps and set off in the direction in which they had gone, but after we had driven about four miles we had to turn back as we had no idea where to go to look for them, and there was no point in getting ourselves lost too.   I had hoped that if they were in serious difficulties they would have lit a signal fire which would guide us to them, but although the country was more or less flat for miles we could not see any sign of a fire, and so we had to turn back, lighting small guide fires here and there as we went.

After we had had some supper we took our torches and strolled around the outskirts of the camp and to our surprise found that we were surrounded on all sides by wild animals that had come to investigate the invaders of their haunts.   We counted altogether more than twenty pairs of eyes, some of which were of hyænas, but many of them of lions.   This discovery, as may well be imagined, did not ease my mind as to the safety of the missing party.

We took the lorry and went out again to hunt for them, but after another fruitless search we had to give up, and I was furious with myself for not having insisted that Captain Hewlett should go with them as neither of them

was a very experienced shot although they had taken a
rifle with them. As there was nothing more that we
could do we went to bed so as to get some rest, and be
ready to start out on another search as soon as dawn
broke next morning, but at 1.15 a.m. we were awakened
by the purring of a motor which was rapidly approaching.
Soon we saw its headlights and in a few minutes they
were in camp.

It turned out that it had taken Professor Reck much
longer than he had expected to re-locate the Langavata
spring, and by the time they had found it and filled the
two water cans which they had taken with them and
returned to where they had left the car, darkness had set
in. Knowing that the moon would be full that night
Professor Reck decided not to try and find the way back
until the moon was sufficiently high to give him good
illumination. But he had overlooked the fact that a
total eclipse was due to take place that evening, and so he
did not have the light of the moon to help him until
nearly midnight ! Meanwhile they had gone to sleep in
the car never thinking that we would even attempt a
fruitless search in the dark, and so had not thought it
worth while to light a signal fire and, being asleep, had
not seen ours.

I was exceedingly relieved to have them safely back in
camp, for I had had awful visions of a sudden and
tragic conclusion to my long-planned expedition, and
after that I gave strict orders that if any member of the
party was ever delayed and could not get back to camp
by the time he was expected, he must try to get in touch
with the others in some way and so save them the
awful anxiety of uncertainty.

Having arrived back so late at night both Professor
Reck and Dr. Hopwood slept late next morning, but I
could not do so as I was much too excited by the

prospect of great discoveries at Oldoway. Soon after dawn I went off to the place where we had found the hand-axe on the previous evening, and before long I found a second perfect specimen, but this time *in situ*.

I was nearly mad with delight and I rushed back with it into camp, and rudely awakened the sleepers so that they should share in my joy. One of the principal objects of my expedition to Oldoway was to see if we could find any trace of prehistoric culture in these richly fossiliferous deposits, and although we had not yet been camped there for twenty-four hours I had found the evidence that we wanted. I felt that even if water difficulties or anything else should force us to leave before any further discoveries were made it would not matter (although it would be a pity) as the necessary link between the Oldoway deposits and those we had been studying in Kenya had been found.

Soon after we arrived at Oldoway one of my Kikuyu workmen reported sick, and on October 1st, less than a week after our arrival, he was so seriously ill that I feared he would die. As I had arranged to be in Nairobi anyhow on October 7th in order to meet my wife and Donald MacInnes, who were travelling out in company with my parents, I thought that the best thing to do was to start back at once and take the sick man to hospital, and so I left at dawn on October 2nd taking my mechanic Ndekei and the patient, and leaving the rest of the party to continue work at Oldoway in my absence.

As we travelled, the sick man became weaker, and I decided that I must get him to hospital as quickly as possible, and so I drove more or less without a stop until 10 o'clock that night by which time I had reached Barikitabu, about half way to Nairobi. Here I halted to cook a meal and sleep for a short time. Leaving again next morning at 4.0 a.m. I managed to arrive at Nairobi hospital by 2 o'clock in the afternoon, having covered the whole distance from Oldoway in a little more than a day and a half. It was a very tiring journey, and I several times wished I had a second driver with me, but once the patient was in hospital I was able to enjoy a good rest, as I had several days to spare before my wife and MacInnes arrived.

I found that Mr. V. E. Fuchs, who was supposed to be returning to Oldoway with me, was in hospital, and I went to see him there. The doctors assured me that he would be quite fit again before long and might even be well enough to start back with me on October 10th, as in fact he did. Apart from rather numerous punctures and tyre bursts, he and MacInnes and I had a fairly uneventful journey back to Oldoway, while my wife and baby stayed at the base camp at Limuru. A friend of my wife's, Miss Kendrick, had come out to Kenya with her, and was going to stay with her at Limuru, and, as my parents were also now in their house there, I knew that I need have no worries about the safety and welfare of my family while I was away at Oldoway.

We found so very many fossils and Stone Age implements at Oldoway that it was soon obvious that we could not possibly expect to transport them all back to Nairobi together, and so I was forced to send back a lorry loaded with cases of specimens about every tenth day, and on its return journey it brought stores, petrol, and our mail. Petrol was our most urgent need as we were having to use a considerable quantity every week in connection with our water supply, for we were not only in need of water for cooking and washing but also for the plaster of paris work in connection with the preservation of fossils.

Every third day ten men had to be away from camp for twenty-four hours getting water. About 4 o'clock in the afternoon one of the lorries would start off for Langavata and would reach the nearest accessible point after about an hour. Then the water party would take all the empty four-gallon cans, and also bedding and food for the night, and, leaving the lorry, would walk up a difficult and rocky path to the spring about three miles away. (Later on we cleared a track along part of this distance, and so were able to get the lorry nearer to the water, and that saved much time as next morning the full cans did not have to be carried so far.) Having reached the spring two men would immediately start collecting the water which trickled from the side of a small rocky cliff, while the rest of the party made preparations for the night. It took approximately thirty-five minutes to fill each four-gallon can—there were two trickles of water so that two cans could be filled simultaneously—and the process of filling the cans continued by lamplight until the early hours of the morning.

As soon as it was light nine of the men would each shoulder a four-gallon can and walk with it to the lorry and return, while the tenth man prepared breakfast. After breakfast a second journey with water cans had to be made, and finally a third, when the bedding had to be carried as well, and it was usually nearly 3 o'clock in the afternoon by the time the lorry was ready to start back to camp. By that time each man had walked about eighteen miles. (Later, when the motor track had been extended we only had to walk about nine miles.) It was arduous work, and made our water supply very expensive, but we had to have water and there was nothing else we could do.

Occasionally we got the water from the Mugurigine rock-pools instead, but the lorry could not be got any nearer to the water there than at Langavata, and the distance from camp was greater. Moreover, the

Mugurigine water was not nearly so good, as it was stagnant, although it had the great advantage of being plentiful so that the cans could be quickly filled.

Oldoway proved to be a veritable paradise for the prehistorian as well as for the palæontologist, and I found that there were Stone Age relics in almost every level in the old lake deposits that were exposed in the side of the Gorge. This fact by itself was very important as, by collecting series of implements from the different levels I was able to study the slow and gradual evolution of the tool-making techniques which had been employed, and in the end I obtained a very complete sequence of evolutionary stages of the hand-axe culture. But that was not all. The ancient lake deposits contained many bones of animals that had lived in those far-off days, and so we were able to find out exactly what the fauna of the time had been. In this connection we made some truly startling discoveries.

During his expedition in 1913 Professor Reck had discovered the remains of a number of extinct species, some of them new to science, and to these we now added a good many more. Perhaps one of the most sensational discoveries was the finding of the remains of a curious cousin of the elephant known to science as the Dino-therium. Fossil remains of this very curious elephant—which had short downward curving tusks in its lower jaw instead of straight or upward curving tusks in its upper jaw—had been found previously in many parts of Europe and also in Africa in deposits which belonged to a geological period long before tool making man appeared on the scenes ; but no one had ever suspected that this species of elephant had survived anywhere long enough to be the contemporary of man. In fact, when I announced the fact that we had found teeth and other relics of Dinotherium in association with humanly flaked stone implements, the report was received in Europe with frank incredulity, and it was not until the discovery had been confirmed by similar finds in Kenya during the later part of the same season that the evidence was accepted.

As far as the age of Professor Reck's human skeleton from Oldoway was concerned the evidence on the spot certainly seemed to support his view, and since the nature of the evidence was such that it was really a purely geological problem I—as a prehistorian—gladly accepted the geologist's verdict that the evidence quite clearly had been correctly interpreted by Professor Reck in 1913, and so I wrote a letter to the British scientific journal, *Nature*, withdrawing my earlier attack. Subsequently it was found that the geologists had been at fault and the skull was shown to be of the same age as those from Gamble's Cave.

But if Oldoway was in some ways a scientists' paradise it was the opposite in others. The shortage of water and the necessity for its strict rationing would under any circumstances have made life unpleasant, but the discomfort was greatly increased by two other factors. Almost the whole time that we were camped there a strong wind blew incessantly and it carried with it vast quantities of fine black dust that filled every corner of the tents and could not even be kept out of the mess tent.

If you spread some semi-liquid sun-melted butter on a piece of bread it would be covered with fine black dust before you could get it to your mouth. If you poured out a cup of tea or coffee in a few minutes it had a fine black scum of dust on its surface. You breathed dust-laden air, your nostrils were filled with dust, you ate dust, drank dust, slept in dust-ridden bedding, and in fact everything was dust, dust, dust! The heat of the sun was terrific; and if you had a tendency to perspire at all you did so very freely, and the dust mingled with the sweat to make your body filthy. And yet water was so scarce and so expensive that a proper wash could only be indulged in when either Langavata or Mugurigine was visited in connection with a water fatigue.

In spite of the absence of water in the Oldoway Gorge, it was the home of many lions and not a few pairs of rhinoceros, for within the Gorge there was far better cover than anywhere else for miles around. Presumably these animals went long distances for water when they needed a drink, or else possibly they had accustomed themselves to doing without water for months at a time, as so many other African animals that live in semi-desert conditions have done. At any rate, there were lions and rhinoceros in plenty, and I considered it advisable for each party working in the gorge to be armed as a precaution, although only once was it necessary to use the rifles in the gorge. On that occasion Captain Hewlett had to shoot two lions.

Over by the waterhole at Langavata things were different, and once when Captain Hewlett and Professor Reck were on duty with a water party they had a pitched battle with some lions, while on another occasion I was charged point-blank by an angry rhinoceros, and had to kill it in self-defence. This particular rhinoceros turned out to have a terrible festering wound on its shoulder, which had embittered it against humanity, and it charged me without provocation from a distance of about ten yards, it presumably did so to revenge itself for the wound it had received from some hunter months, or even years, before.

I had another unpleasant experience one night—with hyænas. These animals are usually very cowardly, especially when in ones or twos. I had been out to shoot meat for the camp, and was returning fairly late in the evening with a dead hartebeest on board the lorry when the clutch gave out completely, and the lorry would go no further. I had three natives with me, and I immediately sent off two of them on foot with the only lantern I had, to take a message to the others telling them what had happe.ied and asking for spare clutch plates to be brought to me next morning. After the men had gone the two of us who were left collected what little fuel we could find and lit a small fire and cooked ourselves some steaks from the hartebeest.

I had not intended that anyone should come out from camp that night, but later on the car arrived bringing the spare clutch plates and some bedding in case I wanted to stay where I was. Alternatively I could have gone back to camp and come out to do the repairs next morning, but I decided to spend the night in the lorry so that Ndekei (who stayed with me) and I could start work on the clutch as soon as it was light next morning. The others went back to the camp in the car.

Towards 11.0 p.m., while Ndekei and I were sitting by our dying fire and just thinking about turning in, I thought I heard footsteps nearby, and in a few minutes we realised that anything from a dozen to twenty big spotted hyænas were circling round us and drawing in closer and closer. I was not unduly alarmed, as hyænas are seldom dangerous, and it was obvious that it was the carcase in the lorry that was attracting them, but as a precaution I got ready my rifle and gave Ndekei the shotgun and waited to see what would happen. Then quite suddenly with awful growls and howls the whole pack charged in on us simultaneously. I do not think they meant to attack us so much as to frighten us away so that they could get at the meat, but I am not sure. Anyhow, it was an unpleasant moment and we both fired at them as fast as we could. One hyæna was killed outright and one wounded mortally, and the starving pack fell upon these two, just as wolves are reputed to do, and dragged them off to devour them, leaving us alone for the rest of the night.

Before I went to Oldoway I was under the impression —which is shared by many other people who have lived in Africa—that nothing except vultures would eat hyæna flesh, but I found that other hyænas would always devour a hyæna carcase, and what is still more surprising, I discovered that leopards were very fond of hyæna flesh. The latter discovery was not made at Oldoway itself, but at Apis Rock some months later, when we camped and carried out excavations in the big rock shelter there.

Towards the end of November the water problem at Oldoway was becoming more and more acute. The spring at Langavata showed signs of drying up altogether, and so we had to abandon our work and prepare to leave, as without water we could neither live, nor even use our lorries which consumed more water in their radiators than they did petrol in their engines. We had already collected and despatched to Nairobi over a hundred cases of specimens, so we were well content and really rather glad at the prospect of a change from the unceasing winds and dust that we had endured for the past two months.

The journey back to civilisation was not accomplished without a good deal of trouble. In the first place we found that we could not possibly get everything that we had in camp into the three lorries and the car, and in consequence we had to leave one tent standing with a variety of articles in it which were to be fetched by a trade lorry which I hoped to hire at Loliondo. Even so all the motors were decidedly overloaded.

Next day after we had travelled thirty-six miles the clutch of one of the lorries broke down and we had to camp for the night, while Captain Hewlett and I put in new clutch plates. The car, however, which was being driven by Fuchs, with Professor Reck as a passenger, had been well ahead of the lorries when the breakdown occurred, and so we became separated from them.

Next morning I decided to travel on as fast as I could to Loliondo in order to make plans there for a trade lorry to go down to Oldoway and collect the load of equipment that we had had to leave behind. The other two lorries, one driven by Captain Hewlett with Dr. Hopwood as passenger, and the other driven by MacInnes, were to follow on at their own pace and meet me there. When I reached the waterhole at Len Lemoru I found Professor Reck and Fuchs, and, as they wanted to examine the geology of various places ahead, I told them that they could go on and camp at Barikitabu which I hoped we should all reach by nightfall. This proved to be an unfortunate decision, owing to quite unforeseen mishaps.

Some time after I had reached Loliondo the lorry driven by MacInnes arrived, but there was no sign of the other lorry. I imagined that possibly they had had a puncture or had damaged a spring, but as Captain Hewlett was a very competent mechanic and was carrying all kinds of spare parts for his lorry I did not worry unduly, but decided to wait until he came. By 4.30 in the afternoon, as there was still no sign of the missing lorry, I took MacInnes back with me in one of the other lorries to find out what had happened, and discovered that they had had a breakdown at 7.30 in the morning, but had been too far behind MacInnes' lorry to be able to attract his attention. To make matters worse, it was a rear-wheel hub which had broken in half and we had no spare hub with us at all, so that there was nothing to be done but fetch a new hub from Nairobi, 230 miles away.

We left Captain Hewlett and Dr. Hopwood all the water we had and food, and hurried back to Loliondo, intending to push on from there to Barikitabu and catch up with Fuchs and Professor Reck who were supposed to be camping there. With the car I would be able to travel much more rapidly than by lorry, and I planned to take it and go straight on to Nairobi to get the necessary spare parts and bring them back.

By the time we got back to Loliondo it was pitch dark and the section of the road from there to Barikitabu was so appalling and our lights so dim that I dared not risk going on in the darkness with the chance of breaking the springs of our lorry and so causing further serious delays, so I was forced to camp, and at 5.0 a.m. we started off again as hard as we could go.

I thought that I had made it clear to Professor Reck and Fuchs that, *whatever happened*, they were not to go beyond Barikitabu before I arrived, but when we got in at 11.0 a.m. I found a note saying that they had gone on to Narok to examine the geology there. I was not at all pleased about this, as I had counted on taking over the car and rushing ahead with it to Nairobi, and there was now nothing left to do but push on with the lorry as fast as possible.

When I was still about ten miles from Narok a leak in the radiator became so much worse that it would no longer hold water at all, and I was afraid of serious over-heating. So I had to stop and take down the radiator and put in a spare one that we had with us. This took some time and delayed us still further, and we did not eventually reach Narok until 6 p.m., where we found Fuchs and Professor Reck at the District Commissioner's house.

By this time a very heavy storm of rain had started, but after a somewhat hasty meal MacInnes and I set off in the car to travel to Nairobi. The rain continued without ceasing and the road became a terrible sea of mud. We had chains on all four wheels of the car, but

even so we skidded from side to side of the road in an
alarming manner and on several occasions left the road
altogether, but fortunately not at places where there was
a precipice below us. We had to get out and push again
and again, and in so doing we were soaked through and
covered with mud from head to foot. But we struggled
on and by 4.30 a.m. we had reached the base camp at
Limuru, tired out and filthy, and very glad of a few
hours' rest and some food.

I was up again by 7.30 a.m. and went on into Nairobi
to buy the hub for the broken-down lorry, and as I drove
this short distance on good roads I found that our terrible
night journey with its many skids off the road had
damaged the car. In particular the steering gear was
strained, and I had to have some repairs carried out
before I could start back, as I did not want to take the
risk of further breakdowns before getting back to
Captain Hewlett and Dr. Hopwood. By midday everything was in order once more, and I went back to
Limuru, picked up MacInnes, who had been resting so
as to be able to take over the wheel for the return
journey to Narok, and we set off.

The road was still in a very bad condition owing to the
storm on the previous night, and we did not reach Narok
until 10.15 p.m., and less than an hour later Fuchs had
taken over from us and started to do a night journey
over the very uneven track to Loliondo and thence to the
broken-down lorry, which was thus rescued on the
fourth day after it had come to grief.

The total of the various expenses that were incurred
as a direct result of not having a spare hub with us was
over £30, although the hub itself cost only a few shillings
in Nairobi. It is this type of unforeseen incident that
makes it so necessary to have an emergency fund on an
expedition such as ours.

CHAPTER XXI

AFTER ATTENDING THE MEETING of the British Association for the Advancement of Science in Johannesburg in 1929 I conceived the idea of starting an annual semi-popular scientific meeting in East Africa, and as the project had been favourably received by various people with whom I discussed it, I put forward a definite proposal to the Council of the East African and Uganda Natural History Society that it should organize such a meeting.

In 1931 I was a member of the Council and I again brought the suggestion to the notice of my colleagues and a decision was made to hold a two-day meeting in December, and to confine it to the reading of papers dealing with archæological and anthropological problems. I was very anxious to see the scope of the meeting widened to include all branches of science, but it was felt that as this first meeting was by way of being an experiment it would be better to restrict its scope.

As we had two distinguished scientific visitors in the country, Professor Reck and Dr. Hopwood, the date of the meeting was arranged for a time when they would be in Nairobi, and could contribute papers, and on December 14th and 15th the first annual scientific meeting, open to the public, was held at the Coryndon Memorial Museum, Nairobi.

The papers on the first day were devoted to subjects connected with prehistory and on the second to various aspects of tribal custom among the Masai, the Kikuyu, the Nandi, and the Kavirondo. The whole meeting was very much more successful, and better attended by the public, than we had dared to hope, and since then it has been an annual part of the programme of the Natural History Society.

Owing to the world-wide economic depression which has affected Kenya Colony very seriously indeed in the last few years, the attendances have lately been very small, as many people who would otherwise attend have been unable to afford to travel to Nairobi for the purpose, but I hope that with better times things will improve. The scope of the meeting has been gradually widened, and papers dealing with meteorology, forestry, botany, ornithology and economic entomology have lately been included in the programmes, and I hope that the time will come when we shall be able to invite the British Association to hold its annual meeting in East Africa in the same way that South Africa was able to invite that Association to join in 1929 in the annual meeting of the South African Association for the Advancement of Science.

Whether this dream of mine is fulfilled or not during my lifetime remains to be seen, but I am sure that the general public of Kenya, African as well as European— for we have no colour bar at these meetings—will grow more and more interested in all kinds of scientific problems connected with the life of the country, and that if only the idea of these annual meetings can be safely nursed through its infancy it will become a popular feature in the intellectual activities of East Africa.

In the interval between our return from Oldoway and the date of the scientific meetings, and also afterwards up to the end of December, I took Professor Reck to see many of the more important of our archæological sites in Kenya, and together we re-examined a number of the geological problems connected with the elucidation of the past climate and geography of the country, and then at the end of the year Professor Reck left us to return to Europe via South Africa. Dr. Hopwood had started back to England a short time before to resume his duties as the National History Museum in London, and the first part of our season's programme was over.

Before starting any fresh work I decided that I must spend some time sorting out much of our Oldoway material and also arranging an archæological exhibit in the Museum in Nairobi, so the month of January was spent in this way, and it was a welcome rest from the strenuous existence of camp life.

One of the most remarkable and disconcerting discoveries made at Oldoway had been the finding of the remains of Dinotherium in deposits containing Stone Age tools, for that cousin of the elephant was supposed to have become extinct during an earlier geological period, and I was very anxious to see if I could find evidence elsewhere that would support this Oldoway discovery. I knew from the work of Dr. Felix Oswald, who had collected fossils for the Natural History Museum in 1913, that there were fossil beds of approximately the same age as those at Oldoway in the vicinity of Victoria Nyanza, and so in February I set off with Donald MacInnes to make a preliminary investigation in this region with a view to choosing a place for more detailed work. As a result of our tour of inspection I decided to make a camp at Kanjera, about eight miles to the west of Kendu Bay on the Kavirondo Gulf of Lake Victoria, and we finally pitched our camp there on March 14th.

During our preliminary visit MacInnes and I had received a very warm welcome from the Kavirondo school teacher at Kanjera, William Adidi, and he now suggested that we should camp on some grassland near

the school so that he could be near at hand and help us in
any way he could.   To this suggestion I readily agreed,
because I could not speak the local language at all while
William Adidi could speak Kishwahili, and also knew a
little English and a little Kikuyu, and so could be most
useful to us in our relations with the local inhabitants.

The school was about three miles from the shore of
the lake whence all our water would have to come, but
after Oldoway this seemed to be very close.   Had we
camped any closer, life would have been made intolerable
by the mosquitoes which breed in millions in the reedy
backwaters by the lake shore.   As it was, mosquitoes
were an absolute menace all the time that we were
camped at Kanjera, and sometimes they were so bad
after dark that it was really difficult to feed ourselves at
supper time.   We used to wear long trousers tucked into
Wellington boots to protect our legs, and tie towels
round our heads leaving only the mouth, nose and eyes
exposed, but even so we were terribly bitten, and on one
occasion one of us killed over a hundred mosquitoes on
his face during one meal.

Whereas the constant trouble at Oldoway had been
" not enough water " here our trouble was too much of
it.   Between us and Kendu Bay—where there were a few
shops and a market where eggs could be bought at a
shilling a hundred and bananas at the rate of six hundred
for a shilling and excellent fresh fish at the rate of $\frac{1}{2}$d per
pound—there was an unbridged river that had to be
negotiated every time we wanted to send in for anything.

When the water in the river was at its normal level it
was possible to drive a lorry across one of the fords
without getting the engine flooded, but whenever the
river was above the normal—as it was most of the time
we were at Kanjera—the water, even at the ford, came up
over the engine and flooded the carburettor, the air

intake and ignition, and then the motor had to be pushed and hauled and pulled through to the far bank and the engine cleaned and dried before it would start again.

Fortunately the district was very thickly populated and there was never any lack of helpers when the car or lorry had to be pushed across the river. In return for doing this the natives usually were given a lift on into Kendu if they wanted it, or if we were returning to camp, a lift in that direction to natives going home after attending the market.

The tribe inhabiting this district is one of the so-called Nilotic group, and they call themselves Jaluo. In former times the men wore no clothing at all, the married women's dress consisted of a minute apron in front and a " tail " behind, while unmarried girls wore nothing at all. There is every reason to believe that this nudism did not in any way lead to promiscuity or to sexual abuse, which, if anything, has become much commoner since the introduction of dress.

In many parts of Kenya where the women of the tribes were habitually clothed according to the custom of their tribes, it is only those women and girls who have come into contact with missions or other educational establishments that have taken to wearing cotton dresses. But in Luo country, since the coming of the white man, the traditional nakedness has very rapidly disappeared and to-day nearly all the women, whether associated with a mission school or not, have taken to wearing a cotton dress.

The interesting thing, however, is that this adoption of dress does not seem to have altered the attitude of the Luo people to nakedness in the very least. They never used to consider nakedness as unseemly nor had they any feelings about being seen nude by members of the opposite sex, and I found that the same idea still holds in spite of the fact that nearly every man and woman is now dressed. Consequently men and women, old and young, will go down to the lake or to the river and take off all their clothing in order to bathe, nor do they even mind doing so in the presence of strangers. And although I have seen very many of these nude mixed bathing parties I have never seen a single indecent act or gesture at them.

At the ford where we used to cross the river on our way to Kendu, it was a common thing to find parties of men and women splashing about in the water with nothing on, and my Kikuyu workmen were absolutely horrified by what appeared to them to be intolerably indecent exposure. The Kikuyu have a very strict set of rules concerning behaviour of this sort, and although a young man may bathe naked in the presence of young women, the reverse procedure is strictly taboo, and mixed bathing undreamed of. The Kikuyu go even further than that, and young men may not undress and bathe with senior men without incurring severe penalties, the rule in this case being that you must not expose yourself naked before any man who is sufficiently senior to you to have daughters of marriageable age, and whom you might, in theory marry, one day.

To my Kikuyu workmen the habits and customs of the Luo tribe were a source of constant wonder, but it was comparatively seldom that they found anything to praise. They considered that their method of hut-building was unworkmanlike, their habit of eating fish disgusting, their mourning customs ridiculous, and their treatment of their children shocking. Very occasionally a Kikuyu child rolls into the open fireplace in the hut and gets badly burnt, but in Luo country this is a very common occurrence ; in my few short stays among the Luo I had been asked to treat more burnt babies than I have seen during years among the Kikuyu. A Kikuyu woman will very seldom leave a really small baby alone and go away for any length of time, but the Luo mother seemed to think nothing of leaving quite small babies alone in the huts for hours at a time, and again and again when they come home they find that they have fallen partly into the fire or against some hot embers and are burnt more or less seriously.

All around Elmenteita, baboons are a serious menace to the crops of the Kikuyu squatters and do a great deal of damage to maize and sweet potatoes, and one day a woman who was at one end of her field saw a troop of baboons invade the far end and start pulling up the maize. She had her infant about eighteen months old on her back, but as she wanted to be free to chase the baboons off she put it down on the ground under the shade of a tree while she ran up the field.

Suddenly she heard the baby screaming horribly, and looking back she saw a big male baboon attacking it. She rushed back, but was not in time to prevent the child from being very seriously mauled. The poor woman brought her baby down to our camp at once, and my wife and I administered what first aid we could, but it was obvious that we could do nothing ourselves, and so I got the car ready and took the mother and child straight in to Nakuru hospital twenty-eight miles away. One of the big canine teeth of the baboon had pierced the thin skull of the child and damaged the brain, another had penetrated deep into the body in the region of the liver, and a third wound was dangerously near a lung, and I believe had actually punctured it. In addition there were about ten other flesh wounds. In spite of the long and bumpy journey the baby was still alive when we reached hospital, and the doctor fought for its life for six weeks before at last it was out of danger, and it finally made a complete recovery, much to the joy of its parents and grandparents and to our satisfaction.

But I must return to Kanjera camp. We had come to this district in search of evidence to corroborate the discovery of Dinotherium remains in deposits belonging to the Stone Age period, and it was not long before we had found fossil remains of this strange animal under circumstances which entirely supported the Oldoway discoveries. In addition, we found very important but fragmentary pieces of fossilised human skulls and a jaw fragment, the latter at a site called Kanam West.

As the story of the controversy which they raised and the conference which was subsequently held at Cambridge to discuss them has been told in two other books of mine, and, *as the question of their exact age is still in dispute*, I will not discuss it in detail here. They are in fact, still *sub judice*. It is sufficient to say that in my opinion they represent the oldest known remains of the species *homo sapiens*, and/or its direct ancestors, and thus represent the most ancient real ancestors of present-day man so far discovered. This view has recently been challenged, and the whole matter must remain in abeyance until such time as we obtain further evidence, which I am confident we shall do, in time.

Some miles away from Kanjera there is an island called Rusinga and I had often wished to visit it and discover whether there were fossil deposits on it. One day the opportunity came to go over by motor boat with Major Buxton, the District Commissioner, who was making one of his periodical administrative visits. He very kindly offered to take us with him, and he left us camped on the island for a few days and then sent the motor boat back to fetch us. We found that there were extensive exposures of fossiliferous deposits, and it was soon clear that they belonged to a much earlier geological age than that with which we were primarily concerned ;

they belonged in fact to the Miocene period and were comparable to the deposits at Koru which Dr. Hopwood had studied in 1931.

In the normal course of events I should not have spent much time at Rusinga, for, although I was interested in all kinds of fossils, I had my own work to do and could not afford to study strata that had no bearing upon the problems which I was concerned with. But during our first visit to Rusinga we discovered the remains of some Miocene anthropoid apes, and this immediately altered the situation. We believe that man and the great anthropoid apes are descended from some common simian ancestor, and such ancestor must have been present in some part of the world in Miocene times. If the conditions in East Africa were favourable for anthropoid apes, as our discovery showed to have been the case, they might very well have been also favourable for an early sub-human ancestor of man, and it therefore became imperative to study the Miocene deposits at Rusinga Island very carefully and to collect all the material that we could. So, during the time that we were camped at Kanjera we went over to Rusinga whenever we could obtain the use of a motor boat for the weekend, and we made a number of important finds, which are still being studied.

During the time that we were at Kanjera my wife was often in camp with us, leaving our baby daughter at Limuru in the care of Miss Kendrick. Then, after a time, my wife would return to Limuru so as to let Miss Kendrick experience a little camp life. Apart from the mosquitoes, conditions in camp here were not too unpleasant, and compared with Oldoway it was paradise.

When we were at Oldoway some months before I had noticed a very fine rock shelter at Apis Rock, and I had made up my mind to return there and carry out excava-

tions. I was also very anxious to revisit Oldoway, and
if possible to take Mr. E. J. Wayland, the Director of the
Geological Survey of Uganda, with me, in order to
re-examine certain geological problems. I therefore
decided to close our work in the Kendu area in June and
prepare to return to the Oldoway region again.

Before we left I arranged to go over to Uganda to
visit Mr. Wayland and discuss the projected second visit
to Oldoway with him, and I set off in one of the lorries
accompanied by Miss Kendrick, Donald MacInnes and
his mother, who was then on a visit to East Africa. The
first part of the journey was over very bad roads, and it
was not until we had crossed the boundary into Uganda
that the road became good.

Uganda is justly famed for the excellent condition of
most of its highways, and the road from Kenya boundary
to the Protectorate capital is one of the best, but we had
the misfortune to come unexpectedly upon a patch of
roadway on which repairs had recently been started, and
the surface was here very loose, and, without any warning, the lorry skidded badly and, leaving the road, turned
over and came to rest in a patch of cultivated land with
all four wheels in the air.

Although everything must have happened in a
moment, the time from the start of the skid to the
moment when we came to a standstill seemed an eternity
to me, and I was vividly conscious of the whole proceeding. As we started to skid I hoped that we should
merely leave the road and not suffer any serious damage.
Then I felt the offside wheels leave the ground and
realised that we were tipping over. Slowly, ever so
slowly, *so it seemed*, the lorry moved over. As the angle
became more acute I felt myself slipping down on to
the driver and was quite powerless to prevent it ; then
gradually we went over further and as the hood of the

lorry cab was crushed in there was a sickening noise of splintering glass and snapping woodwork, and then all seemed to be over.

I had an awful vision of the lorry catching fire before we could extricate ourselves, and two thoughts rushed through my head—" Will anyone discover and recognise the precious specimens which we have on board and recover them ? " and " We shan't reach our destination to-night."

Mercifully, although petrol was leaking badly and the engine was still running, no fire started, and slowly and painfully we extricated ourselves and looked at the wreckage. All of us were damaged to a less or greater degree, but no one was injured seriously. It is a remarkable fact, for which I cannot now find any adequate explanation, that before we rescued the medical chest and attended to our bleeding wounds and bruises we dragged out our cameras from the wreckage and took photographs. This done, we gave first aid to each other's wounds, and then set to work to get the lorry back on to its wheels again. This task proved to be much easier than I had expected, but the damage to the steering and radiator was such that there was no hope of moving the lorry under her own power.

Not very far away was a little Indian trade store, the owner of which had a ramshackle old lorry and we persuaded him to take us on to a place called Busia where I knew there was a garage. We were all considerably shaken and our nerves definitely on edge, but the Indian driver absolutely refused to drive slowly, as he wanted to get back to his business as soon as possible, and so we were rushed along at about thirty-five miles an hour when we would have preferred to go at about a third of that pace. The mental agony that we endured during that journey was so great that our physical wounds were almost forgotten.

The relief of standing on firm ground once more at Busia was on the other hand spoiled by the fact that for the first time since the accident happened, the pain of our cuts and bruises made itself really felt. The garage arranged to send out and tow our lorry in and also provided us with a car to take us on to the township of Sinsa, where there was a good hotel and a doctor, and there we remained for several days recovering from the shock while the lorry was made fit for the road once more.

After we had returned from this fateful trip to Uganda we went to the base camp at Limuru and there made final preparations for the last part of the season's programme—the second visit to Oldoway, and the excavation of the rock shelter at Apis Rock.

From the point of view of Stone Age cultures Apis Rock was an excellent site and we found, in all, six different occupational levels with different stages of culture and obtained some very valuable material some of which enabled us to fill in blanks in our previous knowledge of the culture sequence. We were, however, seriously disappointed in one thing. I had hoped to find that the lowest deposits at the shelter would contain an occupation level with tools of the hand-axe culture, and possibly some skeletal remains, but the Apis Rock rock-shelter had proved to have never been occupied by the race which made the hand-axe culture.

After we had been at Apis Rock for a few days we noticed that there were a few hartebeests and giraffe about and that they often went off in a north-westerly direction, presumably for water, since neither of these two species can exist without water. We therefore prospected in that direction, and found a series of waterholes with an abundant supply. These pools were about ten miles from Apis Rock, and it was much less expensive to get water from them than from Mugurigine, but the water itself was foul. It was comparatively clean to look at—like weak china tea—but it tasted of a mixture of sulphur and soda, and I have never had to drink or use a more nauseating fluid. But there was nothing else that we could use, for I could not afford the petrol for fetching the water from Mugurigine which was more than twice as far away, and over very much worse country, and so we had this vile water for the rest of our stay at Apis Rock.

Its effect on all of us was bad, and as it was impossible not to use water in the preparation of some of our meals we used to dread meal times. I would have given anything for a still with which to distil some pure water, but we had nothing to make one with.

We had several unusual incidents with wild animals at this camp. Hyænas became a nuisance and started raiding camp at night and carrying off pots and pans and boots, and so Mr. Turner made a gun trap for them, and the first night that it was set it went off while we were having supper. It was only about thirty yards from the supper table, and we were somewhat surprised that a hyæna should come so near while we were talking. So we left the table and went over to the trap and found that instead of a hyæna there was a dead leopard.

After that the trap killed several hyænas which were raiding camp, and then a most unusual thing happened. The gun trap had been set with a small bore rifle so arranged as to shoot through the neck any hyæna that entered.

One morning about 5.0 a.m. I heard the gun go off and I immediately went to see what had been killed, and very much to my surprise saw a big lion lying on its side by the trap and lashing its tail. I went back to camp and called MacInnes and Turner, and by the time we got back to the trap the lion was completely still, and I thought it was dead. We approached it cautiously, however, and when we were quite near, it suddenly came to life and with an angry roar tried to charge me. I retreated keeping my face towards the "King of Beasts," and in doing so I caught my heel on a bit of projecting rock and sat down somewhat violently facing the angry animal. Fortunately the lion was paralysed by its wound and was unable to charge properly, and we very soon put it out of its pain.

The trap had been specially prepared for hyænas and the entrance made so narrow that we thought nothing larger than a hyæna could possibly force its way in, but somehow this lion had succeeded—it must have been very hungry—and had received the bullet through the side of the neck instead of through the spinal column, which is where the bullet would have hit a hyæna.

After about two months at Apis Rock we packed up and started back to Limuru, as my funds for the season were exhausted and our health was also in too bad a state to allow us to continue much longer. From Apis Rock we journeyed in the first day to Len Lemoru, and as soon as we got there I went to look at the waterhole and found that it still contained a little water. Having removed the scum we had tea made from this liquid, and it tasted so wonderful after the Apis Rock water that I decided to camp for the night so that we could enjoy a good meal which did not taste of sulphur and soda.

And so back to Limuru base camp to pack up and return to England. My third Archæological expedition was over, and also the first thirty years of my life.